NO SHORTCUT TO CHANGE

No Shortcut to Change

An Unlikely Path to a More Gender-Equitable World

Kara Ellerby

NEW YORK UNIVERSITY PRESS

New York

NEW YORK UNIVERSITY PRESS
New York
www.nyupress.org

© 2017 by New York University
All rights reserved

References to Internet websites (URLs) were accurate at the time of writing. Neither the author nor New York University Press is responsible for URLs that may have expired or changed since the manuscript was prepared.

ISBN: 978-1-4798-9360-7 (hardback)
ISBN: 978-1-4798-1716-0 (paperback)

For Library of Congress Cataloging-in-Publication data, please contact the Library of Congress.

New York University Press books are printed on acid-free paper, and their binding materials are chosen for strength and durability. We strive to use environmentally responsible suppliers and materials to the greatest extent possible in publishing our books.

Manufactured in the United States of America

10 9 8 7 6 5 4 3 2 1

Also available as an ebook

For my parents

Sharyl Ellerby,

Rick and Karen Ellerby.

Thank you for always supporting my journey.

CONTENTS

ACKNOWLEDGMENTS

Writing this book was one of the most terrifying yet gratifying endeavors I have ever undertaken. It was achievable with the professional and personal support of so many wonderful people in my life. I would like to offer my acknowledgment and sincerest gratitude in recognizing that writing this book was only possible because of how others have supported me and my work.

I have had many mentors and this book should be read as a dedication to—and acknowledgement of—the vital and powerful feminist scholars from whom I have learned, and who have created a welcoming and inclusive subfield where my work was made possible. It started at the University of Arizona School of Government and Public Policy, where these ideas began to form. To V. Spike Peterson—whose gifted research and writing, sharp sense of humor, and unwavering support have shaped my career so profoundly—I offer my deepest thanks. You are the kind of scholar and produce the kind of scholarship I aspire to.

I would also like to thank Gary Goertz for his support in offering both feedback on my ideas and the space to develop and present them. Thank you for being an open and thoughtful mentor. I would also like to thank Suzanne Dovi for her earlier support during my graduate work, which kept me in academia when I was ready to leave—I will never forget that.

I thank my graduate school cohort for the great conversations, helpful feedback, and support through countless papers and my dissertation, and for all those JT references and fun we had. Thanks go to Ruth Alminas, Trina Running, Tiffany Harper, Diane Forster, and Zack Shipley.

I also thank Laura Sjoberg, Ann Tickner, Jenny Lobasz, Jacqui True, and Mona Lena Krook for support on parts of this project and encouragement to keep working on them.

I must thank everyone in the Department of Political Science and International Relations at the University of Delaware for creating such a welcoming scholarly environment. I felt supported and encouraged to write this book and appreciated the helpful insights and ideas from my colleagues. This especially includes Gretchen Bauer, Claire Rasmussen, Matthew Weinert, Elaine Salo, Alice Ba, and Daniel Green. I also thank Lynn Corbett, Barbara Ford, and Nancy Koller for keeping me on track and sane during this process and for always being so helpful.

I also owe a large debt of gratitude to my wonderful research assistants, including Susan Weaver and Sara Jann. These intelligent, fierce women helped me complete the onerous tasks of finding and organizing data, and reviewing and editing early drafts. It is such a pleasure and honor to have such smart women advisees. I would not have finished this project without them.

My family has been critical in making this possible as well. Thanks to my hero, my mom Sharyl whose strength inspires me. To my dad and stepmom Rick and Karen for unending support and motivation. Thank you to my grandparents Jan Littrell and Dick Ellerby, and siblings Ryan Ellerby, and Kyle and Shelly Ellerby. I also would like to thank my parents-in-law Masako and Katsuro Hamada for taking care of Kai while I finished the project; I could not have finished this book without your help! I would also like to thank Jimmy Howard and Jacqueline Winslow for listening to early ideas of the project and always having such enthusiasm for them.

I especially want to thank my husband, Koji, for his "get it done" support. Your belief in me and my work—and your calm demeanor—were always just what I needed. You are a great partner and your humor and steadiness keep me level. And finally I would like to thank my son, Kai, for giving me a big new reason to care about and hope for what sort of future we are creating.

LIST OF ACRONYMS

AU: African Union
CEDAW: Convention on the Elimination of All Forms of Discrimination against Women
CSW: Commission on the Status of Women
DRC: Democratic Republic of Congo
EU: European Union
FAO: Food and Agricultural Organization
GBV: gender-based violence
GPE: global political economy
IFI: international financial institution
ILO: International Labour Organization
IMF: International Monetary Fund
IO: international organization
LGBTQ: Lesbian, Gay, Bisexual, Transgender, Queer
MDG: Millennium Development Goal
MENA: Middle East and North Africa
NGO: non-governmental organization
OECD: Organisation for Economic Cooperation and Development
PFA: Platform for Action
ROSCA: rotating savings and credit association
SAP: Structural Adjustment Plan
SDG: Sustainable Development Goal
UN: United Nations
UNDP: United Nations Development Programme
UNIFEM: United Nations Development Fund for Women
UNSCR 1325: United Nations Security Council Resolution 1325
USAID: United States Agency for International Development
WEF: World Economic Forum
WILPF: Women's International League for Peace and Freedom
WHO: World Health Organization
WMD: weapon of mass destruction

1

Add Gender and Stir

"The twenty-first century must be the century of inclusion and that has to include women's equal leadership and participation. We will not realize our goals for building true citizen democracies, ensuring peace and a development that is sustainable and for all, if we fail at inclusion."[1]
—Michelle Bachelet, UN Women

The last forty years have been marked by unprecedented changes regarding women's rights. States all over the world have adopted and continue to adopt policies to include more women in governments, economic activity, and legal codes, often in the name of promoting "gender equality." This includes the adoption of sex quotas in parliaments to ensure greater representation; the creation of bureaucratic agencies dedicated to women's issues; and the implementation of efforts aimed at increasing numbers of women as national leaders and judges. States are also adopting more women-friendly property laws to ensure single, married, and widowed women have access to land and livelihoods on their own terms. Finally, states are passing laws criminalizing acts of gender-based violence, including sexual assault, domestic violence, human trafficking, and sexual harassment. The scale by which such policies have been adopted is impressive—the result of the tireless efforts of women activists working to pressure governments, international organizations, and their own "fellow" citizens to acknowledge the importance of gender equality.

But even as states have adopted so many woman-centered policies, and amid a growing awareness of and support for "gender equality," some troubling global consistencies remain. In practice, nearly all of these policies have yet to be fully and adequately implemented. Globally, women still account for just 22 percent of parliament members, only slightly higher than ten years ago. Only 14 percent of current prime ministers or presidents are women. One in three women worldwide have experienced, or will experience, assault and domestic violence in their lifetimes, and there is evidence to indicate that violence against women may actually be increasing.[2] Despite significant progress, women still account for the majority of the world's poor and consistently lack access to land, credit, and higher-paying jobs in both developed and developing countries. Why then—despite numerous efforts made by states and global international organizations to promote policy shifts to better include and protect women—does women's exclusion, lack of prosperity, and lack of security remain so pervasive? Why has a growing global awareness of "gender equality" not yet translated into significantly more women in government, greater economic well-being for more women, or less violence against women at global levels? Equally important, why are all these policies situated as policies for "gender equality"? This book seeks to address these questions.[3]

The central problem of this book is the problem with "gender equality," as it is used in international policy and political practice. I seek to engage the word "problem" in two ways. Crucially, this is not a book arguing that gender equality is bad or should end. Rather, it means to problematize the idea of, and policies and practices framed as, gender equality. When something is a "problem," it does not necessarily mean it is an issue to be resolved; it can also mean to "unsettle" or to more deeply consider, understand, and thus explain. In this case, the goal here is to problematize—or better understand and explain—gender equality and how it has become taken for granted in the context of policies aimed at including more women. To problematize gender equality means to ask: How did gender equality come to be the "catch-all" for any policy meant to address discrimination against, and exclusion of, women?

Using a more conventional understanding of "problem," this book illustrates that the "problem" with gender equality is that woman-centered policies do little to disrupt and challenge gender (as ranked patterns of masculinities and femininities), or facilitate substantive equality (as valuing femininities and masculinities equally, or significantly promoting women's emancipation). The promotion or adoption of sex quotas, women's policy agencies, greater employment and property rights, and violence against women legislation are normalized as part of "gender equality" to end discrimination and better include women. But, a more accurate description for what is happening is a global "add-gender-and-stir" campaign based on liberal feminist logics of individuality and anti-discrimination, and sex-based, essentialist ideas of "gender." This campaign has pursued and promoted policies that add women to exclusionary institutions such as governments, legal codes, and state practices. But through analyses of these policies and practices and their implementation, it becomes clear that an accurate understanding of what "gender" really is remains an issue.

To call this a global add-gender-and-stir campaign is to highlight four central issues: 1) these policies all work within a liberal feminist framework of emancipation of women; 2) these policies treat women and gender as substitutable terms; 3) these policies and practices have been co-opted by and work within a neoliberal world order; 4) these policy efforts should be studied in conjunction. In regard to the fourth issue, it is important, for example, to assess sex quotas alongside changing credit laws and sexual assault policies because, when one begins untangling the research on the status of these policies, similar patterns emerge among them all. The next several chapters build the case for why it is time to stop using the phrase "gender equality" in reference to any woman-centered policy adopted by states and promoted by global institutions.

It is an important moment for women's rights. It has been over twenty years since the monumental Beijing Declaration and Platform for Action on Women in 1995. We have seen the "end" of the Millennium Development Goals in 2015 and the start of the Sustainable Development Goals, and it has been over fifteen years since United Nations Security Council Resolution 1325 on Women, Peace, and Security was adopted. Thus it seems like an opportune time to critically engage this global effort to promote women in particular ways. To be sure, many women have benefited from the changes in policies and practices that were sparked by these landmark initiatives—and the world is a better place because more states are doing more to address women's issues and needs. But this book challenges the assumption such policies engage gender or promote equality by elucidating how gender—understood as socially constructed and differently valorized scripts of masculinities and femininities—is not sufficiently challenged or destabilized by policies focused primarily on women. And equality is not sufficiently achieved by simply "adding" some or a few women to male-dominated institutions.

Part of the reason for this can be found in the language used for such policy prescriptions—essentially, what we call them and how we talk about them. For example, if a "gender" quota in parliament is considered an indicator of gender equality, then having the quota becomes a satisfactory benchmark for a "gender-equal" state. And in this process, two important patterns have emerged: gender has become a "short-cut" expression, a way to acknowledge the socially produced, differently valorized realities of men and women, without the deeper critical analyses explaining why such realities persist. Additionally, "gender" and "women" have become synonymous terms, often used interchangeably as though they have the same meaning. In order to critically engage these policies, we need a new way of thinking and talking about what is going on in efforts to promote women.

In this capacity, this book offers a critical renaming and reframing of gender equality policies and practices by engaging these efforts as part of a liberal feminist norm of *women's inclusion*. The goal in renaming and reframing gender equality as women's inclusion is to offer a cohesive yet critical examination of woman-centered policies. By challenging (implicit and explicit) assumptions that any effort to include more women *is* an effort to advance gender equality, one begins to see how *gender is actually women* and *equality is actually inclusion* and *women's inclusion has inherent limits*.

Critical feminist conceptualizations of gender and equality inform the analyses in this book, which focuses on the global adoption and diffusion of multiple policies and practices in the pursuit of women's rights and interests—*women's inclusion*—and how such rights are pursued within a rubric of "gender equality." This movement for "gender equality" relies on a narrative in which gender and women are interchangeable terms. It also relies upon a liberal feminist logic of emancipation through addition. But liberal feminist policies are insufficient to fully engage women's subjugation (and the subjugation of many men and other marginalized groups). Indeed, liberal feminist policies are actually (re)enforcing gendered binaries that other feminisms see as the root of oppression and subjugation.

The reality is, despite significant changes in state-driven approaches to address women's exclusion and subordination, pervasive gendered logics continue to inform and shape policy adoption and implementation. Furthermore, equality has come to mean a variety of thresholds that do not necessarily call for equal numbers of women and men or equal access to material and symbolic power. By introducing "women's inclusion" as an alternative naming for these global policy shifts, later chapters in this book present an alternative discourse and assessment. It is my hope that this will facilitate the work of scholars and practitioners to illustrate for larger (and especially non-feminist) audiences why it is a problem to call any policy promoting women "gender equality."

The following sections of this chapter layout the main arguments, key terms, limits, and organization of the book. The next section explains the meanings of "gender" in this book. Then, I turn to the framing of analyses, centered on five interrelated reasons that efforts to promote women's inclusion, evidenced in these policy practices, have limits in emancipating anyone.

Add *Gender* and Stir

Cynthia Enloe advocates for a "feminist curiosity" in understanding how gender operates in global politics: this means to look deeper at the lived experiences of women (and men) and begin to understand how a particular idea or practice becomes taken for granted.[4] While this study engages primarily with global ideas and how they are promoted as state-level policies, it still uses a feminist curiosity to understand an array of policies and practices aimed at improving women's lives. It is through careful examination of how gender shapes policies, how different women experience such efforts, and how scholars make sense of the conditions under which these policies work, that one begins to understand how including more women in gendered institutions has been normalized to mean "gender equality."

While often policies, including legislation criminalizing violence against women, sex (gender) quotas, and legislation affecting women's property rights, are treated distinctly in academic work (and as part of different subfields), a central argument here is these policies all embody liberal feminist sensibilities regarding causes of women's subordination and solutions to fixing it.[5] As further examined in chapter 2, liberal feminism identifies women's oppression to be rooted in institutionalized discrimination and legal barriers that deny women access to the same rights and opportunities as men; once these barriers are removed women can then be fully equal. Such policies are pursued via the state, as the state plays a central role in becoming "the neutral arbiter to ensure women's equality."[6] This approach is often referred to as the "add-women-and-stir" approach because it treats women's oppression like a recipe: one does not need to change the whole recipe, just add women to it. In other words, liberal feminism assumes one can change the composition of the institution without needing to also change the way said institution operates. Because women and gender are now often used interchangeably (and problematically), I argue what is happening is actually an add-gender-and-stir campaign, in which gender is used as a shortcut, a technocratic term for including women without really discussing how gender shapes the experiences of both women and men within such institutions. *Gender, as a shortcut, became a way to acknowledge power without talking about the production of power.*

As other forms of feminism have identified, there are limits to just adding women, particularly in how liberal feminist approaches do not focus on the power of gender or gendered social structures as a central cause of women's oppression. While "patriarchy" is often the term used to illustrate gender as a male-dominated and identified social structure, this term does not adequately engage how systems of subordination are not just about male domination, but also about racist, imperialist, and heterosexist forms of domination as well. To engage how social structures promote domination through multiple yet intersecting systems of oppression, I use the term "kyriarchy," defined as "interlocking structures of domination" to name the sexist, racist, heterosexist, and imperialist system(s) of subordination central to understanding how gender equality has come to represent add-women/gender policies.[7] Given the neoliberal world order in which such policies are being pursued, adding women and calling it an effort to advance gender equality actually works with an already powerful liberal narrative of individuality, universality, rights, and anti-discrimination. Discussions of kyriarchy and structural oppression are marginalized, and critiques of liberal feminist pursuits and policies are treated as counter to the feminist movement.

This norm of "women's inclusion," as an alterative naming and framing, situates these efforts to better include women within a neoliberal world order of the last forty years, under which woman-centered policies have been promoted. Three key aspects of women's inclusion focused on in this book include: an emphasis on *women's representation in government, recognizing women's economic rights,* and *protecting women from violence.* These ideas are central to understanding how gender equality has been normalized to embody "adding women" as "addressing gender" because it elucidates the trade-offs in promoting liberal feminist policies centered on women without adequately disrupting masculine/feminine (and other) binary logics and practices. Neoliberal world order relies upon the subordination of women and other marginalized groups to function, and policies normalized as gender equality construct a narrow narrative in which including *some* women becomes "enough." Liberal feminism seeks to reform existing institutions by addressing the sex composition of them. More radical discussions by critical feminists (among other critical thinkers and activists) of dismantling neoliberal capitalism have been artfully silenced or marginalized through state and international organizations' recognition of liberal feminist efforts to reform sexist institutions.

What this means is that while formal barriers *are* being systematically addressed, informal practices and sexist (as well as racist, heterosexist, and imperialist) beliefs limit the effectiveness of removing such barriers; and thus, women's exclusion and marginalization persist. And these informal practices and ideas are *endemic* to these formal institutions and practices excluding and marginalizing women. It also means many policies, feminist in origin, have actually been co-opted and promoted in troubling ways by powerful global institutions and states because women's inclusion is considered paramount to better state development and progress. To say it differently: when global organizations and states argue for sex quotas, property rights for women, and ending violence against women, they do so, not necessarily for social justice, but because women's inclusion is considered important to neoliberal economic growth, development, and prosperity. Inclusion has become a strategy for reinforcing gendered binaries and is complicit in neoliberal world order through the reproduction of difference.

According to this rhetoric surrounding efforts to increase women's inclusion, women are an important means to a more just, prosperous, and secure end. But the trade-off is that these policies, and the discourse surrounding them, do not adequately engage persistent exclusion and marginalization of many women or subordinated groups other than women. In thinking of this norm as one of women's inclusion, along with critical engagement with such policies, one may begin to broaden the possibilities and discourse around what gender equality actually means or could mean. In order to understand how women's inclusion has become such a powerful norm, one must first engage with the slight-of-hand in which gender and women have become synonyms, obscuring the radical origins and intentions of gender in global practices.

Gender = Women

One of the most powerful ways in which the limits of add-women policies are obscured is via the "gender = women" narrative. As many feminists have argued, gender is not synonymous with women.[8] But despite a consistent reminder that gender is not just about women, in practice these terms are used interchangeably and this conflation has had important effects. Gender has become a ubiquitous global term: it is listed on official forms and in government and organizational documents, and is a staple term for how we talk about ourselves—a lexicon for discussing difference: gender equality, gender mainstreaming, gender-based violence, gender gaps, gender equity, gender parity, gender inclusiveness, and the list goes on. All of these concepts, in practice, are actually referencing only women (and, sometimes, biological sex). They are also in some way tied to a campaign in which adopting certain woman-centered policies has been normalized as evidence of a more "gender-equal" world. But in centrally focusing on policies aimed at including more women and calling it gender, what we understand to be "gender"—as a feminist, and thus political, concept and tool of analysis—is obscured. This matters because gendered binaries remain central to making sense of why woman-centered policies are not having a greater global impact, and help further understanding about how these policies may actually essentialize women in ways that do not adequately promote emancipation. Associating such policies with gender equality negates a more political and feminist understanding of gender *and* equality.

As the concept of gender is central to the ideas and arguments presented in this book, this section explores its meaning, historical development, and properties. To do so, let me first begin with a critical feminist definition of gender: the socially constituted and hierarchical structures and behaviors organized via practices of masculinities and femininities.[9] Gender, as it is commonly used today in policy prescriptions and scholarly analyses, no longer encapsulates this definition and thus loses its radical feminist origins. This has consequences for how activists and scholars study and advocate for feminist change. In order to challenge this narrative, one must first distinguish between terms such as "female," "woman," and "femininities," which carry distinct connotations for feminist scholars. Indeed, making the distinction while noting their interdependencies, and illustrating the power produced via these ideas has been a central feminist research agenda in global politics and in academia more generally.[10]

"Male" and "female" have historically been offered as the only way to distinguish sex differences and were assumed as based in biological or "natural" differences. "Feminine" and "masculine" were terms used to describe behaviors associated with these "natural" differences well into the twentieth century.[11]

The term "gender" was then offered in the 1970s by feminists to "insist on the fundamentally social quality of distinctions based on sex."[12] It was central to the feminist project to challenge the essentialist and deterministic ideas about "natural" differences between men and women because these were used to justify women's exclusion and subordination. Thus gender became a feminist tool to illustrate how masculine and feminine ideas and practices were *socially constructed* though pervasive "scripts" specifying men and women's behaviors.

"Women," as a concept, may be used interchangeably with "female" to describe biological sex, but it can also be used in a way to indicate some socially constructed features of being female. In this sense, "woman/ women" is a good way to talk about how femininities may shape femaleness—sort of a "gender lite" idea.

A key aspect of "feminist" gender is understanding that it is relational. As historian Joan Scott articulated, women and men are defined in relation to one another, the "relational aspect of normative definitions of femininity."[13] In other words, "masculine" is defined by that which is not "feminine" and vice versa—one does have not meaning without the other.

What is key about any feminist understanding of gender is that it is also an analytical tool, not just a category. "Analytical gender" focuses on how masculinity and femininity are a system of meaning, which produces, and is produced by, global politics.[14] In this sense, analytical gender is a tool that seeks to *politicize, historicize*, and *de-essentialize* the subjugation of women and other marginalized groups. It *politicizes* subjugation by focusing on the inherent power relations built into the male/female, masculine/feminine dichotomy. It illustrates how "the personal is political" and illuminates how women's lived experiences of oppression are best explained as part of larger global processes.[15] It *historicizes* the subjugation of women by challenging the idea that "things have always been this way" through critical analyses on how kyriarchical structures of oppression, such as states and capitalist economic systems, relied upon masculinized practices to work the way they do.[16] And, in conjunction with historicizing, feminist gender *de-essentializes* difference by questioning the apparent "universalness" of the category of "woman," and the "naturalness" of segregation and subjugation of women. It does so by focusing on the socially constructed scripts of masculinities and femininities (re)produced in societies and understood as equally applicable to all. This includes challenging a sex-gender binary, illustrating how they are actually co-constituted, in that bodies do not exist free of gender and gender is produced via bodies and institutions.[17]

Ultimately, a feminist approach to gender understands it to be a powerful organizing force in social life and global politics: *gender does things.* It shapes behaviors, informs our logics, bounds our agency, and structures our relationships. As Anne Sisson Runyan and V. Spike Peterson articulate, *the power of gender* "fosters dichotomization, stratification, and depoliticization in thought and action."[18] The goal here is to expose and explore the power of gender in the construction of policy discourses and objectives about women among states.

Why does it matter that we use gender when we often mean women? As I stated, gender can be a useful concept for exploring how the power dynamics of masculinities and femininities have produced the subjugation of many, not just women. When "gender" is taken to mean "women," it produces a more superficial and narrow discussion about policies aimed at including more women.[19] This is important for two reasons. The first is when gender means women we render silent and invisible conversations and analyses about the dominance of masculinities, maleness, and men. We also render silent conversations about the multiple categories of "woman"—that women carry other equally important identities such as race, class and sexuality that impact their everyday lives. It means we focus on analyzing why women (as a universal category) are excluded, why (some) men dominate, and why we privilege most masculinities over most femininities. More importantly, the obscuring of gender in the discourse surrounding the diffusion of woman-centered policies means we talk about how and why these work or do not work in a particular way. Much of the work on large-scale diffusion of national machineries, quotas, and violence against women policies tends to focus on what accounts for their adoption and which states seem to have better policies.[20] But lurking under that conversation is the reality that women are still more excluded than included, and these policies are rife with poor implementation. These practices are not universally working and the variation hidden in such studies reveals important insights when using a "gender lens" rather than a woman-centered one.[21] These revelations are primarily about how gender binaries—masculinities and femininities—still shape implementation and are not destabilized by including women. Male dominance is challenged, but masculinity less so.

The world still seems to advocate women's inclusion using very gendered logic—arguing women as more honest, caring, family- and community-focused, and peaceful, to articulate the reasons for their inclusion. But why do we not expect men to have such characteristics and why do we ostracize women who do not? Binary thinking simplifies necessarily complex issues, but there are costs. Ultimately, the goal of this study is to advocate for a repoliticization and more critical feminist engagement with gender in analyses and policy prescriptions, and a reframing of liberal feminist policies as advocating for women's inclusion, not gender equality. This book is part of a long tradition of critiquing the troubling relationship between (liberal) feminism and neoliberalism.[22] This book adds to this field by focusing on how liberal feminist practices were normalized to mean gender equality and the limits such a concept of gender equality has. Nancy Fraser recently called feminism "capitalism's handmaiden," and liberal feminism, in many ways, facilitates some contradictory patterns of including women while excluding gender (and race, class, sexuality and geography) from the conversation.[23]

"Adding women" via women's inclusion has not been highly transformative because it does not centrally address structural causes of gender inequality—kyriarchical (sexist, racist, heterosexist, and imperialist) structures. As V. Spike Peterson has noted, "One can add women or refer to gender without disrupting orthodox methods or altering foundational questions" and in this way, *adding women's bodies to institutions, adding their perspectives to policies, and adding women as a category of analysis to our studies does not adequately elucidate or challenge how gender shapes such "additions."*[24] A useful analogy is women's inclusion serves as a bandage for a much larger wound of global gendered, raced, classed, heteronormative, and imperialist binary logics and their power in shaping people's lives and political processes more generally. While bandages matter in treating symptoms, they do not necessarily treat the disease, which would require different policy "prescriptions." In this case, policy prescriptions that challenge gendered (read: raced, classed, heteronormative, and imperialist) ways of thinking and gendered institutions and organizations in both formal and informal capacities would better challenge the disease of kyriarchy. Furthermore, these policies actually have reinforced, not just challenged, gender differences and in the process perpetuate a neoliberal world order that continues to subordinate women and other marginalized groups.

It is important to keep in mind there are many types of feminism and many of these types have long engaged in more critical assessments of gender, kyriarchy, and capitalism.[25] This problematizing of "gender = women" is not a new endeavor, and as long as liberal feminism has been promoted, so have critiques been made about it. Sandra Harding in 1987 noted how "add-women" approaches to social science research still kept "androcentric standards firmly in place" resulting in partial or distorted analyses. Sandra Whitworth has written about the depoliticization of gender via gender mainstreaming in the United Nations where including women is actually used to "accommodate existing policies or practices, not transform them."[26] Anne Runyan and V. Spike Peterson argue empowering women has happened alongside "deepening global crises," in which women are a means to an end while gender equality has a narrow meaning of "elevating women."[27] But despite these critiques, international organizations (IOs), states, and many academics continue to call anything including more women "gender equality" and focus primarily on how to better implement such policies and practices by focusing on variable-oriented metrics of "what works."

By focusing on *how* gender equality was normalized via a broad set of narrowly envisioned practices, one can begin to make sense of their limits. These practices are narrowly envisioned because they work within a liberal logic in which including more women is equated with emancipation, despite evidence indicating this is not happening. The goal is then twofold: for those advocating and working for women's advancement and empowerment to change the discussion of what such policies are and can accomplish—that is, to make it known these policies are only a starting point to gender equality, not the end. And the second goal is to push for a (re)imagining of what gender equality could mean both theoretically and in practice.

Some may offer the alternative argument that if these policies were better implemented, then they would lead to gender equality, which follows a liberal feminist logic. While better implementation should be a goal for many of these policies, I contend that it will still only result in better women's inclusion, not gender equality. Gender equality would, at minimum, require a world that values and prioritizes femininities, reproductive and unskilled work, nonviolence, and a host of other feminized values and practices the same way we value masculinized values. One can challenge male domination, which many of these policies do, without challenging masculinities. Said differently, one can change the compostition of the game without significantly changing the game itself. A critical feminist gender equality would challenge binary logics of gender and other socially constructed identities in their entirety, queering the concept and focusing on how it intersects with other identities so what is categorized as within, between, and outside such categories as masculine/feminine gets blurred to the point of no longer existing.

A critical feminist definition of equality would also centralize oppression's multiple faces, of which gender is only one face: one that centers issues of race and ethnicity, (neo)imperialism, class, and sexuality in efforts to dismantle rigid kyriarchical structures upon which neoliberal capitalist order relies.

The Problems with Gender Equality *and* Women's Inclusion

To make coherent sense of all the empirical evidence on add-women/add-gender policies requires a renaming of this global phenomenon as women's inclusion in order to bring analytical gender back into the discussion. When one no longer takes for granted that efforts to include women—via quotas, violence against women policies, and property rights—are gender equality, then *gender* becomes the key explanation for poor adoption and implementation. Gender becomes the key explanation for why states and global institutions co-opt these policies. Gender also becomes the key explanation for why these policies do not adequately disrupt patterns of masculinity and femininity and other social identities. This section further develops five key issues with "gender equality" that a renaming and reframing can expose. The first issue, discussed at length in chapter 2, is poor implementation of woman-centered policies. Despite adopting many policy prescriptions, states and organizations have yet to meet the targeted goals for women's inclusion. In other words, nearly everywhere in the world, women's inclusion still lags. Additionally, poor implementation is indicated in how some states either actively do not adopt these policies, or more commonly, implementation appears to lack resources and political will.

Most large-N quantitative studies focus entirely on this first issue, focusing on correlations between policy adoption/implementation and particular variables that explain variation—variables often framed as "gender equality." These large studies then become the "common knowledge" in understanding how to include more women. However, correlation is not causation and while variables may explain how to better include more women, they do not usually explain *why* certain factors matter in the ways they do. For example, research indicates sufficient resource allocation affects the "success" of many of these policies being implemented. But this begs the question: Why are sufficient resources not allocated in the first place? Additionally, if "political will" matters so much for implementing violence against women policies or quota implementation, why isn't there sufficient political will among the powerful to fully implement women's inclusion? It is precisely at this point in analyses in which gender as an analytical tool is indispensable in making sense of these patterns of cumulative state adoption.

The second issue with gender equality focuses on women's "bounded agency," or how informal beliefs and practices shape the implementation of, and women's experiences within, their inclusion. Women exercise their power and authority despite being bounded by male- and masculine-dominated institutions. Often the resistance women face in such institutions is not formal, but the result of interactions with other human beings who carry their own (often sexist) beliefs and ideas. Political scientist Somita Basu, in her work on agency and security, cites Karin Fierke's definition for agency as "the potential for the individual or state [or any institution] to influence their environment as well as to be influenced by it." Basu explains that "agents are both constrained and enabled by structural factors," such as "rules and resources."[28] In other words, women influence their environments but these interactions do not exist in a cultural or political vacuum. Rather, agency is exerted in a bounded environment. Those "bounds" are often informal, and include people and their beliefs, informal norms and rules, and institutional memory or standard operating procedures. While these "bounds" may change as a result of an agent's actions, they are often strongly, even if not entirely obviously, gendered, and they indicate a pattern of behavior-shaping policy implementation. For example, while women wield power in political office, exercise their rights to work and own property, or challenge abusive home lives, they do so despite serious informal beliefs about women's competency or what actually constitutes "violence" against women.

The third issue with gender equality and women's inclusion focuses on the ways in which women's inclusion reinforces and is reinforced by gendered binaries and gender roles. Gendered binaries can be understood as the categorizations of masculinized and feminized values in which masculinities are valued over femininities. Gendered binaries are not just about male/female or man/woman, but the values we associate with sex differences. These binaries include strong/weak; rational/emotional; breadwinner/homemaker; protector/protected; independent/dependent; public/private—all in which the latter are associated with masculinities while the former with femininities.[29] These binaries then shape behaviors and gender roles, in which men and women become associated with particular behaviors based on such binaries. This is strongly linked with women's bounded agency, as many of the informal beliefs and practices result from assumptions about gender. But this reason elucidates more deeply how beliefs and practices are tied to particular "scripts" and expectations about men and women.

Importantly, masculinities and femininities are multiple and while hierarchies generally privilege masculinity over femininity, there are hierarchies within each, including subordinated masculinities.[30] While gendered binaries are fluid, shaped by time and place, and women may be masculinized and men feminized, generally the expectation is for men to produce the script of masculine and women feminine. These gender roles remain immensely powerful and, despite that many of these policies are adopted to challenge gender roles, often the justification for and implementation of woman-centered policy actually buttresses gendered logics and roles. For example, women in office are often expected to act differently (read: according to traditional ideas about women). One major force shaping many of these policies is found in prevalent heteronormative assumptions about families, in which women's roles shape their access to resources and power.

The fourth issue, also deeply interdependent with gendered binaries, is the poor engagement with the complexities of gender as an intersectional identity shaped by race and ethnicity, class, sexuality, and geography.[31] In other words, we are seeing a failure to ask "which women" are helped and hurt by these policy efforts. Kimberlé Crenshaw coined the term "intersectionality" to denote the need to think about how different types of discrimination interact, particularly for women of color.[32] She wrote: "I used the concept of intersectionality to denote the various ways in which race and gender interact to shape the multiple dimension of Black women's . . . experiences" and it is about "the need to account for multiple grounds of identity when considering how the social world is constructed."[33] Intersectionality is meant to capture the idea that people are constituted by multiple, complex, and intertwined identities. These complex identities inform and shape our experiences. One does not experience sex void of also experiencing race, class, sexuality and "place"—we sit "at the intersection of many categories."[34] Intersectionality means one does not treat identities as a mathematical equation, adding and subtracting identities to understand one's experiences. While some identities may change in salience in particular contexts, social identities inform one another. Intersectional analyses have been important in the feminist movement for challenging white women's feminism and Western dominance. It exposed how experiences of women of color were not the same as many white women because race impacts one's sex and gender in fundamental ways.[35]

While many of these policies discussed in this book have helped women, they may only help a small number of women, sometimes reinforcing class and racial distinctions by rendering these identities invisible in conversations and analyses about "gender equality." For example, women's inclusion in government institutions usually promotes elite women, and sex quotas may not engage how race and ethnicity inform representation. Additionally, policies promoting women's land ownership often rely upon heteronormative assumptions about marriage, which is cost-prohibitive for many and problematic in more complicated kinship arrangements.

The final issue with gender equality focuses on the combined effects of these previous issues in how women's inclusion does not adequately engage all the ways "gender equality" and its liberal feminist policies have been co-opted by global institutions and may actually re-enforce gender differences and a gendered, neoliberal world order. Rather than promote women out of justice and equality claims, global institutions and states advocate for these policies because of sometimes-problematic beliefs about women's inherent nature, or in the name of state productivity and stability. Women play a central role in neoliberal world order because this system relies upon inequality to function, and gendered logics and practices are one way to generate inequality. What I mean is that neoliberal world order requires cheap, disposable labor, and pliable, manipulatable governance: there have to be some "haves" and many "have nots" to generate economic wealth for some individuals, corporations, and states. This neoliberal system of inequality is generated through devaluing particular social identities and particular geographical locations. This is most evident in the association of women's inclusion with "good governance" and economic growth.

In terms of "good governance," the idea is that women make for more stable and less corrupt regimes *because they are women*. As evidenced in chapter 4, women are valued as government agents because of assumptions about their femininities as honest and community-oriented. Women's inclusion is also a central tenant of current economic growth discourses, in which the latest slogan is "gender equality is smart economics." But when these policies are promoted as gender equality, they do little to challenge a gendered, raced, classed, heteronormative, and imperialist world order. In other words, gender is often reinforced when states and IOs promote women *because they are women*. Ultimately, the global order relies on and perpetuates masculinized and feminized gender roles to meet other ends that may ultimately subjugate women and other marginalized groups.

Outline of the Book

This book traces the normalization of gender equality by focusing on how woman-centered policies and discourses adopted over the last forty years are better described as women's inclusion. In order to do this, the book first presents the problem(s) with gender equality in chapter 2. This chapter outlines the empirical trajectories and limits of various policies and how they have been pursued in the name of "gender equality." It then introduces women's inclusion and explains why it is a necessary intervention to the rhetoric of gender equality. Women's inclusion—framed as a liberal feminist norm embodying the ideals of *representation, recognition,* and *protection*—is key to later chapters, which deal more specifically with representation of women in government, the recognition of women's economic rights, and the protection of women from direct violence.

Chapter 3 maps out how gender equality came to be associated with policies to "add women." It traces the normalization of gender equality in global discourses over the last forty years by examining the language used to outline how states should address women's exclusion. It identifies dual, yet dueling, narratives regarding women's inclusion. The first narrative is a quite radical and feminist narrative identifying the need for a new world order to challenge the current one that has perpetuated domination of women and other marginalized groups and states. The second narrative treats women as a means to a more peaceful, prosperous, and secure world. In this second narrative, gender is a technocratic "shortcut" to acknowledging women's subordination without deeply interrogating its structural causes. The development of these two narratives are traced through the texts of the four United Nations (UN) women's conferences (1975, 1980, 1985, and 1995), as well as the Geneva Conventions, Convention on the Elimination of all Forms of Discrimination against Women (CEDAW), Declaration on the Elimination of

Violence against Women, and United Nations Security Council Resolution 1325. Women's inclusion is articulated through efforts to promote women's representation, recognition, and protection, although often vaguely and without clear mandates for all involved.

Chapter 4 focuses on the push for greater representation of women in government via several practices to "add women" to all branches of government—including sex quotas, policy agencies, and more recent pushes to increase the number of women heads of government and judges. In focusing on discussions about what conditions seem to better predict women's inclusion, similar patterns emerge in which women are more likely to be in government where the offices are less competitive, where women are insulated from the public, and when women are well-connected politically. The chapter ends with an overview of the treatment of women's inclusion and representation as a "good governance" strategy, which, rather than challenging gender roles, actually relies on them to explain why women are good for government.

Chapter 5 focuses on the recognition of women's economic rights via policies to improve women's employment, property, inheritance, and credit rights. This is done under the rubric of "women as smart economics," in which various international organizations promote women's inclusion in formal economic activities because it is good for growth and development. But this instrumentalist treatment of women's inclusion in formal economic activity is shaped by employment segregation, the type of legal system in a state, and heteronormative assumptions about family structures and resources. Ultimately, the focus on adding women as smart economics has reinforced masculine/feminine dichotomies within the global neoliberal order. To illustrate this, the end of the chapter focuses on three central issues with current economic models, including the gendered nature of microfinance, the "productivity trap" in what "counts" as work, and the centrality of gendered patterns of crisis and austerity in global capitalism.

Chapter 6 turns to policies to protect women from direct violence. This includes domestic efforts but also on a broader, global scale, especially in "post-conflict" environments. The movement to increase women's personal security is evidenced by state adoption of violence against women policies, but also efforts to implement United Nations Security Council Resolution 1325 on Women, Peace, and Security. What emerges from the push for violence against women legislation in states and conflict environments is the consistent need for an active feminist movement, women's policy agencies, and imposition of women's inclusion by other actors. A deeper look into these explanations exposes persistent ideas that violence is a women's issue and a "private affair." These ideas shape implementation and reinforce beliefs about masculinities and domination. Ending violence against women in everyday life and post-conflict situations are promoted as an important growth and development strategy—fighting violence against women is, again, "good governance." But such links between violence and political economy obscure the ways in which economic development itself has actually destabilized gender via the feminization of economies; subsequently, violence is actually used to re-stabilize gender, contrary to the logic of women's empowerment through development. This problem of governance is also evident in post-conflict peacebuilding in which violence against women is being "securitized" and even fetishized by the global community, which shapes women's narratives of violence.

The book's conclusion, in addition to summing up the ideas and problems discussed throughout, focuses on a few other important points not fully addressed in earlier chapters. One is the violent backlash these policies generate. Clearly men and maleness are being challenged in some capacity; otherwise there would not be a need to lash out, usually with violence, against those advocating for policy changes. The second point is to further consider what policy ideas out there now among states could be considered as tied to "gender equality." In this capacity I reference policies to add legal genders, protect reproductive justice, and challenge militarization as possible examples of where "gender equality" should head.

Methodology for the Book

To problematize gender equality and understand women's inclusion, this book engages, in a broad sense, a critical feminist methodology. I understand methodology to mean "the intellectual process guiding reflections about the relationship" between epistemology, ontology, and methods.[36] More specifically, my epistemology (understanding of knowledge) is that knowledge is gendered, or shaped by the subjectivities of masculine/

feminine binaries in ways that obscure women's lived experiences. While the analyses here are situated primarily at the state and global levels, I engage a social ontology and reject the usual statist ontological assumptions of states as individual and autonomous actors.[37] That is, I am interested in how particular relationships between states and women have been fostered through particular policies and practices, and how these relationships are deeply shaped by (gendered) power dynamics and hierarchies. To do this, the book engages feminist, constructivist, poststructuralist, postcolonial, comparative, and quantitative theories and research. I do not present original data, but rather have generated deep and complex analyses based on the plethora of already existing research and data on "gender equality."

This book draws on a variety of methods (tools of research).[38] In chapter 2, I rely primarily on descriptive statistics, illustrating how these policies and practices have diffused over the last forty years. To build these figures, I use data and databases from various sources, including International IDEA's Quota Project database; United Nations Secretary-General's database on violence against women; Uppsala Conflict Data Program; Transitional Justice Institute; Women, Business, and the Law database; and the Inter-Parliamentary Union, among others. I also draw on data produced by other researchers. This chapter also includes a critical feminist analysis of research on gender equality in the social sciences, particularly political science. In addition, chapter 2 presents the theory and elements of women's inclusion, drawing heavily upon democratic and feminist theory. Chapter 3 uses textual and critical discourse analysis to explore how women's inclusion has produced particular policy outcomes and meanings through a careful reading of United Nations documents produced over the last forty years. Textual analysis is the interpretation of meanings produced through particular texts.[39] Critical discourse analysis, similarly, may use texts to understand how language is used to produce particular realities, often reflecting particular power dynamics. In this case, these texts produce gender equality to have particular meanings and values, manifested in certain policy objectives.

Chapters 4 through 6 use an analytical gender lens—here understood as a critical reading—of current research on different aspects of women's inclusion. The analyses "read between the lines" of large-scale studies to locate and elucidate how "gender" operates. This means not only examining the findings about what factors (variables) promote women's inclusion, but re-reading through a gender lens and asking *why* certain variables may matter. For example, violence against women laws are more prevalent in states that have an active feminist movement, but why?[40] Underlying this variable of a feminist movement are informal beliefs about violence against women being a "women's issue." There are no institutional rules that women must, or men cannot, advocate for violence against women policies, but informally this happens. In these chapters I also engage with an array of case-specific studies on these policies and their effects. It is through in-depth analyses of the politics of policy adoption and implementation, where similarities emerge that may not be captured in large studies, and explanations for findings in large-N studies are actually fleshed out. This is also where I explore these informal practices that are not captured by variables, but directly impact them.

Conclusion

It is important to note, up front, the potential pitfalls in engaging in a critical feminist critique of feminist ideas and movements. Although what follows here is a critical analysis of this campaign aimed at helping women over the last forty years, it is not meant to diminish the work of feminist activists to force states to deal with women's exclusion and increase their rights and perspectives. Rather, it is to shift the discourse surrounding such efforts and to reconsider what women's inclusion can accomplish.

There are two potential "traps" I have tried to avoid in writing this book. The first trap is how to offer critique without obscuring the "success" of such policies. While advocating for women's inclusion is essential, it is often treated as the end goal, rather than one means to a more gender-equitable end. Even if one does not agree with my claims that these policies will not promote gender equality, it is still useful to have the empirical claims and analyses about why certain variables matter and how binary gender persists. One wishes to avoid being criticized for focusing on what is not working, when some things have improved for some women. These policies should be treated as both successful and unsuccessful; my argument is to shift the discourse on what sort of success is being achieved by calling it "women's inclusion" rather than "gender equality."

While it is important to continue to push states to better implement these policies, it is also a critical moment to imagine what the next forty years of feminist policy activism can look like. What is gender equality in practice if the world is already working on women's inclusion? What will it take to adequately challenge gendered logics and intersectional oppression?

The second potential "trap" is how this critique could be co-opted by those wishing to reverse, challenge, or turn back the movement. These policies have helped countless women: *women and the world would be worse-off without feminist activist efforts and these policies.* Woman-centered policies can and do work, but they work to challenge male domination more than promote gender equality. Such policies focus on the presence of men and the dominance of their preferences in governmental and legal institutions. This is evidenced by the increased desire on the behalf of states and international organizations to be seen as women-friendly and "gender aware." No one can interpret this as a failure or as an unnecessary aspiration. But there is room for improvement and room for more critical feminist ideas and approaches to what constitutes equality in such an unequal world.

The goal is to preserve the term "gender equality" for policies that do more than add women—for policies that fundamentally challenge how we think and organize ourselves in this world, and not just based on sex and gender, but other identities that fundamentally shape our experiences of both. At minimum, it would include efforts to value equally what is considered "feminine" or perhaps more importantly, dissolve binary thinking so as to better engage the continuums informing people's lived experiences. Women's inclusion should be treated as an important step, but only a step, and often a troubling one, in a larger movement to challenge the unequal structural forces of sex, race and ethnicity, class, sexuality, and geography that organize and valorize humans in unjust and unequal ways. By reframing the discourse on sex quotas, policy agencies, property and employment rights, and violence against women legislation by associating them with women's inclusion rather than gender equality, one can shift the discourse to focus on what these policies can (and do) accomplish and why they are not sufficient to destabilize a global, kyriarchical, neoliberal world order.

2

Gender Equality and the Illusion of Progress

The term "gender equality" remains a key phrase in the global discourses on progress, democracy, security, and development. It is even now a Sustainable Development Goal (number five). Gender equality is also a popular variable and topic of discourse in research about women and women's rights, even among critical feminist scholarship. Research on "gender equality" in a global context comprises a robust research agenda; for both scholars and policy analysts, this has been the case since the late twentieth century.[1] This research offers useful insights into how women may be better included, focusing on both formal and informal institutions shaping women's access and opportunities. But, as I will argue throughout this book, much of this work is based upon uncritical and essentialist ideas about gender, equality, and progress that are rooted in larger assumptions of liberal feminism and neoliberalism, which ultimately affect the interpretation of theories and results.[2]

When one looks to define, measure, and discuss gender equality, there are a variety of possible means to do so. One may look at policies meant to enact it; particular variables in quantitative models; or index measures to rank states. This chapter engages all these means for approaching gender equality, though with an emphasis on the policies and practices that states adopt. This chapter introduces the reader to these policies and practices further discussed throughout the book, and illustrates empirically how widespread they have become. It focuses on policies and practices in three key areas: promoting women in government, encouraging their inclusion in the economy, and protecting women from violence. To promote women in government, states have created women's bureaucratic agencies; states and political parties have also adopted sex quotas to promote women in the legislature. There has also been an increased effort in many states to promote women into top positions as judges and heads of government. To promote women's economic rights, states have changed employment, property, and credit laws. And finally, states have adopted policies addressing different forms of violence against women, including intimate partner and domestic violence, trafficking, sexual harassment, and sexual assault. These violence against women policies have been further extended to conflict zones and in efforts to promote peace, which are also discussed. This chapter seeks to complicate the meaning of gender equality more generally and the problematic ways it is theorized and measured. It then introduces women's inclusion as an alternative framing of these policies. It explores the theoretical foundations of women's inclusion—representation, recognition, and protection. It concludes with a discussion of the issues of promoting women's inclusion in a neoliberal world order.

The Global Promotion of "Gender Equality"

The patterns of adoption and diffusion of policies aimed at promoting women all follow similar trajectories. In the 1970s, few states had policies to increase women in government, ensure their economic well-being, or criminalize violence specifically targeting women. But slowly a few states began to adopt such practices through the 1980s and, by the mid-1990s, many more states had adopted such policies, often after encouragement through international conferences and conventions. In most cases these policies are found in well over 50 percent of states and for some practices of women's inclusion, such as women's policy bureaus and violence against women policies, nearly all countries have adopted such protocols. This section explores the data on women's inclusion, including the global trajectories of change over time.

Women's Representation in Government

Perhaps the most well-studied policies and practices focus on the promotion of women in government. These include women's policy bureaus, which serve to promote women's issues at the national level as part of the executive branch of government; sex quotas in legislatures; and the growing practices of promoting more women judges, cabinet ministers, and heads of government. Over one hundred countries have sex quotas or women's policy bureaus. The percentages of women legislators have quadrupled since 1960 and doubled since 1995.[3] Today the number of states without any women in the legislature has dwindled to only six (mainly island nations and oil monarchies). In the early 1990s this number was at least double and perhaps as much as four times as high.[4] The number of women in ministry-level positions has steadily increased since the mid-1970s and there has been a sharp decline in all-male cabinets from 70 percent in 1979 to about 17 percent in 2009 to about 8 percent in 2015.[5] The world has had more female leaders in the last fifteen years than the rest of modern history combined. The number of female judges is also on the rise. Studies indicate many of these women in power believe their presence has changed the priorities of their party and the government to the benefit of women.[6] A look at figure 2.1 illustrates these upwards trends.

Starting in the early 1990s, diffusion dynamics changed in terms of the types of states adopting quotas and the types of quotas being adopted. Between 1990 and 1994, equal numbers of democratic and non-democratic states adopted quotas and half of the non-democratic states had recently experienced a democratic transition prior to adoption.[7] While party quotas remain the most common, both legislative and reserved-seat quotas emerged during this time. The diffusion of sex quotas gained momentum beginning in 1995. And between 1995 and 1999, twenty-seven states adopted quotas. While most states with quotas were democratic, nearly one-third of them had only recently become democratic. Additionally, 40 percent of the quotas adopted during this time were legislative and reserved-seat quotas, which have stronger mandates than party quotas because they are legal mandates.

Beginning in 2000 there is a significant shift in the nature of the diffusion. It is at this point that primarily non-democratic states began adopting quotas—many of which had experienced a prior transition (nearly 40 percent). Thirty-four states gained some form of quota between 2000 and 2004; two-thirds of these states were non-democracies. Roughly 56 percent of the quotas adopted in this time period were either legislative or reserved-seat quotas. Since 2005 the adoption of quotas have tailed off, but sex quotas appear to be having greater impacts on increasing women in government, especially since 2005.[8] Today, over one hundred countries have an electoral quota, and nearly 120 states in the global system have some form of sex quota.[9]

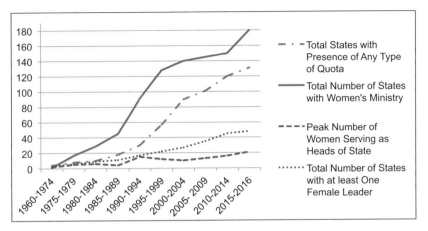

Figure 2.1. Global Trends in Women's Representation. Source: This chart has been developed using data from Krook 2009; Paxton and Hughes 2014; International IDEA, Inter-Parliamentary Union, and Stockholm University 2016; and Christensen 2016.

There is less information available about women judges, though current projects are underway to collect it. Among OECD countries (Organisation for Economic Cooperation and Development), the average percent of women serving on high courts is 23 percent, though the range is from 0 to 60 percent.[10] The European Union did a self-study indicating 50 percent of its judges were women.[11] Larger studies beyond OECD find the same average of 23 percent women on high courts.[12]

The number of women in the executive branch quadrupled in the 1990s and 2000s and 75 percent of female presidents and prime ministers joined the office in the last twenty or so years.[13] In total, from 1960 to 2010, seventy-nine women were national leaders in fifty-eight countries. These women have primarily served as prime ministers and twelve countries have had multiple women leaders (one-third of the nations with women leaders had more than one national leader).[14] As of 2016, twenty-four women were leaders of their countries, nine women were heads of state, and fifteen were heads of government, totaling about 14 percent globally.[15]

Recognizing Women's Economic Rights

Women's economic rights include policies meant to increase women's access to material resources, such as employment, inheritance, credit, and land. Recognition of women's economic rights often receives less attention in global politics (and in the study of global politics) than women's representation in government and the protection of women from violence. But the growing emphasis on the links between women's "economic empowerment" and states' economic growth and development have been a cornerstone of both developed and developing states, especially in the last twenty years. As the International Labour Organization (ILO) stated in their 2015 annual report: "There is a need to re-focus attention on gender equality and women's economic empowerment as an issue of fundamental human rights and a key driver for global progress."[16] The World Bank's 2012 *Gender Equality and Development* cites important gains made among women in the last several years in indicators such as education and poverty rates. The "gender gap" in education is disappearing and even reversing: two-thirds of states have "gender parity" in primary education and in one-third of states, girls actually outnumber boys.[17] Education is considered a key aspect of improving women's overall access to material resources and employment.

Globally, poverty rates have declined and the number of people living on less than $1.25 a day has decreased from 1.8 billion in 1990 to 1.4 billion in 2005.[18] Women's participation in the labor force has also increased over the last forty years, where the gender gap has narrowed from thirty-two to twenty-six points from 1980 to 2008—and by 2008, women accounted for 40 percent of the global workforce.[19] Fertility rates are also on the decline and women's life expectancy has increased in developing states by twenty to twenty-five years, so women now outlive men "in every region of the world." The report outlines the changes in these terms:

> Women's lives have improved greatly over the past decades. Enjoying even higher education, women have greater control over their life choices. They use those choices to participate more in the labor force; have fewer children; diversify their time beyond housework and childcare; and shape their communities.[20]

Over the last forty years the recognition and adoption of policies to promote women's economic rights is considered a key aspect of these changes. The idea is that working, owning property, and having access to credit greatly benefits women, their families, and their state. Based on this logic, a growing number of states have passed laws to improve women's access to property, credit, and employment. A recent report on women's property rights found that one-half of the limits on women's economic rights in the 1960s were removed by states by 2010.[21] This means out of their sample of seventy-five countries who restricted women's property, credit, and work rights in the 1960s, only forty-seven still had some restraints and twenty-eight had removed all legal restraints.

Figure 2.2 indicates that since 1960 there has been a steady increase in the number of policies adopted by states meant to improve women's property and financial rights. This means that in the 1960s women had few legal rights to employment, credit, or property. The greatest increases are in a woman's right to get a job without male permission and property rights for both married and unmarried women. The figure indicates that there have been over one hundred policy changes increasing women's property rights among states since the 1960s. The findings indicate that out of one hundred countries, sixty-three states have adopted one or more policies granting married women control over property and forty-seven have changed or added polices granting unmarried women more property rights. Nearly sixty states have also adopted one or more policies granting women the right to work and open a bank account without male permission, and about the same number have adopted laws requiring equal inheritance access for daughters and sons.[22] According to the United Nations, many states increased women's property and inheritance rights to equal men's between 1990 and 2010, especially in Western and Central Europe, the Americas, and parts of Central and East Asia.[23] The scholars who collected the data used in figure 2.3— Mary Hallward-Driemeier, Tazeen Hasan, and Anca Bogdana Rusu— noted there were positive trends in promoting women's economic equal rights nearly everywhere in the world. They also noted how Eastern Europe and Central Asian states did not have many legal barriers to begin with (those states probably accounting for the pre-1960 numbers), and OECD states, which began with severe inequalities, removed all of them by 2010.[24] In the United States, for example, a woman had to bring a man to cosign credit applications and had her wages "count" sometimes as much as 50 percent less than a man's until the Equal Credit Act in 1974; further, until a court decision in 1981, men could take out second mortgages on houses without their wives knowing.[25]

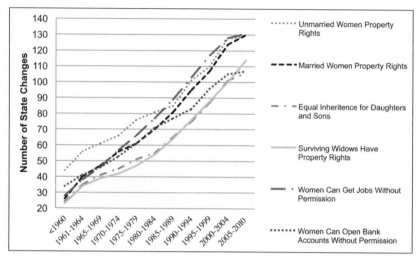

Figure 2.2. Changes in Women's Property and Financial Rights Policies from 1960–2010. Source: This figure was constructed using data from the World Bank *Women, Business, and the Law* website. The dataset is titled "Historical Data: 50 Years of Women's Legal Rights," available at wbl.worldbank.org. The data cover one hundred economies from 1960 to 2010, so the data are a sample and do not include all cases, though a look at the countries indicates a fairly representative sample based on level of economic development, legal system type, and region.

Today, most countries have outlawed sex-based employment discrimination, such as prohibitions against night work, overtime, and the types of work women can do. And while in 1975 only one-third of countries had equal pay laws, this increased to 86 percent by 2005.[26] Today, nearly one-half of working-age women are in the labor force. Updated data on women's economic rights indicate most states are finding ways to ensure women's access to employment, property, and personal finances.[27] Figure 2.3 illustrates that out of 114 countries measured, most guarantee unmarried women have property rights. And nearly two-thirds of states ensure married women have access to property rights, equal inheritance for sons and daughters, and that married women can work and have their own bank accounts. A 2013 report from the World Economic Forum, which measures "gender gaps" in countries based on economic participation, education, health, and political empowerment, found that of one hundred countries studied since 2006, 86 percent of them have

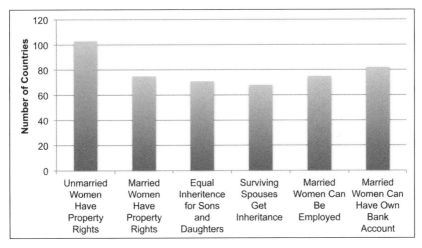

Figure 2.3. Number of Countries with Women's Economic Rights Laws as of 2015 (N = 114). Source: Figure configured using data from Hallward-Driemeier, Hasan, and Rusu 2013a.

diminished gaps, indicating that many women have improved access to employment opportunities, more credit, and more property and economic access.[28]

Protecting Women From Violence

The final of these common areas of "gender equality" policy is the effort to eradicate violence against women domestically and in post-conflict situations. The violence against women movement has been a multi-faceted and arduous battle to get states, organizations, and everyday citizens to recognize and report violence directed specifically at women and girls, and to give women and girls resources to leave such violence. Today most states have passed at least some policies criminalizing violence against women (about 95 percent) and among these a significant minority have addressed all four main forms of violence against women (sexual violence, domestic violence, sexual harassment, and trafficking of women). As the pervasiveness of violence against women became more visible, states and the international community felt pressure to address the epidemic. A look at figure 2.4 indicates they have taken steps to do so, in large numbers.

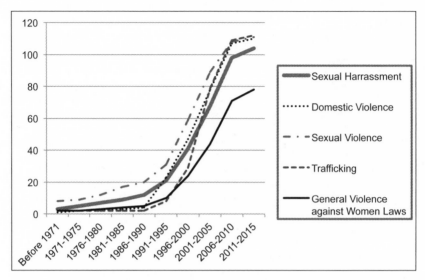

Figure 2.4. Global Diffusion of Violence against Women Legislation. Source: The data for this chart was collected from UN Women's (2016b) *Global Database on Violence against Women.*

Figure 2.4 illustrates that states did not begin to adopt violence against women legislation in significant numbers until the mid-1990s. As scholars have noted, while violence against women was definitely part of the transnational women's movement in the 1970s, activists faced resistance through the 1980s and it was not until the mid-1990s that states began to systematically criminalize this violence.[29] Figure 2.5 indicates 42 percent of countries have legislation dealing with all four forms of violence against women and another 26 percent have three categories—meaning that today, two-thirds of states in the world have institutionalized violence against women policy within their legal systems. According to the UN, 119 countries have passed domestic violence laws and 125 have laws prohibiting sexual harassment.[30]

This movement to elucidate, publicize, and penalize violence against women has been essential in providing women with better legal and cultural tools to talk about and address their experiences. The promotion of these policies and practices has been important in challenging the public/private dichotomy that rendered violence against women "personal," "private," and an accepted part of life for many women. It also led to the

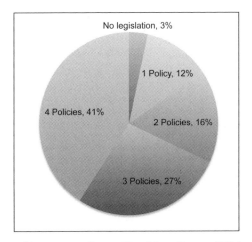

Figure 2.5. Percent of States According to How Many Forms of Violence against Women Are Criminalized (N= 147). Source: Data collected from UN Women's (2016b) *Global Database on Violence against Women.*

opening of battered women's shelters and resource networks important for women to have means to remove themselves from lives of violence. It also gave women legal tools to fight harassment in the workplace.

Figure 2.6 presents another aspect of the diffusion, which is the changing government response to violence against women. Political scientists Mala Htun and S. Laurel Weldon created a "Government Response Index" to violence against women that focuses on five categories of possible response: services for victims, legal reforms, programs targeting vulnerable populations, training for violence against women professionals, and prevention programs and administrative reforms.[31] Using these categories, they created an additive ten-point scale and assessed seventy countries at four points in time. What this interpretation of their data indicates is not only are more specific policies being adopted, but governments are increasingly dealing with violence against women using a multi-pronged approach via policies, training, services, and programming. In 1975 most states had no government response, but by 2005 this drops to only four states without a response in place. Additionally, the number of states who are addressing violence against women via multiple avenues has also increased, with almost half of their cases scoring a seven or higher. In a similar fashion to the adoption of sex quotas, where the degree of the mandates has increased over time, a similar argument can be made here: the strength of the mandate, indicated by higher index scores, also appears to be diffusing.

There is specific data on trafficking of women worth examining as well.[32] In 2003, the UN adopted the *Protocol to Prevent, Suppress, and Punish Trafficking in Persons, Especially Women,* the first "globally legally binding instrument with an agreed definition of trafficking in persons."[33] The first report assessing the protocol's impact, *Global Report on Trafficking in Persons,* found the Protocol to be having an impact, at least at the policy level. When the Protocol was passed in 2003, only one-third of the 155 states for which data was available had any legislation against human trafficking. The report goes on to identify how over one-half reported "at least one human trafficking prosecution," and seventy-three countries reported "at least one conviction." Importantly, the report also identified that among convicted traffickers, women were convicted at much higher rates than all other crimes in many countries (though many states did not record such information). The report indicated this was the first time such a question was being addressed in regards to trafficking.[34] According to the United States State Department, today 158 countries have signed and 110 countries have ratified the treaty.[35] As of 2016, one hundred countries have criminalized trafficking in their domestic legal systems.[36]

Violence against women legislation has targeted the home, the workplace, and public spaces more generally. More recently policies and practices have targeted "extraordinary" violence in conflict and post-natural disasters. Because women's access to traditional "security" remained male-dominated and male-centered, especially during conflict, this area became a central focus for women's activism and in 2000 culminated with the adoption of the United Nations Security Council Resolution 1325 (UNSCR 1325). UNSCR 1325 acts as an internationally binding policy to acknowledge and remedy women's exclusion from traditional security apparatuses and discourses. This move was motivated, in part, by the pervasive sexual violence in armed conflicts in the 1990s. Women in conflict, with the support of the international community, publicized how rape was actually used as a weapon of war. Conservative estimates suggest 20,000 to 50,000 women were raped during the 1992–1995 war in Bosnia and Herzegovina, and 250,000 to 500,000 during the 1994 Rwandan genocide.[37] While do-

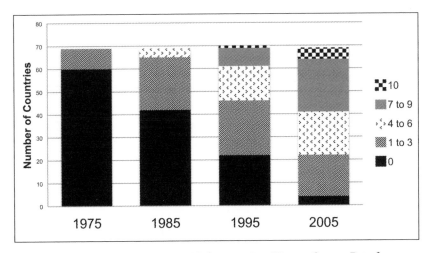

Figure 2.6. Government Responses to Violence against Women. Source: Data from Htun and Weldon 2012.

mestic violence against women policy and women's security during conflict are often not treated as similar issues (though much scholarship today emphasizes their link), the efforts to publicize and challenge the acts of violence against women during war would not have happened without the efforts to end violence against women in states.[38]

Resolution 1325 matters in the context of violence against women because it focuses on women's protection and is entirely about how to include more women in security practices. It has the same logic (add-women/gender) and politics (compromises with major powers) of inclusion that made general violence against women policies possible. The goal in treating UNSCR 1325 as a policy instrument to address violence against women, and thus another part of women's inclusion, is to identify the similar explanations for adoption and implementation, as well as the limits to its effectiveness.

Through a careful reading of UNSCR 1325, one can argue that it too promotes inclusion in many of the same ways identified more generally in this book. The underlying goal of including more women is that their inclusion will help promote peace and security, and the Resolution outlines the well-known ways in which to accomplish this.

In an assessment of all civil conflict-related peace agreements beginning in 1991 through 2014, using the rubric of inclusion set forth in

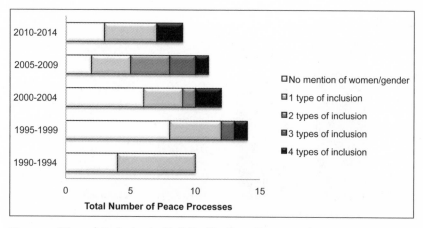

Figure 2.7. Women's Inclusion in Civil Conflict Peace Processes. Source: Figure constructed using data from the following: Harbom, Högbladh and Wallensteen 2006; Högbladh 2012; Bell and O'Rourke 2010; United Nations 2014.

UNSCR 1325, the results show similar patterns as the general violence against women legislation.[39] More and more peace processes are including provisions regarding women's inclusion over time, as illustrated in figure 2.7. In addition to an increase in the overall number of peace processes promoting women's inclusion, more peace processes are including multiple aspects of this inclusion, including representation, recognition, protection, and incorpation.

The first measure of increased women's inclusion in peace processes is the changing ratio of those peace processes that make *any* provisions for women. In the early 1990s more than half of peace processes included at least one category of inclusion; this dips between 1995 and 2000, and remains rather low until 2005. After 2005 there seems to be a sharp increase in the number of peace agreements acknowledging women's inclusion—nine of eleven processes. This again declined since 2010, with six of nine agreements including provisions for women's security, though the number of processes promoting women's inclusion appears more entrenched in global peacebuilding endeavors, though clearly not fully entrenched by any measure.

Figure 2.7 also shows that not only is the number of agreements with any provisions for women increasing, but agreements seem to also include more dimensions of inclusion. Prior to 2005 most peace agreements included only one dimension (predominantly, recognition of women as a special group), but by 2005 over one-half included more than one category of women's inclusion in peace processes. Security for women is addressed using multiple strategies. But in the last five years, the majority of those with provisions for women have only included one category and of these, three had to do with protection from sexual violence (in the cases of Central African Republic, Democratic Republic of Congo, Mali, and South Sudan, representation was included as well). Among these that include all types of inclusion, the "quality" seems to have increased after 2005, as most of those with provisions for women include multiple properties. The Sudan-Darfur, Ugandan, and the Philippines' peace agreements contain all the categories. This illiustrates that the violence against women movement has even affected strategies in the post-conflict context. But, as will become evident in the next sections, women still remained more excluded than included in peace processes despite the consistent and powerful lobbying of those working around UNSCR 1325.

What all of these figures and data show is that states have been doing a lot to try to deal with women's exclusion, domination, and insecurity. These changes have resulted from the hard work of women activists pressuring international organizations to prioritize and publicize, and states to respond to, these demands. The value of having such laws should not be underestimated, for countless numbers of women have been served through such legal protections. But despite all these policies and practices, and our attempts to understand and improve gender equality, both the efforts and discussions surrounding them need some critical feminist attention. When one looks more deeply into "the numbers," their limits emerge. While one may anticipate it takes time for policies to have effects, in most cases these policies and practices discussed throughout the book have been part of state legal codes for at least fifteen to twenty years. However, despite such entrenchment, their implementation and effects have yet to make momentous impacts. Many women still face significant discrimination and insecurity nearly everywhere in the world.

Gender? Equality?

Despite all of these efforts to include women, the concept of "gender equality" has its problems. More generally, even with the diffusion of

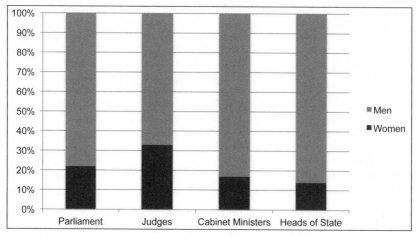

Figure 2.8. Global Averages of Women and Men in Public Offices, 2014. Source: UN Women 2016a; Christensen 2016.

sex quotas, the creation of women's policy bureaus, and the promotion of women in the executive and judiciary sectors, the global numbers still tell a rather unsatisfactory story: women represent about one in five parliamentarians, one in three judges, one in six cabinet ministers, and one in ten heads of state (see figure 2.8). Only twenty-four women are currently heads of state/government, but most nations have never had a female leader.[40] Only thirty-four countries have more than thirty percent women in parliament, while only twenty-one countries have 30 percent or more women cabinet ministers.[41] These numbers both represent declines from 2014, where thirty-five states had more than 30 percent women in parliament and twenty-eight states had more than 30 percent women cabinet ministers.[42] Despite the fact the percentage of women in parliament has doubled in the last twenty years, the global rate is only 23 percent.[43] And despite yearly increases in the number of women cabinet ministers, globally, women only account for 17.7 percent of all government ministers; this is only an increase of 3.5 percent since 2005.[44]

Generally, while women are participating in greater numbers in the economy nearly everywhere, their "productivity" and earnings remain much lower than men nearly everywhere. The pay gap globally is 24 percent, ranging regionally between 14 percent in the Middle East and

North Africa, to 33 percent in South Asia.[45] In all regions of the world women still do more unpaid work than men.[46] And "women work more than men once all productive (housework, care, and market) activities are taken into account."[47]

Poverty, too, remains highly sexed. In one UN study, out of twenty-five developing states (primarily in Africa and Asia), in twenty-two of them women were more likely to live in poverty *because* they are women; another study specifically on Latin America found similar results.[48] And this does not take into account wealth distribution within households in which women were much less likely to earn a cash income (18 percent versus 57 percent), so women may also live in poverty even in a household that is not considered poor.[49] Despite the fact 1.6 billion women depend on farming for their livelihoods, in all developing regions they own significantly less land, ranging between 5 to 18 percent.[50]

Even macro measures of economic rights of women indicate little substantive change over time. The World Economic Forum's 2014 *Gender Gap Report* notes that no country has closed the "economic participation gap." The report also notes on average "only 60 percent of the economic outcomes gaps . . . have been closed."[51] The World Economic Forum estimates to fully close the gap in the workplace will take until 2095 at the current pace.[52]

In terms of women's global employment trends, they actually appear to be stagnant and, by some estimates, getting worse.[53] Today women's labor force participation lags behind men by 27 percent (50 percent versus 77 percent) and this gap has only decreased 1 percent since 1995, primarily after the 2008 global economic crisis.[54] The International Labour Organization's 2012 report, *Global Employment Trends for Women*, noted that while the "gender gap" in unemployment had remained constant from 2002 to 2007, after the global crash it actually increased.[55] Twenty-nine million women's jobs, lost as a result of the 2008 economic crisis, have not yet been recovered, and the crisis "appears to have worsened gender gaps in unemployment across all regions." Women's employment rates, which steadily increased in the early 2000s, actually reversed after the global financial crisis and are not anticipated to grow until after 2017.[56] Global estimates illustrate the ratios of employment for men and women—at 72.7 and 47.9 percent, respectively—and in North Africa, women's employment rate is 19.6 percent.[57]

Among women who are employed, they consistently make less money, are more likely to be in lower-wage sectors of the economy, and participate in more vulnerable forms of employment than men.[58] In developing regions, approximately 75 percent of women's employment is in informal work.[59] The situation is less promising for women in the Arab states, where 25 percent of women of working age participate in the labor market, compared with 73 percent of men. Labor force participation rates tend to be higher among women in sub-Saharan Africa because women are more often than not working in the informal sector.[60] Over-representation of women in low-wage work translates to less pay and pensions later in life; in France and Sweden women will earn 31 percent less than men over their lifetimes, in Germany it is nearly 50 percent and Turkish women will make 75 percent less.[61]

Also, despite "progress," violence against women remains a *global epidemic*. While organizations consistently identify lack of data on prevalence and enforcement, the World Health Organization (WHO) produced its own report identifying how so many women's lives are shaped by violence on a daily basis: one in three women *worldwide* experience intimate partner violence during their lifetimes—and this average is fairly consistent across regions.[62] If one takes into account non-partner sexual violence, the average increases to 35.6 percent— ranging from 27 percent to 45 percent. The World Health Organization cites some of the long- and short-term effects of this violence: 38 percent of murdered women are murdered by intimate partners; women experiencing violence are injured 42 percent of the time; these women have lower birth-weight babies, are twice as likely to experience depression and have abortions, and are more likely to contract HIV/AIDS and syphilis. Indeed, as some have noted, "violence against women appears to be becoming both more common and more egregious."[63]

A UN report found 40 to 50 percent of women in the European Union (EU) and 30 to 40 percent of women in the Asia-Pacific region had experienced sexual harassment in the workplace.[64] This trend extends to girls in school as well, where 83 percent percent of girls between eight and eleven experienced some kind of sexual harassment. Another study in New Delhi found over 60 percent of women experienced harassment between two and five times in the previous year.[65] The prevalence of violence according to age remains about 30 percent, though it does appear to drop to around 20 percent in women fifty-five and older.[66]

There is some variation in levels of violence regionally, with the highest levels reported within Africa, the eastern Mediterranean, and Southeast Asia, while the lowest levels were in the Western Pacific, Europe, and the Americas. However, less standardized reports find varying levels in Europe as well from 30 percent in France to 63 percent in Lithuania.[67] Overall, higher-income countries have lower rates of domestic violence, but the range of variation is 13 percent from lowest to highest.[68]

According to the World Health Organization's latest report on violence against women, sexual violence among non-partners ranges between 5 and 12 percent.[69] While they cite that these results were not as robust as results on domestic violence, it is likely indicative that most sexual violence occurs within the contexts of relationships. Interestingly, the report also finds that while domestic abuse rates appear lower among higher-income states, sexual assault is actually higher than in lower-income regions, at over 12 percent.[70]

But violence against women is also an epidemic during, before, and after conflict. During conflicts in Bosnia, Rwanda, and Sierra Leone, sexual violence was epidemic, and this appears to be continuing and is documented in every active conflict today. In Syria, for example, women cited fear of rape as the number one reason for fleeing.[71] The 2013 UN Secretary-General's report on *Sexual Violence in Conflict* states: "It is increasingly evident that sexual violence has been used to forcibly displace populations, internally and across borders, in places such as Colombia, the Democratic Republic of the Congo, Libya, Mali, and the Syrian Arab Republic." But this list goes on to include basically all states with active conflicts today (including Afghanistan, Bosnia, Liberia, Libya, Myanmar, Somalia, South Sudan, and Yemen). The report notes a link between sexual violence and "flawed disarmament" in the DRC, Central African Republic, Cote d'Ivoire, and South Sudan.[72] Thus, post-conflict sexual violence also remains rampant.

Despite global efforts, "gender equality" in these policy areas has a long way to go. And while better implementation may promote women's participation in government, and the economy, and reduce woman-centered violence, calling these practices "gender equality" ought to be challenged as well.

Destabilizing Discourses on Gender Equality

This discourse of gender equality is not limited to particular policies promoted in its name. It is also ubiquitous in academic and policy research on women. This section focuses on the scholarship and measurement of "gender equality" and illustrates the problem with gender equality as an academic and practitioner-based narrative. The indicators, measurements, and the subsequent narrative of gender equality are problematic for four reasons: 1) this discourse often uses the term "gender" as a synonym for "women" or "female," obscuring how masculinities and femininities are not adequately disrupted by many of these policies; 2) this narrative uses "equality" in under-specified ways, promoting low thresholds both numerically and substantively; 3) this narrative of gender equality poorly engages gender as intersectional—that is, steeped and inseparable from identifies of race, class, sexuality, and geography; 4) and finally gender equality is used as a theoretical "shortcut" that bypasses and obscures the complex and diverse ways gender roles and binaries shape people, institutions, policies, and thus politics. When gender equality becomes a measurable indicator, it obscures analytical gender and how masculinities, femininities, and other identity-based binaries contextualize and explain sociopolitical phenomena. This leaves readers, researchers, and practitioners to "connect the dots" between sex variables and gender as an essential explanation. Without this discussion of feminist (analytical) gender, gender itself becomes an essentialized measure primarily meaning women.

Political scientists Mona Lena Krook and Jacqui True, in their critique of norm life cycle models, focus on "global gender equality norms." While they note this is a "slippery concept," they go on to focus on women's political participation and women, gender, and development policy. The two policies they track through the United Nations include women in decision-making and gender mainstreaming. In a similar vein, political theorist Judith Squires, in her book *The New Politics of Gender Equality,* does not explicitly define gender equality but focuses on the "parity of participation" via gender quotas, gender mainstreaming and women's policy agencies as indicative as gender equality measures.[73] In both of these cases gender is a modifier for quotas and mainstreaming that substantively focuses on efforts to add women, and could more appropriately be named "women" mainstreaming. These authors use analytical gender in their assessments of what these policies offer, but because they do not adequately define or explain gender equality, quotas and mainstreaming become substitutable with gender equality. Additionally "gender" as a modifier for quotas and mainstreaming, where "women" would more aptly apply, also renders gender and women as synonyms.

Political scientist Mary Caprioli's research on the relationship between gender inequality and internal conflict finds states with higher levels of gender inequality are more likely to experience civil war. While she does not actually define gender, she identifies how structural violence against women is informed by how gender determines "roles, power relationships, responsibilities, expectations, and access to resources."[74] But it is the measures of gender equality that warrant further discussion.

The measures for gender equality in her research (and that of others) are fertility rates and percent of women in the labor force.[75] The idea is these measures capture gender discrimination and inequality, so high fertility rates result from gender discrimination and are associated with other negative impacts on women. But these measures are "shortcuts" for understanding complex ideas about women's reproduction and labor. The percent of women in the workforce is understood as empowering by "improving livelihoods and increasing women's self-esteem, social status . . . and decision-making power."[76] But one could argue these are both low bars for gender equality and make some essentializing assumptions about women, equality, and work. Are women with fewer children equal to men? More importantly, are masculinities and femininities valued differently as a result of fewer children?

First, to assume more women in the labor force as an indicator of gender equality is based on some problematic assumptions about globalization and why women have joined the workforce. While some women have joined for their own sense of autonomy and independence, many more women join the workforce out of economic necessity—in both developed and developing states. To claim that more women in the formal workforce is an indicator of gender equality assumes the following: 1) women feel empowered by the work they now do (which, given the increased flexibilization of labor and erosion of long-term stable career employment options for women and men, this seems a broad generalization to make); 2) women working in the formal sphere signifies an improvement in livelihood (while this is surely true for some, as wages stagnate and prices continue to increase globally, there is little guarantee women's incomes may drastically improve their or their families' livelihoods) and; 3) women working have more empowerment (there is an important link between the increasing role of women in the workforce and a corresponding increase in levels of violence against women).[77] While some working women have improved their lives and increased their civic engagement, many poor women work many jobs, both formal and informal, and would probably challenge how their employment signals their equality.

Additionally, the causal chain between lower fertility rates, which is measured as three or fewer children, and gender equality is not a straight or obvious path. One must assume women have more than three children because of patriarchal pressures, such as religion, or they do not have adequate access to birth control or little negotiating power in relationships.[78] But these assumptions are not adequately developed in explaining the measure. Caprioli explains that because women are expected to reproduce, this lowers occupational aspirations, allowing for fewer opportunities. The "fertility rate is thus a direct measure of gender equality and a proxy measure for education, employment and social standing."[79] Fertility rates may allude to women's access to resources and agency in relationships, but without a more complex and less deterministic discussion of these links, how they are informed by gender and what is meant by equality, fertility rates are a direct measure of fertility rates, not gender equality.

More importantly, both measures are also implicated in imperialism, population control, and globalization that undermine any conception of gender equality. While there are vital reasons to promote women's control over their own reproduction, as Caprioli identifies, using fertility as a measure of gender equality is also implicated in the politics of forced sterilization. Historically, while women have fought for reproductive justice, it was not just to control their own reproduction but also to make sure women's reproduction was not controlled by states and global institutions. Because fertility rates have been linked to issues of population control, fertility is shaped by issues of race and ethnicity, class, and imperialism, further challenging it as a measure of gender equality. Based on the logic that women's reproduction is tied to better employment, opportunity, and state development, global institutions and states have pursued forced sterilization policies for several decades.[80] Betsy Hartmann, a scholar of population control and gender, documents this pattern. She cites how in Peru in the late 1990s, with the support of United States Agency for International Development (USAID), President Fujimori's regime sterilized over 200,000 Quechua women. There was also widespread forced sterilization in the 1980s in Bangladesh and extensive evidence of several countries sterilizing women with HIV in the last decade. Even in 2011 USAID wanted to compensate poor women for "voluntary sterilization," but as Hartmann points out, "paying poor people to be sterilized . . . distorts the whole notion of reproductive 'choice.'" She writes how this practice and discourse of blaming poor women of color for overpopulation is back "in vogue." Forced sterilization has also been used in the United States, primarily among Latina, black, and immigrant women; it has been used as recently as 2010 in the California prison system.[81] Ultimately, while in some cases fertility rates may measure women's greater access to "empowerment," it can also be a measure for women's oppression and racialized and imperialist oppression. When women's fertility—particularly that of racially marginalized and poor women—is regulated by governments and IOs in the name of state development, it is the antithesis of equality.

Political scientists Ronald Inglehart and Pippa Norris, in their well-known book, *Rising Tide: Gender Equality and Cultural Change around the World*, identify gender equality as a scale of beliefs based on the World Values Survey, which offers a series of categorical questions about employment, education, and children based upon categories of men and women.[82] While potentially such questions are tapping into issues of gendered divisions of labor, "sex inclusion" would more specifically capture the measures at hand. The authors do not actually define gender equality beyond one's stronger disagreement with phrases such as "men make better political leaders than women," and approval of single women "wanting to have children." Thus, if a person is okay with single women wanting children and women leaders in power, then this signals a commitment to gender equality. But this renders gender equality a "shortcut," obfuscating *why* someone thinks women are better or worse leaders or *why* acceptable motherhood is contingent on marriage. These beliefs can only be explained using analytical gender to explore masculinities, femininities, and heteronormativities, which is not captured in a scale question. What the questions here capture are degrees of sexism and heterosexism, and while sexism is related to gender equality, these are not logical equivalents.

In a more recent article titled "Trends in Global Gender Inequality," sociologists Shawn Dorius and Glenn Firebaugh define gender equality as when females constitute 50 percent for any given characteristic.[83] This very technocratic understanding of gender (in)equality identifies equality as a number—a 50–50 split in access to, or representation of, a particular good or quality. Their study relies upon UN measures of literacy ratios, primary and secondary school enrollments, proportion of legislative seats held by women, and proportion of women wage earners not in agriculture. Their logic here is important: "Because we are interested in *gender* inequality, we focus explicitly on domains where men and women can be compared; thus we focus on education . . . as opposed to fertility or maternal mortality." The authors do not actually ever define gender, though they note that gender inequality exists when "men (or women) enjoy a disproportionately large share of some valued good such as political power." In this study gender means comparing what men have to what women have, but what their data indicate are actually sex comparisons, not gender comparisons. More problematically, the authors argue such research can only be done in institutions where both men and women exist (since fertility is out), which is particularly troubling because it implies women's fertility and mortality rates are not indicative of inequality or gender.

Political economy and development research often uses the term "gender" where "sex" would better encapsulate their meaning. In a recent article titled "Globalization, Gender, and Growth," economists Ray Rees and Ray Riezman clarify that "gender" is in their title so as to distinguish between factories that use male versus female labor.[84] The article "Gender-Specific Human Capital, Openness, and Growth" uses sex-disaggregated rates of school enrollments as its main data source in order to understand economic growth.[85] Another study of "gender equality in employment" measures equality via female-to-male employments ratios, similar to Caprioli.[86] In all of these cases gender is used when sex would more accurately describe the measure, and equality is measured via numerical comparative ratios. These use a "shortcut" for gender and equality and do not adequately discuss how masculinities and femininities shape sex segregation in employment and education.

In a recent review article on "Gender Inequality and Economic Growth," David Cuberes and Marc Teignier claim: "gender inequalities *may* reflect discrimination against women, but they could also be the outcome of *society's preferences towards gender roles, or even women's rational choices . . . we are silent about whether gender inequality reflects pure discrimination or optimal choices.*"[87] What is troubling here are the sexist assumptions permeating such claims: there are many men and women who do not "prefer" certain gender roles; society's preferences are neither ahistorical or a social "given"; and finally, women's "rational choices" are not exogenous but endogenous to socioeconomic outputs. This means women make rational choices within and because of their socioeconomic situation, never separate from it. Ultimately, society's preferences and women's choices are both shaped by gender discrimination.

These studies of "gender inequality" do not adequately engage gender: to understand the causes and effects of sex on economic growth requires a more in-depth discussion about how masculinities and femininities inform preferences and how gender roles are constructed in particular ways so that economies function. For example, a feminist gender analysis of economic growth would focus on why economists do not "count" reproductive labor in calculating a country's gross domestic product (GDP) and other economic indicators.[88] Or why there is a preference for women in low-wage "caring work" like education, nursing, and childcare.

Sociologists Jocelyn Viterna and Kathleen Fallon look to the link between "gender-equitable" states and democratization.[89] They argue "women's democratic movements are the mechanism by which states may become more gender-equitable." But later in the article, the authors seek to understand how states become more "women-friendly." This represents a "gender = women" narrative, in which gender equality literally means women-friendly. Their indicators include women's representation in parliaments and state response to the demands of women's groups. They acknowledge their variables of interest do not deal with all the ways states are gendered but then argue, "If these foundational gendered changes are institutionalized . . . they will have positive influences on other aspects of the state apparatus." While adding women to parliament and responding to their demands are key issues in building democratic institutions, one could challenge the degree to which these are either foundational or gendered. This implies the liberal feminist logic that the foundation, or most basic principle, to confronting women's exclusion is to add women to its institutions and respond to women's demands. While these are absolutely essential for any democratic or democratizing state, acknowledging these assumptions as liberal feminist assumptions is useful for clarifying the claims being made here about what the authors assume democracy, gender, and equality to actually mean.

International Organizations and Gender Equality

Global organizations also use gender equality in problematic ways. Gender equality has become a central theme of global poverty platforms, including the now-completed Millennium Development Goals (MDGs) and new Sustainable Development Goals (SDGs). Millennium Development Goal 3 (MDG 3), initiated in 2000, was to "promote gender equality and empower women" through parity in education, political participation, and economic empowerment. However, the only target for this goal was to "eliminate gender disparity in primary and secondary education, preferably by 2005, and in all levels of education no later than 2015."[90] While, according to the United Nations Development Programme (UNDP), the ratio of female-male primary school enrollment has reached 97 percent globally, sex disparities have been rectified, not gender disparities. While gender identities and roles presumably must be challenged for sex disparities to change, how these have been challenged is not the central focus, it is just assumed to have already happened. Again, gender is a shortcut for the more challenging discussion of how masculinities and femininities shape the conditions under which girls and boys are encouraged to go to school, but this analysis is left out of the discussion when gender and women are taken to mean the same thing.

The other indicators, or measures, for MDG 3 include the share of women in wage employment in non-agricultural work and the proportion of women in national parliaments. As in Caprioli's measurement of gender equality, the proportion of women in the workforce is used here as an indicator of equality, as is the number of women in parliament.

While gender is important in understanding women and girls' exclusion from education, public office, and employment, gender in the context of this goal only means women, and gender equality is measured by better efforts to include women in employment and public office. But there is no specificity on what would adequately constitute a threshold for this equality. Yet based on recent reports, *any* increase in the number of women in office is considered having met the goal. The UNDP's 2014 *Millennium Development Goals Report* suggests that the MDG targets "have been *met*," stating: "In January 2014, 46 countries boasted having more than 30 percent female members of parliament in at least one chamber." More women are now holding some of the so-called hard ministerial portfolios—such as Defense, Foreign Affairs, and the Environment.[91] Thus the target for promoting gender equality, in terms of political participation, is considered met—as in completed. Fewer than 25 percent of states have over 30 percent women in parliament, and gender equality is thus achieved?

Sustainable Development Goal 5, "Achieve Gender Equality and Empower All Women and Girls," is much more expansive than MDG 3, as indicated by table 2.1. Several of these targets are in line with the policies explored in later chapters, emphasizing how such policies are considered key aspects of "gender equality," including: improved access to government and representation; economic resources and rights; and the elimination of violence against women. The broader list of goals is an important signal of all that needs to be addressed to improve women's daily lives. While there are very important targets here that—were they fully implemented—would increase women's access to important resources, one cannot help notice the language of the goals. Despite the goal of gender equality, there is no mention of men or masculinity, emphasizing that focusing on including women in the Sustainable Development Goals *is* the UN's attempt to achieve gender equality.

The World Bank is perhaps one of the worst offenders in their indiscriminate use of gender. Their "gender" page on their website begins: "Women can and do play a vital role in driving the robust, shared growth needed to end extreme poverty." In this case gender is already specifically focused on women. Their "focus areas" include "gender and the private sector," "gender-based violence," "gender in extractive industries," "girls education," and gender in specific regions—"gender in Africa," "gender in East Asia and the Pacific," and so on. All of these sectors could have easily replaced the word "gender" with "women" and more accurately described the central emphasis of projects and ideas. Reports on gender equality (such as the World Bank 2006 report) do not define the term, but rely on sex ratios in employment and education as indicators (as in MDG 3). Other reports seem to assume readers already know what is meant by the term.

TABLE 2.1 Sustainable Development Goal Five "Achieve Gender Equality and Empower All Women and Girls"; emphasis added.

5.1 End all forms of discrimination against all *women and girls* everywhere	5.6 Ensure universal access to sexual and reproductive health and reproductive rights as agreed in accordance with the Programme of Action of the International Conference on Population and Development and the Beijing Platform for Action and the outcome documents of their review conferences
5.2 Eliminate all forms of violence against all *women and girls* in the public and private spheres, including trafficking and sexual and other types of exploitation 5.3 Eliminate all harmful practices, such as child, early, and forced marriage and *female* genital mutilation	5.a Undertake reforms to give *women* equal rights to economic resources, as well as access to ownership and control over land and other forms of property, financial services, inheritance, and natural resources, in accordance with national laws
5.4 Recognize and value unpaid care and domestic work through the provision of public services, infrastructure and social protection policies, and the promotion of shared responsibility within the household and the family as nationally appropriate	5.b Enhance the use of enabling technology, in particular information and communications technology, to promote the empowerment of *women*
5.5 Ensure *women's* full and effective participation and equal opportunities for leadership at all levels of decision-making in political, economic, and public life	5.c Adopt and strengthen sound policies and enforceable legislation for the promotion of gender equality and the empowerment of all *women and girls* at all levels

This is not to say the World Bank and other financial institutions are not focusing on some social construction of sex and gender. The World Bank consistently acknowledges women's domestic responsibilities matter and women do more care work than men. They even cite the power of "social norms" in prescribing such differences. But acknowledging this differential and citing it as a problem based on social norms is where the analyses end. Masculinities, femininities, and kyriarchy figure nowhere in exploring these social norms, though sometimes they do refer to "traditional" values.

There is a body of scholarship on the "slippery concept" of gender equality relevant for this argument to reframe the politics and policies of gender equality to one of women's inclusion.[92] Political scientists Emanuela Lombardo, Petra Meier, and Meike Verloo illustrate how hegemonic discourses on gender equality are shaped by processes to "fix," "shrink," "stretch" and "bend" it to meet needs of policy-makers.[93] They note how gender equality has been shrunk into meaning legal non-discrimination, "only women" in certain European contexts, and "bent" to fit within other goals, particularly economic growth policies like childcare. As will become evident in later chapters, gender equality embodies a "shrunken" use of gender and it has been "bent" and used in larger liberal policy objectives, particularly among global actors. The authors note these processes "depoliticize and de-gender" gender equality by obscuring "hierarchies of power," or the gender dimension was "reduced, neutralized, or abolished."

But the authors then reference violence against women policies and economic development policies as implicit examples of gender-equality policy. They argue these processes occur within certain feminist hegemonic discourses (taboos) privileging certain interpretations of policies while marginalizing others. One of these "taboos" is the possibility of overcoming patriarchy (which they identify as interrelated with the merits of incremental change). They find a "blind spot" in some research where interpreting this bending and stretching as having "negative effects that reinforce patriarchy first." In other words they find it problematic when feminist scholarship is doubtful of the benefits of some of these "gender equality" policies.

The issue here is the need to clarify the feminist ontologies informing research on gender equality—its meaning and how to implement it. In this case, the authors still adhere to a concept of "gender equality" as a set of policy practices that actually exist, even though they do not define their understanding of gender equality. Their work suggests a liberal feminist ontology in which policy objectives and state practices can eradicate patriarchy. From a more critical feminist perspective (including the one taken in this book), these policies and practices may actually reinforce certain patriarchal values (like gender binaries), and may be counter-productive to eradicating oppression if they continue to inform processes oppressing women. In other words it is crucial to challenge the assumption that adoption and implementation of women's inclusion and add-gender/women policies will logically result in gender equality.

Introducing Women's Inclusion

Why the need to (re)frame gender equality? And why should women's inclusion replace this narrative about gender equality? The purpose in engaging woman-centered policies and practices as women's inclusion rather than gender equality is that it encourages different theorizing and a different set of assumptions about current practices and policies promoted as gender equality. It encourages scholars and practitioners to use gender as an analytical tool for a more critical engagement of the trade-offs of such policies. This section introduces women's inclusion as a liberal feminist concept. It first presents the key tenets of liberal feminism, and then outlines the meaning and theories of what is meant by women and inclusion. It then presents the key politics informing women's inclusion—*representation*, *recognition*, and *protection*—that embody much of the policy efforts of the last forty years. It finishes by offering a critique of women's inclusion as a liberal feminist norm and how it has developed in neoliberal world order.

Despite that many of these policies discussed earlier have been promoted based upon a variety of feminist ideas, they all work within the liberal feminist concept of women's inclusion.[94] While socialist, liberal, and radical feminists have promoted some similar policy objectives, such as violence against women policies and wage equality, these policies are usually rationalized via liberal feminist logics. According to Judith Lorber, liberal feminism is considered a "reformist" model of feminism because it advocates for reforming sexist institutions to create gender equality. Including more women in an institution so it has "gender balance"—or equal numbers of women and men—signals, according to the liberal feminist perspective, the elimination of discrimination against women and thus ensures their emancipation.[95] It focuses on rights, equality, and rationality. These are key aspects in liberal democratic thinking more generally, and has a long history, articulated in Mary Wollstonecraft's *A Vindication of the Rights of Woman*, in the late 1700s.[96] Although it has a long history, liberal feminism emerged as a powerful ideology in the 1960s during what is considered the "second wave" of the United States feminist movement. Second-wave feminism included other forms of feminism, such as socialist and Marxist feminism, radical feminism, black, and multicultural feminism (among others); however, liberal feminism prevailed as the dominant paradigm for "feminist emancipation" both in the U.S. and globally.[97]

Liberal feminism emphasizes men and women are no different; rather, women are bound by discriminatory constraints.[98] "Liberal feminists believe that these impediments to women's exercise of their full rational capacities can be eliminated by the removal of legal and other obstacles that have denied them the same rights and opportunities as men."[99] Their work has emphasized removing discriminatory legal barriers to increase women's rights so women may live more robust lives, including better access to work that was void of harassment and more women's representation.[100]

The goal of liberal feminism is to make sure one's sex and gender do not determine one's access to resources and public life, but as political scientist Marysia Zalewski articulates, this emphasis on creating policies based on assumptions that women and men can be the same is translated into "why can't a woman be more like a man?" Thus, if women are not treated as feminine and have access to male-dominated resources and opportunities, they too can be equally successful.[101] Historically, because women's exclusion was justified based on assumptions of women's natural (and always-inferior) differences, emphasizing that women are like men was an important and radical strategy. It also worked with the already powerful discourses of liberal democratic values emphasizing individuality and rationality—women too were rational beings just as capable as men.

Women's inclusion embodies these liberal feminist ideas. The term is meant to encapsulate policy efforts to include/add women in both formal and informal "institutions."[102] It is based on the fact that women are primarily excluded from many institutions as historically and currently structured. Women's inclusion is named to foster a particular discussion. It has two key terms: women and inclusion. First, I use "women" in an attempt to find a middle ground between a "biological"[103] concept of female and a critical feminist understanding of gender as associated with masculinities and femininities. "Women" indicates more than female (body parts) but less than gender (masculinities and femininities).

The other term is "inclusion," which is meant to capture the liberal democratic ideals of how women's rights and interests have been pursued the last forty years. Inclusion is often framed in the language of rights and democratic practices in the context of liberalism or liberal world order, as even non-democratic states still use such ideas and language.[104] The logic underlying inclusion is to "widen and deepen democratic practices" and women's inclusion specifically focuses on the efforts to eradicate women's exclusion. Indeed, Iris Marion Young identified inclusion as a democratic norm that those within a democracy should be able to shape its political outcomes.[105] Philosopher Charles Taylor argued "liberal democracy is a great philosophy of inclusion" and for many it remains the most inclusive form of government in history.[106]

Women's inclusion rests upon two important liberal assumptions: 1) women have inalienable rights; and 2) inclusion is progressive and group-based exclusionary practices are not good for states or democracy.[107]

The first assumption underlying inclusion is the idea that women have inalienable rights. This builds upon the classical philosophers and liberal thinkers of the Enlightenment—Immanuel Kant, Thomas Hobbes, John Locke, and Thomas Paine—who argued the existence of natural rights of men. Inalienable rights are those that cannot be removed, and are grounded in natural law beyond governments and laws or customs. These natural rights, codified in the United States Declaration of Independence, became a cornerstone for the human rights movements of the twentieth century and are central to the Universal Declaration of Human Rights adopted by the United Nations General Assembly in 1948. The Preamble states:

Whereas recognition of the inherent dignity and of the *equal and in-alienable rights of all members of the human family* is the foundation of freedom, justice and peace in the world . . . Whereas the peoples of the United Nations have in the Charter reaffirmed their faith in fundamental human rights, in the dignity and worth of the human person and in the *equal rights of men and women* and have determined to promote social progress and better standards of life in larger freedom (emphasis added).

Article 2 then makes clear that "everyone is entitled to all the rights and freedoms set forth in this Declaration, without distinction of any kind, such as race, color, sex, language, religion, political, or other opinion, national or social origin, property, birth, or other status." In other words: inalienable rights belong to humans and women are human and thus entitled to said rights.

Nevertheless, as activists Charlotte Bunch and Samantha Frost have made clear in their analyses of the "women's rights as human rights" movement of the 1990s, women's rights were given secondary status within the human rights movement.[108] As further explored in chapter 3, "women's human rights" developed via transnational networks and international conferences bringing women together. Bunch states this engagement with human rights required a "double shift" in thinking: "Put quite simply, it has entailed examining human rights framework through a gender lens, and describing women's lives through a human rights framework." This double shift has been important in the justification of pursuing violence against women legislation in particular, but also quotas and policy agencies. While historically these human rights documents use "men" and "human" interchangeably, the women's rights movements capitalized on these ideas in their women's-rights-are-human-rights campaigns in the 1990s in order to point out how women were excluded from these "human" rights.

The second assumption underlying inclusion contains two related parts, the first being that the exclusion of women is considered bad for state development, economics, and democracy. The second part is that inclusion itself is progress/progressive. This idea that exclusion is bad for states is based upon the logic that women are important for economic development and democratic governance *because they are women*. Global institutions and powerful countries highlight what women add when they are included. This often focuses on increased accountability and transparency to government institutions (explored in chapter 4), women's financial contributions to gross domestic product (GDP) and growth through formal employment (chapter 5), and increased productivity due to women's safety and security (chapter 6).

The corollary is that inclusion is considered progress and progressive. Political scientist Anne Phillips argues democratic states are revitalized (to be given new life or invigorated) when they include women.[109] When women are better integrated into legal codes, government offices, and formal employment, such institutions are thought to be more accountable to women who now actively participate and consult in such institutions. Also, when women are included it may make institutions more transparent because those "inside" rather than "outside" institutions may have more information about how historically sexist institutions work, so they can promote more transparency. By this reasoning, women should be included, not just as voters, but as leaders, as well as workers and full citizens. The policies and practices discussed in subsequent chapters explore how women's inclusion promotes women as leaders, workers, and citizens.

Women's inclusion is about more than women in government, or violence against women, or women's property and credit rights. Women's inclusion is about the ideas linking all of these policy efforts, ideas situated within a liberal, liberal feminist, and neoliberal world order. Three key ideas essential to both liberalism and liberal feminism are *representation, recognition, and protection*. These ideas are based on already existing language and ideas of women's inclusion developed over the last forty years. They have informed the policies and practices adopted by states over the last forty years and discussed in later chapters. For this reason, it is important to explore the theoretical reasoning underlying them.

Representation

Representation is a key component of women's inclusion. Women's increased access to government and their right to run for office are central to ensuring more progressive, democratic, and even economically efficient states. Representation, although usually used in the context of women's access to legislative branches, has been used more recently to promote women in both executive and judicial branches as well. Women decision-makers, as discussed in chapter 4, are often treated as a key "variable" for the promotion of other aspects of women's inclusion, including their economic rights and violence against women legislation. In this sense, promoting women in government, and to ensure they may act as representatives for other women, is the lynchpin of women's inclusion and will have effects on all other efforts.

In her book, *Feminism and Politics*, Anne Phillips identifies four main reasons it is important to include women in governing: promoting women as role models, a sense of justice, the importance of women's interests, and a revitalized democracy. While I addressed the link between inclusion and revitalized democracy above, inclusion is also linked to her first three reasons women are important, including the importance of women as role models, different interests they represent, and the exclusion of women as unjust.[110]

The "role model" aspect of representation focuses on how women in government serve as role models for women to be able to participate by increasing self-esteem, as well as encouraging women that government is not just a "man's world".[111] Role modeling is connected to the concept of shared identity, for women will look to other women as role models because they presume some sort of shared interests due to gender roles. It is difficult and time-consuming to break down institutional barriers, and to know someone else has altered the system by proving "it can be done" can be a powerful catalyst for other women's participation.

Phillips also states it is important to include women because they perhaps have different interests that need to be represented:

> Women occupy a distinct position within society: they are typically concentrated, for example, in lower-paid jobs; and they carry the primary responsibility for the unpaid work of caring for others. There are particular needs, interests, and concerns that arise from women's experience, and these will be inadequately addressed in politics that is dominated by men.[112]

Phillips's next reason is the justice argument—it is unjust and unfair to allow "men to monopolize representation."[113] Since women account for (usually) over 50 percent of the population, democratic principle would establish that representation reflected this, but only in Rwanda and Bolivia do women account for 50 percent or more of the legislative body, lending merit to the fact that the democratic system, in practice, is unequal.[114] Ultimately, because of this numerical inequality, women have actively promoted policies aimed to change their governments.

This echoes Iris Marion Young, who argued that, as part of a deliberative democracy, decisions are only democratic if those affected by the decisions are included in the process of decision-making.[115] Such beliefs and evidence have shaped the norm of including women to the point that the inclusion of women has become an *objective* of democracy. In addition to creating democratic institutions and laws (free elections, infrastructure for rights and liberties, access to economic opportunity), democratic and democratizing countries are also addressing the *composition* of these institutions.

Recognition

Recognition is another key tenet of liberalism and liberal feminism and thus women's inclusion. The idea that group identities ought to be recognized by the state and its apparatuses, so as to guarantee more full citizenship of recognized groups, is paramount to a liberal state. Charles Taylor argues recognition works in two important ways. The first is under the "politics of universalism" in which there is a "vital human need" to be authentic and to be seen as equal even when different, which applies to all citizens. The second is a "politics of difference" in which every person should be recognized for her or his unique identity.[116] Taylor argues recognizing difference is important because difference is what has been ignored and often assimilated. As groups refuse to be second-class citizens, they do so based on ideas of "universal equality" and "universal dignity." Taylor notes the tensions between universalism and difference in liberal states and how apparent "neutrality" of certain positions based on universalness are indeed not neutral because of their treatment of difference, which is to allege "blindness" towards it, which is not the goal for recognizing difference.

While Taylor is specifically talking about multiculturalism and race, his discussion is important for liberal feminism because it too has an inherent tension in promoting the universalism of women as human beings while also trying to recognize women as a systematically different group. Political theorist Nancy Fraser cites recognition as a key aspect of today's feminist movement. She defines recognition as the recognition of difference and acceptance of difference without having to assimilate to the "majority or dominant cultural norms."[117] But this recognition of women-as-different is done in a liberal context of universal claims about citizenship, so women are treated as simultaneously different *and* the same. Liberalism is built on ideas of universalness of human beings (inalienable rights), so institutions that allow or promote universal access are thus deemed equal. This is important because policies that add women or gender reflect this paradox: because women are different they should be specifically included, but because women are also part of a universal category of human or citizen, the institutions do not necessarily need to change, just the composition. Thus, recognition of women is central to their promotion in any aspect of public life and so it has become a central aspect of women's inclusion.

Protection

The final idea underlying women's inclusion is "protection." This word and the ideas behind it permeate much of the movement for women's rights, particularly anti-discrimination policies but also violence against women policies. Protection of women and their rights stems from two logics. The first is the protection of rights and liberties, considered a cornerstone of liberal democratic thought. The "protection" of rights is considered key to the pursuit of inalienable rights and "is a key element of a liberal political order."[118] Because people are born with natural rights, the role of government is to protect those rights. For example, in the United States, the Fourteenth Amendment's "Equal Protection Clause" clarifies no state can deny any person "the equal protection of the laws." Protection of rights has been used to articulate anti-discrimination policies globally.

However, protection also has a particularly gendered meaning in that this idea of protection has long been used as a tool of women's oppression. The common adage of "protect women and children" is a powerful idea used to maintain sexual divisions of labor and life and was based in liberal distinctions of the public and private. Political scientist Ann Towns, in *Women and States*, provides useful insights into understanding how this protection-of-women narrative developed via Western liberal practices. She outlines how the development of Western "civilized" states focused on how the category of "woman" and her exclusion from the "political realm" were central to state-making and defining states as "civilized" in the nineteenth century.[119] Politics became part of the public sphere, in part, by justifying a two-sex belief system using secular scientific reasoning to exclude women based on emerging categories of masculinity/femininity, Men and the state came to represent reason, force, and modernity, while women came to represent weakness, emotion, and tradition.[120] This sort of organization, or "civilization" was used to justify women's exclusion *by protecting them* to maintain their value to the "public good" through being devoted to gendered tasks such as child-rearing.[121]

Over the last forty years the global community has pretty much agreed women should be protected from violence directed at them because of sex and gender. This is an implicit acknowledgment that women's experiences with violence, which were historically treated as "private matters," or "spoils of war," were excluded from cultural and legal redress. As women exposed the emotional, economic, and physical "costs" of violence against women, most states could not ignore how their security apparatuses perpetuated and even exacerbated this exclusion and marginalization. As will become clear throughout, while protection is not usually associated with inclusion, the underlying logic about bodies, individualism, and rights within liberal feminism privileges protection of women. Said differently, policies and practices to protect women from violence are centrally about adding women to exclusionary laws about bodily harm both domestically and internationally. In this sense, violence against women is a framework for women's inclusion in security practices and discourses.

The Limits of Women's Inclusion in a Neoliberal World

All of the policies and practices explored in subsequent chapters are part of a global add-gender-and-stir movement to include more women. Women's inclusion has become a mainstream global effort because it embodies liberal feminist logic, which is tolerated and even co-opted within neoliberal capitalism. But before illustrating how women's inclusion fits in a neoliberal world, it is first important to identify what neoliberalism means in the context of this book. David Harvey identifies neoliberalism as "a theory of political economic practices that proposes that human well-being can best be advanced by liberating individuals' entrepreneurial freedoms and skills . . . by strong private property rights, free markets, and free trade."[122] From this, I derive neoliberal world order to mean one that privileges open-market economies, minimal government involvement in economic activities, and the importance of certain liberal values like individualism, security, and competitiveness, and institutions that protect such values.

International relations scholar James L. Richardson, in *Contending Liberalisms in World Politics*, identifies neoliberalism as a "liberalism of privilege," based upon rationalist assumptions of the primacy of the individual and necessity for the freedom to maximize one's own utility.[123] The point here is there has been a shift, beginning since the 1970s with Chicago School–economics and the "Washington Consensus," in promoting a belief that the role of the state is to ensure open markets, but otherwise its interference should be minimized in economic endeavors of individuals and between states.[124] Markets are better providers of goods and needs than states. And the state should promote policies fostering individuals' access and participation in neoliberal states. It is with this in mind that one can begin to understand how liberal feminism would work within such a global framework.

Nancy Fraser notes how the more radical anti-racist, anti-classist, and anti-imperialist feminism of the second wave became "largely stillborn" because second-wave feminism coincided with a shift in capitalism to neoliberal capitalism. And this specifically meant a shift from a politics of redistribution of economic resources to one of recognition and representation. She explains how recognition, steeped in identity politics, displaced redistributive justice and reified group identities. Specifically, efforts to recognize an "identity" obscured links between social or cultural values, like "feminine," and structural practices, such as low female wages. This form of identity politics also assumed that by valuing devalued identities, redistribution would subsequently follow, which has not happened.

More importantly Fraser argues this focus on recognition stifled dissidence and discouraged criticisms, such as intra-divisions based on race, sexuality, and class. She argues the effect is "to impose a single, drastically simplified group-identity which denies the complexity of people's lives, the multiplicity of their identifications, and the cross-pulls of their various affiliations."[125] In this sense, the contestations and struggle for authority, power, and representation are obscured, and dominant factions (largely, elite white factions) continue to dominate feminist policies and politics.

"Woman" has become a universalistic stable category for inclusion, based on ideas that women are both different and the same as men. Women have fought to be recognized as citizens, workers, and leaders. But while Fraser identifies this shift to emphasizing recognition and the co-optation of certain ideas within neoliberalism, she treats feminism today as a singular unified movement and idea—feminism with a capital "F," which obscures the power dynamics among different feminisms. What is missing from Fraser's analysis is how the singular idea of "feminism" she identifies as existing today *also* represents the triumph of liberal feminism. Where Fraser publically declares that feminism has become "capitalism's handmaiden," she is obfuscating how liberal feminism has emerged out of second-wave feminisms as the dominant paradigm for today's global "Feminism."[126] Sociologist Hester Eisenstein has made a similar argument that "mainstream feminism" replaced labor feminism and stressed "equality" based on the ideas that women and men were the same, which has been usurped by global capitalist institutions.[127] Eisenstein's "mainstream feminism" *is* liberal feminism and it has become the dominant paradigm for addressing women's exclusion.

The hegemony of liberal feminism as "Feminism" has happened, in large part, because liberal feminism already works with the powerful narrative of liberal capitalist individuality, inclusion, anti-discrimination, and equality of opportunity.[128] Both neoliberalism and liberal feminism seek to remove barriers limiting an individual's right to prosper. Liberal feminism understands sex discrimination as a barrier to women's prosperity and articulates a set of policies aimed at exposing and then removing such barriers. Thus it is not fully accurate to say that second-wave feminism promoted a certain politics of recognition, without delineating that this represents a triumph of liberal feminism. While liberal feminism has in some ways served to justify some of neoliberal capitalism's logics and policies, the shift in capitalism, beginning in the 1970s, also served to privilege and promote liberal feminism over more radical and revolutionary varieties, especially those emphasizing capitalism as imperialist, racist, and heterosexist.

While practices aimed at including more women may be considered progress compared to not having said practices, simply assuming such policies are then "progressive" stunts critical discussion about for whom such efforts represent progress. As part of liberalism and liberal feminism, progress measured as increased numbers of women is treated as universally good. But many of these policies involve serious trade-offs, and may help some women while marginalizing others. These trade-offs may not be fully articulated when scholars and practitioners treat "woman" as a monolithic and universal category. For example, Caprioli's research on conflict and gender equality, mentioned earlier, implicitly assumes women's lower fertility rates and greater workforce participation are signs of women's progress. Mala Htun and Laurel Weldon explicitly identify violence against women policy as a progressive social policy because it empowers women, who are a historically marginalized group.[129] They group violence against women with marriage equality rights, affirmative actions, and quotas for minorities.

But women's inclusion is permeated by the politics of race, class, sexuality, and imperialism. In questioning how practices aimed at adding women are informed by these politics, one begins to see women's inclusion's limits: it is never power-neutral.

Underneath this assumption of women's inclusion as progressive and good for states lurks troubling power dynamics informed by gender and other social identities and how these interact. While including women is beneficial for some women, the universalizing logic that all women benefit from inclusion obscures how women's identities are complex and shaped by race, sexuality, class, and geography. For example, sociologist Rachel Pierotti's work on cultural scripts about violence against women makes some troubling assumptions about the Global South.[130] She identifies global cultural scripts about violence against women as a norm, promoted between the ideas of human rights and gender equality and modernity and development—a liberal human rights issue. But she does not fully clarify who this world society is beyond those in urban areas, who are better educated and have access to media. Yet her data hint at who this world society may be. All her (twenty-six) cases are middle- or low-income states (primarily low) and predominantly in sub-Saharan Africa. Since these are the cases, it would appear world society is those in the Western developed world who have already made this link between violence and gender equality. While she notes developing states also played a role in defining violence against women, the emphasis here represents a cultural script of violence against women as a Western liberal policy that Global South women needed to "learn" to reject intimate partner violence.

Women are not a monolithic category. Race, class, imperialism, and heterosexism greatly impact women's access to inclusion. As political scientist Zehra Kabasakal Arat argues, liberal feminism "assumes that as some members of a marginalized group gain access to some sources of power, the entire group is empowered."[131] But this again obscures how inclusion is often about power politics. Recent research on queer citizenship has noted how inclusion is often steeped in extreme violence and integral to the politics of wars on terror, international aid in the Global South, and neoliberalism.[132] "Queer citizenship" as a form of inclusion is informed by binary logics, constituting subjects as either "grievable and ungrievable," worthy and unworthy of state protection, "folded into life," or "socially dead."[133] Queer subjects are included and then regulated and surveilled by the state and global and local organizations.[134] Amy Lind and Cricket Keating, in a case study of Ecuador's pro-LGBT policy agenda in the early 1990s, notes how the platform of greater inclusion was selective so while sexual orientation is a protected status (since 1998), same-sex marriage and adoption, and abortion are still illegal, which was reinforced in the 2008 Constitution.[135] Thus heteronormativity continues to inform state practices and laws. This is further reiterated in Jessica Scott's analysis of same-sex marriage in which she argues marriage remains a mechanism of heteronormativity and racialization.[136]

This critical research on the "murderous" inclusion of queer subjects is central to understanding women's inclusion because one can see how inclusion may become a strategy of the state, and financial and global organizations, to regulate/police/define/co-opt previously excluded groups and identities. When an identity-based group is "included," the effects can be multiple: they may lose agency in (re)defining identities and priorities for the state; they may become complicit or even active in the subjugation of marginalized people through persistent "othering"; and they may find "pragmatism" a more useful strategy for change, reinforcing rather than dismantling kyriarchical systems of power. All of this applies to women's inclusion. When "woman" is treated as a category for inclusion, it obscures how "woman" has become a privileged identity for inclusion, often at the cost of, and even in opposition to, racialized, sexualized, classed, and imperialized identities.

Conclusion

The world has seen significant changes regarding women in the last forty years. The global spread of woman-centered policies has been an important intervention in promoting women's rights, but even such efforts have not resulted in major shifts in the number of women in government or the economy, or in more women's safety and security. As radical as these add-women/gender practices were in the early 1970s and 1980s, they were also a strategic compromise among many feminist and women's groups. Even getting states to recognize domestic violence and sexual harassment as a problem was a major hurdle, and more radical ways of thinking (that focused on patriarchy as an institutional problem) were dead on arrival because they asked for fundamental changes that male-dominant institutions were unwilling to even entertain, such as their commitments to gender roles or the broadening of the meaning of gender. Feminists had to make compromises to get any policy objectives enacted, sometimes making personal and political compromises in the name of pragmatic activism. These women were successful because they worked within the liberal discourses of individualism, equal rights, and anti-discrimination.

Women's inclusion is a positive strategy for challenging male domination (the fact that cisgender men occupy the majority of positions in a given institution) and male-centeredness (the fact that laws and policies privilege men's realities and interests). But for more radical forms of feminism, the problem is bigger than male-dominated and male-centered institutions. The problem is that male dominance and male-centeredness—and patriarchy—depends upon and reproduces a powerful belief in gender binaries. Policies aimed at male dominance do not necessarily destabilize gender binaries but may actually reinforce or maintain them.

3

Dual and Dueling Gender in Global Narratives

One of the central questions addressed in this book is how "gender equality" has come to refer to certain policy efforts to include more women. How have "women" and "gender" become substitutable terms? Women's inclusion did not emerge from a political vacuum, but it is a result of, in part, dual and dueling narratives about women and their role in states and global economic order. The first narrative is a fairly radical and feminist narrative of systemic and structural inequalities in the world that perpetuate and exacerbate women's subjugation.[1] This narrative focuses on "international economic order" and how inequalities between the Global North and South impact states and women's development. The second narrative is a more instrumentalist narrative in which women are a means to a more equitable, peaceful, and secure world. In this discourse, women's inclusion serves a purpose, which challenges the degree to which states and international organizations (IOs) promote policies *because* women have inalienable rights or deserve equality for the sake of being human. Within these narratives, feminist and women activists strategically engaged states and organizations to publicize and address women's exclusion from governments, laws, and legal frameworks on violence and economies.[2]

Through a tracing of key international documents, one can see how these narratives are produced and produce particular meanings for gender equality. Through a careful reading of the Geneva Conventions, reports on the World Conferences on Women, the Vienna Declaration, the Convention on the Elimination of All Forms of Discrimination against Women (CEDAW), the Declaration on the Elimination of Violence against Women, and United Nations Security Council Resolution 1325 (UNSCR 1325), what emerges are these dual and dueling set of global narratives. These narratives are reproduced in a neoliberal world order that prefers and promotes liberal feminist women's rights and inclusion that adds women without challenging or radically destabilizing gender or the gendered institutions that exclude women in the first place. Said differently, the development of neoliberal world order and free-market economies meant woman-centered policies reflecting individualism, rationalism, universalism, political rights, and discrimination faired better in receiving global support among states and IOs than more radical efforts for a global reordering.

As the instrumentalist narrative of women-as-a-means-to-an-end gained traction through global discourses, one also begins to see the shift in language, where "women" and "sex" get replaced with "gender." Gender then becomes a modifier for ideas like "equality," "gaps," "sensitivity," and "disparities," but without the accompanying analyses of how masculinities and femininities, as well as other social identities, shape and inform said disparities, gaps, and inequalities. While both narratives have resulted in some significant changes for some women, it has also simultaneously obscured and depoliticized the role that gender and kyriarchy play in understanding the global oppression women experience. And the result over time is a privileging of instrumentalist women's inclusion and rights, over the more feminist, radical narrative. This has resulted in the subsequent depoliticization of gender from a feminist analytical concept to a liberal technocratic one.

This chapter outlines how women's inclusion developed over time via the conferences and conventions that gave it meaning and direction. While policy outcomes such as sex quotas and violence against women legislation and economic rights are the substantive outcomes of such work and what one measures to assess women's inclusion, exploring the developing logic underlying women's inclusion—and in particular the key ideas of *representation, recognition, and protection*—are particularly relevant for what women's inclusion has come to mean today and how analytical/feminist gender has been obscured in the process.

Before 1975: Women Organize

While 1975 marks a turning point for the global women's movement against exclusion and the starting point for subsequent chapters, the movement has a much longer history, which I will briefly highlight here. It remains important to identify a long history of women's activism in challenging and changing sexist oppression. As long as women have been oppressed and excluded, they have also been fighting for increased access and rights.

At the global level, one of these key early documents for women's inclusion is the Geneva Conventions, which espouses both recognition and protection of women. According to other Conventions (the Beijing Platform in particular), the Geneva Conventions are important in understanding why women, as a recognized category, are uniformly identified as non-combatant and in need of protection. The Fourth Geneva Convention on the Protection of Civilians in Times of War makes the following case in the "Wounded and Sick" section: "Women shall be treated with all consideration due to their sex." The commentary on why such a provision is included follows:

> What special consideration [should women have]? No doubt that consideration which is accorded in every civilized country to beings who are weaker than oneself and whose honour and modesty call for respect. Apart from this, the principle of equality of treatment as between enemies and nationals is involved. Women of the enemy's side will be allowed to enjoy the same advantages as women patients who are nationals, as well as any other favourable distinctions to which they are entitled by reason of their race, or because of the climate or food to which they are accustomed, in the same way as men of the same origin as themselves.[3]

The language present in the commentary is emblematic of ideas about women in 1949 and permeates much of the Convention in regard to women. It also sets the stage for "othering" women by classifying them as weaker and in need of protection.

The Geneva Conventions build upon both difference and sameness claims made by feminists discussed in chapter 2. On the one hand, women are included under the umbrella of "human" and thus are entitled to rights as men are: women and men are the same, which is a central tenant of liberal feminism. On the other hand, women hold a special and distinct societal role that has long been ignored as part of conflict, and this difference entitles them to special protections, which illustrates a paternalistic logic as well. For example, the Geneva Convention's Additional Protocol of 1977 specifies:

Protected persons are entitled, in all circumstances, to respect for their persons, their honour, their family rights, their religious convictions and practices, and their manners and customs. They shall, at all times, be humanely treated, and shall be protected, especially against all acts of violence or threats thereof and against insults and public curiosity. *Women shall be especially protected against any attack on their honour, in particular against rape, enforced prostitution, or any form of indecent assault.*[4]

That women must be especially protected indicates there is some difference in being a woman worthy and necessitating special discussion. The Geneva Conventions' focus on women's bodily integrity and physical violence ultimately leads to similar ideas in UNSCR 1325. But the logic here that "women are different," is a paternalistic one that actually reinforces women's subjugation, because it assumes women must be protected by the state and men. This will inform violence against women policies in the future. But the Convention became the basis for women's groups to seek conflict-related protection, as this signals some worldwide acknowledgement that there are international laws and some level of universal rights, which legitimized and grounded claims for women's security within an already acknowledged framework, however liberal and paternalistic it may be.

1975–1985: The Decade for Women

The United Nations first declared 1975 as the International Women's Year, which is considered a critical juncture in international women's rights.[5] This culminated in the UN-declared "Decade for Women" from 1975 to 1985 in which the Commission on the Status of Women (CSW) sought to push the women's inclusion agenda in states. They did this via three World Conferences on Women in 1975, 1980, and 1985, as well as passing the Convention on the Elimination of All Forms of Discrimination against Women (CEDAW) in 1979. The "Decade for Women" demarcates the emergence of a global focus on women's inclusion by centering women's rights and issues that would shape state and global policies in the coming decades. Previous and later conventions outline women's inclusion as part of their larger objectives of human rights, population issues, and peacebuilding; however these conferences and CEDAW really set the stage for addressing women's inclusion and rights as central to states more generally and issues of development and peace more specifically. The reports are titled "Equality, Development, and Peace," emphasizing how women's exclusion permeates all governments, development, and security practices. CEDAW builds upon this language and further specifies many of the ideas of the conferences; it is also considered a binding international treaty holding states to the ideas of women's inclusion. The importance of such reports and conventions should not be understated, for they outlined the ways in which women's lives were affected by global processes, and in that sense were very radical. This section first outlines the first three United Nations World Conferences on Women, in the context of representation in government, recognition in the economy, and protection in state security apparatuses. These conferences and subsequent reports offer insights into the ideas and language of women's inclusion as it became a global issue for states.

All the UN conference reports outline "Programmes" or "Plans of Action," which include actions to be taken by states, international organizations, and within the United Nations. The reports are all more than two hundred pages specifying dozens of substantive resolutions. These cover a broad range of issues, though I will centrally focus on the resolutions promoting women in government, including women in the economy, and granting women security from direct violence (broadly defined).[6]

The first United Nations World Conference on Women held in 1975 in Mexico City marks an important point during which women began to globally and publically outline their demands. And states responded. The report contents are radical in their acknowledgement of structural forms of women's oppression, such as reproductive labor and family dynamics; the role colonialism, imperialism, and apartheid play in women's oppression; and the autonomy of women's bodies from physical harm. Buried deep in the report is the comment that less than 10 percent of delegations to the United Nations General Assembly and United Nations conferences are women, and less than 5 percent of member representatives are women, seeming to indicate this was a report produced and signed primarily by men.[7] While these declarations were ones women had been articulating for decades, that states were now part of the discussion is why this time is so vital in understanding the development of women's inclusion.

Representation

Including more women in government is a consistent theme throughout all the reports, and issues of representation are repeatedly emphasized, though policy objectives are never explicit about how to actually increase women's representation. "Political participation" is one of the main sections for national action plans for every report, highlighting that, "despite the fact that, numerically, women constitute half of the world, in the vast majority of countries only a small percentage of them are in positions of leadership in various branches of government."[8] The 1975 report outlines the need for "national commissions" to ensure "active participation by women," which includes the right to vote and run for public office. The section goes on to identify "special efforts" for states, and while quotas are not specifically mentioned, most of the efforts call on governments to pursue "special activities" or "temporary measures" to increase "recruitment, nomination, and promotion of women" and to have specific goals for the following decade for increasing women in elective offices.

The 1980 report continues to emphasize the need for special activities and asserts that "special governmental instruction should be issued for achieving equitable representation of women in the different branches of government."[9] Political parties are also called to nominate more women though there is no mention of sex quotas in any office at this point. One shift in the 1980 report is the emphasis on "national machineries" for women, which is repeatedly highlighted as a useful and productive strategy for states and coincides with a large number of states creating these women's bureaus.

By 1985 the report calls on states to "intensify efforts" to promote "equality of participation" of women in executive, legislative, and judicial branches and decision-making processes more generally. The report also recommends that states should set up offices in each department, headed by a woman, to monitor "equitable representation."[10] The possible policy outputs that could be enacted, however, are not specified.

Generally, what the reports highlight is the need to add women to exclusive and elusive branches of government, and special measures would be encouraged, though it is not clear what these special measures, in practice, would be. National machineries and a network of offices specifically focusing on women and their promotion is as specific as the reports get. Crucially, none of these reports explicitly call for sex quotas, but what they do is either recognize a deficit of women in public office, or call for an increase in women's representation through special measures. This has broadened the meaning of women's participation from its historic association with voting to also include women holding office.[11] As further discussed in chapter 4, national machineries (women's bureaucracies) were adopted wholesale during this "Decade for Women" and representation became a key issue of women's inclusion.

Recognition

Recognizing women as a group entitled to more inclusive participation, especially in capitalist economies, permeates discussions about women in national economies and women in development in all the reports. The politics of recognition emphasizes the importance of explicitly acknowledging women, as a group, who remain excluded and marginalized by global economic processes. Centrally, the reports emphasize the need to address deficits for women's full economic participation through better inclusion, *not* redistribution of resources. Neither is there a discussion of dismantling an imperialist, sexist, racist, and classist capitalist system. The reports focus on the need for more actual women in economic activities and greater access to exclusionary economic industries and practices.

Curiously women in national economies and women in development were (and are) treated as somewhat distinct issues—primarily based on geography and levels of economic well-being. When documents refer to "women in national economies," they are talking about developed states—the Global North. When documents refer to "women in development," they are focused on economic issues in the developing world, or the Global South.

The reports consistently identify the need for more "equality of opportunity" and promotion of non-discrimination legislation to help women participate more fully in the economy.[12] The 1975 report focuses on how women's work activities were not "counted" in official economic data (which remains the case today, and is further discussed in chapter 5). It advocates for more women in management, improved training for women's "entrepreneurial skills," and increased access to credit and capital. Additionally it imparts "equal pay for equal work" and maternity protection for women workers. These policies recognize women as a group-based identity experiencing particular forms of exclusion and discrimination.

The report notes two-thirds of economically active women were found in developing states and makes several statements about including "rural women" in development. It also explicitly calls for minimum wages in "cottage industries and domestic labor." It is in this context in which the discourse shifts from women's economic participation to development, which comes to mean women's economic participation in developing states. Multiple sections call for the "consideration of women" in creating and executing development projects.[13] The report also calls for the creation of women's commissions and the need to address how all development programming will impact women.

Recognizing issues of family planning and education appear most often in reference to how to boost women's integration into development in the 1975 UN report. It notes women's integration into development does not happen without improved health, education, and job training, but also in women's decision to have children, and how many children to have. It continues by linking women's greater economic participation to state development, emphasizing the need to change the burden of household labor and lower fertility rates to improve women's lives: "Make available to individuals and couples through an institutionalized system, such as a national family planning programme, such information, service, and means as will enable them to determine freely the number of their children and the intervals at which they will have them."[14] This is a fairly broad view of economic development, one that links greater household equity and access to resources to women's well-being; however it does not specify why such inequalities exist or how they are tied to larger global processes. This narrative sits somewhere between a radical new economic order and an instrumental view of women's inclusion as means to a more developed state.

One of the priority areas for women's employment includes early iterations of sexual harassment: the need for legislative measures to "guarantee women protection against any sexually oriented practice that endangers women's access to or maintenance of employment, that undermines her job performance and thus threatens her economic live-lihood."[15] That this is considered a work-related issue, rather than a violence against women issue is important, because today most sexual harassment policies are adopted as part of employment legislation rather than part of violence against women frameworks.

The 1980 report again emphasizes the same issues of family planning, educational opportunities, and better development programs. It includes the oft-quoted factoid: "While [women] represent 50 percent of the world adult population and one-third of the official labour force, they perform nearly two-thirds of all working hours, receive only one-tenth of the world income and own less than 1 percent of world property." This report has a few new relevant sections on water supply and sanitation, recognizing that women spend up to one-third of their workday getting water.[16] This is worth noting because issues of water access and sanitation are a precursor to poverty eradication policies of the twenty-first century, as with emphasis on improving women's access to education.

Women in agriculture and rural areas are the main focus for develop-ment ideas in the report, which notes that little was done in the previous five years to help rural women and there have been almost no "positive improvements." The report calls for a greater emphasis from states to train rural women to be leaders, to have better agricultural techniques, and to know their rights. There is also a section in this report on "women and development assistance programs." This section calls for woman-specific programs that are aware of women's unique disadvantages and to include actual women in developing these programs for women.[17]

While there are hints of anti-capitalist rhetoric in exploring why women are poor, these sections on women and development become increasingly politicized over the course of the reports. This is indicated by the increased use of "reservations" from states in the Global North to particular themes in the reports. By 1985 the focus on development continues to identify the same issues of improving work conditions and access to work within developed states. But the report takes a decidedly different tone of power politics in which the United States repeatedly "reserves" its positions and declines to support certain phrases. These contested phrases emphasize how core-peripheral issues of development are a source of women's inequality and use the term "coercive practices" in describing powerful states' behaviors. The Holy See also repeatedly rejects resolutions on family planning and fertility programs.[18] By 1985 women's positions are increasingly an issue in core-periphery politics by which neoliberal and conservative agendas collide and shape discourses. This results in a direct challenge to and rejection of the more radical structural discussions of subjugation of women (and men) in poor developing states. Overall, the development sections in all the reports contain lofty and vague goals and do not offer many concrete ideas for how to improve women's economic well-being. This coincides with Nancy Fraser's assessment that a politics of recognition replaced a politics of redistribution that centers women's subjugation in capitalism.[19]

Protection

Protection is manifested in policies specifically aimed at protecting women from direct violence. While violence against women was a minor issue in the 1975 report, for both domestic policy and in the context of conflict-related violence, domestic violence against women issues gained prominence over the next ten years. It even became one of the most emphasized issue areas of later reports; however at the same time, conflict-related violence against women remains off the agenda until much later.

In the 1975 report, there is a section on trafficking but no explicit mentions of domestic violence, sexual assault, or sexual harassment. Issues of physical or direct violence against women are not central to this report and remain absent from national action plans. Within sections on "family," the report notes the need for legal equality but nothing specific about violence. And while sexual harassment is not specifically treated as part of the section on employment, the report calls for equal treatment of women workers and non-discrimination based on sex or marital status.[20]

The section on trafficking and the exploitation of women and girls focuses primarily on women and girls recruited into prostitution, and the main point of the section is the call on governments to "abolish prostitution."[21] By 1980 abolishing prostitution is no longer part of the discourse, and while the section on trafficking still primarily focuses on prostitution of women and girls, the report removes the language of eradicating prostitution and instead focuses on dealing with traffickers and their networks.[22] This is an important shift in framing: abolishing prostitution can translate to criminalizing paid sex work, which would directly affect women, often poor and racially marginalized women, in ways potentially counter to their empowerment (like putting them in prison). So greater specification indicating sex work as a global enterprise and a complex issue means states may start understanding sex work as not the "fault" of women.

Prominently, in the 1980 document there is also an additional section and set of resolutions on "battered women and violence in the family" that recognizes the problem of domestic and sexual violence, something not addressed at all in 1975. The report calls for family courts and states to adopt measures to "protect the victims of family violence," provide them with resources, and implement programs to prevent abuse, though it does not clarify what prevention means or what it would entail.[23] By 1985 the section on violence is titled "abused women," an area categorized as worthy of "special concern" and it is here the term "gender-specific violence" is first used in these reports. The section advocates for more resources for victims, the importance of generating public awareness of violence against women, and the need for measures to "ascertain its causes and prevent and eliminate such violence."[24] Critically there is no explanation for what "gender-specific" violence means other than violence against women, a theme returning in the 1995 report.

In the context of violence against women in conflict, direct treatment of the issue remains absent from all the reports. The 1975 report recognized the need for women's participation in "peace and co-operation," but the resolutions made broad links between human rights and peace, encouraging women to become leaders in international affairs. It does note women's participation in promoting peace and "friendly relations among nations," but it does not call for more women's access or participation in these processes. Rather it stresses the need to reduce international conflict, including colonial wars, apartheid, and foreign domination.[25] In this sense, the focus of this report is not about violence within conflict or women's experiences of conflict, but that women's well-being is better served when states cooperate. It *does* call attention to women's experiences in particular conflicts, including the Arab–Israeli conflict, Vietnam, and Chile. The resolutions call for global solidarity with Palestinian women and for the international community to assist them in their struggle for self-determination. It calls for the world to prevent another Vietnam and calls for the end to political executions and imprisonment, particularly of women in Chile.

The 1980 report reaffirms women's roles in promoting peace against domination, though it is distinct in including the family as the referent from which to promote peace where "preparation for peace starts" in creating respect and understanding. This is a big shift in linking violence within the private sphere to larger-scale conflicts of the state. This report more clearly identifies that war creates a particular kind of danger for women and children, though does not specify what these dangers are.[26]

By 1985 there are hints at how armed conflict actually affects women, beginning with the shift in language from "women and peace" to "women in areas affected by armed conflicts, foreign intervention, and threats to peace." The section elucidates how conflict threatens the lives of women and children via fear, displacement, and physical abuse, and international protocols protecting civilians ought to be heeded by governments.[27] It also identifies disarmament as a goal, and suggests that women's role in disarmament should be supported. It also iterates women's commitment to eradicating apartheid. Thus violence against women in both domestic contexts and war emerges during the early 1980s as a priority for women's conferences. Though, as indicated by the diffusion data of violence against women policies discussed in chapter 1, states do not start enacting violence against women policy in large numbers until the 1990s, so even at this point it remains more a commitment on paper than an action for most states.

Convention on the Elimination of All Forms of Discrimination against Women

While the Convention on the Elimination of All Forms of Discrimination against Women (CEDAW) is technically included within the context of the "Decade for Women," it stands out as the most critical treaty regarding women's inclusion and rights to date and thus, deserves specific attention.[28] In 1979 the UN General Assembly adopted CEDAW, which had been promoted by the Commission on the Status of Women (CSW) within the UN. This convention is considered the pinnacle document for global women's rights and a binding treaty ratified by nearly

190 states. It principally serves as a formal treaty for many of the ideas that the reports and women's conferences outlined and discussed in the previous sections. What is of particular importance about this document itself is the positioning of women's inclusion as a right of women, situated within a broader context of human rights. It first states, "Recalling that discrimination against women violates the principles of equality of rights and respect for human dignity . . ." and then goes onto define discrimination against women:

> Discrimination against Women shall mean any distinction, exclusion, or restriction made on the basis of sex, which has the effect or purpose of impairing or nullifying the recognition, enjoyment, or exercise by women, irrespective of their marital status, on a basis of men and women, of human rights and fundamental freedoms in the political, economic, social, cultural, civil, or any other field.[29]

This section is followed by six "parts" on discrimination (four of these substantive and two procedural), outlining different areas in which states should act to end discrimination.[30] Part I focuses on how states can pursue measures to end discrimination, including establishing "equality of men and women" in constitutions; establishing legal protection of women's rights; changing laws; ensuring others do not discriminate (such as organizations and authorities). It also makes clear that any "special measure aimed at accelerating de facto equality between men and women shall not be considered discrimination." This has important implications because it means policies like quotas and women's national machineries would not be considered discriminatory, but actually even welcome because women are a disadvantaged group. It also clarifies the need for states to "suppress all forms of traffic in women and exploitation of prostitution of women."

Part II outlines women's rights to inclusion in political participation and representation—ensuring women's right to vote, hold office, and engage in public political life. It specifies women's equal rights to nationality as well. Part III focuses on education, employment, health care, and rural women. Again, it contains many similar resolutions as the world conference reports, though it offers some very concrete issues to be addressed. For example, in education it calls for equal opportunities for scholarships and sports participation, something not specified in the world conference reports.

Recognizing women's economic rights is a key feature of CEDAW. It recognizes women's right to work as an inalienable right. This includes women's equal treatment in remuneration and choice of employment, safe working conditions, and social security. It also calls for prevention of discrimination against women based on marriage or maternity. It articulates the need for equal rights for family benefits, bank loans, and credit. Development planning and the particular problems of "rural women" are also specifically addressed, mentioning access to health care and family planning resources. Part IV imparts countries "shall accord women equality with men before the law," including rights to property and contracts and freedom of movement. Marriage rights are also part of this section, specifying that both sexes have same right to "enter into marriage," choose spouses, be parents, and manage property and resources. It also calls for states to set a minimum marriage age and make marriage registration compulsory.

As stated, this Convention is important because it outlines women's inclusion via anti-discrimination policies as a *right* of women. It succinctly elucidates what the 200-plus-page reports emphasize in women's representation, recognition, and some protection. What is missing is any discussion of violence against women, but given that did not appear on the agenda until the 1980 world conference report, this is perhaps not too surprising. This omission would become the basis for the Declaration on the Elimination of Violence Against Women in 1993.

Advancing Women and Global Order

These reports and the "Decade for Women" tell us a lot about how women's inclusion was envisioned at the beginning of this global surge of woman-centered policy diffusion. These documents identify a particular global agenda for promoting women's inclusion, which will have later impacts on policy options and the ways in which women's inclusion is pursued. To understand the importance of these documents, this section focuses on their meaning in the context of promoting women in an emerging neoliberal global order. Several points are worthy of further development, including the central focus on the "advancement of women," a narrative in which gender is not yet present; the developing potential for intersectional analyses over the course of the reports; the dual and dueling narratives about women permeating these reports—including one radical narrative of systemic inequalities and oppression and another of instrumental rationality that identifies women as a means to a particular end; the total absence of patriarchy (or kyriarchy) as a structural cause of oppression; and the strengthening liberal language of "progress."

The first point worth emphasizing, because it stands in contrast to later language on women's inclusion, is how gender is not yet part of the discourse. The term "advancement of women" is a central term in these reports and ultimately, the goal for these conferences.[31] This phrase aligns with what is in the text: resolutions to make sure women are better recognized, represented, and protected; to make sure women have the opportunity to participate; and that women's needs and interests are considered in the organization of institutions and rules. The reports focus closely on (biological) "sex" and sex roles and how these shape other domestic processes, such as within the family. Traditional sex roles are acknowledged as a major impediment to women's full participation in social and political life.[32] While CEDAW does not mention advancing women, it does use the language of "equality of rights" between men and women, which leaves the space for dialogue about *both* men and women. Later documents are primarily focused on "gender equality" or even "women's rights," but lose the space for discussion of both women and men because the meaning of gender and woman begin to merge.

The second important development over the decade is a stronger emergence of intersectional discourses, though not necessarily intersectional analyses. For example, the 1985 report uses the term "compound discrimination" in the context of race, class and ethnicity and their effects on women. While all reports deal with the intersectional issues of sex, class, and geography more explicitly through the focus on "rural women," later reports include sections on disabled women, migrant women, and displaced women. The reports emphasize the extra barriers these groups of women face, and the need for governments to provide legislative and material resources for these vulnerable groups. The 1980 report also includes resolutions regarding "women and discrimination based on race," which note the "dual burden" of these identities; however it does not treat them as intersectional as much as it treats them as co-existing.[33] The resolutions mention needing to eliminate discrimination based on sex *and* race without interrogating what this duality actually means for women.

Later reports pay more attention to race and ethnicity, geography, and class, though at a fairly superficial level. This is through acknowledging that race and class matter in understanding women's empowerment, though without any discussion of how or why. Issues of class feature more prominently than race, though the reports remain very heteronormative in assumptions of family structure (by assuming all families include male/female, where the male is head of household). Even though such analyses are lacking, that women are not identified as a monolithic group and are heavily influenced by wealth and race is extremely important in acknowledging women's complex identities. But these different categories of women each get their own "section," so while complex identities are included they are relegated as a piece of, rather than central to, overarching issues of structural subjugation.

The third point is the emergence of a dual and dueling narrative on women. These dueling narratives are central for understanding the development of women's inclusion because they highlight the tensions and trade-offs in promoting feminist ideas at the global level. The first narrative is about structural oppression of both women and states and how these are fundamentally related. Using the term "international economic order," this narrative focuses on unequal distribution of wealth and power between the Global North and Global South, and how this disparity is itself a barrier to women's inclusion and development.

The second narrative is more instrumentalist in how it treats women as a means to a more just, developed, and peaceful end and, because women will help create such a world, states should find ways to better include them. This is a rather pragmatic argument, and both feminist activists and states have used it, though often for different reasons. When feminists argue that women's inclusion is central for more peace or a better economy, they still do so from a stance of social justice, so women's inclusion is both an issue of justice and pragmatism. However, this discussion or belief in justice does not accompany the narrative states and IOs use. Rather, the emphasis is the calculable contribution women can make as women, often steeped in essentialist ideas about women's inherent traits. This narrative obscures the causes of women's subjugation and simply sees the addition of women as a solution to the world's problems.

But this narrative also treats women as different from men, which serves to justify their exclusion. States thus pursue policies to add women, not because they have inalienable rights or it is the right thing to do, but because it will help states develop and "progress." While these narratives are both important in understanding the diffusion of woman-centered policies, they create a tension for feminists. This tension is between pragmatic activism and public policy promotion on the one hand, and the realization that adding women is not sufficient for eradicating kyriarchy, or even gender roles, on the other.

The first more radical and critical feminist narrative links development and oppression between multiple levels of analysis (within the family, the state, between states and overarching structures) and cites a radical shift in global economic practices as a *prerequisite* for women's empowerment. The reports cite how inequality among states continues to grow, and this has bred further oppression of women.[34] The documents call for a "new economic order" based on "equality, sovereignty, and international cooperation and understanding." And this new order was considered a prerequisite for integrating women into development and subsequent "economic progress for all." CEDAW contains the same ideas: "Convinced that the establishment of the new international economic order based on equity and justice will contribute significantly towards the promotion of equality between men and women."

In this same context, the 1975 report explicitly highlighted how many delegations noted "a radical and fundamental economic and social transformation of society was a prerequisite of the improvement of the situation of women."[35] What underlies this discourse is the idea that development is not just economic. There was strong agreement that social, political, and economic issues must be treated equally in order to fundamentally change society for women and men. In this sense, the conference and its findings and discussions were radical and feminist because they made important links between the oppression of women and the inequality among states in the global economy. This discourse of world order and women remains central to all of the reports, though by the 1980s the tone shifts and the link between global inequality and women's oppression becomes more central to the report.

The 1980 report notes how the movement for a new international economic order is even more in limbo than before because of a deepening "crisis in the world economy," hurting developing states and, "world economic crisis had put additional burdens on women." It begins with its definition of equality:

> Equality is here interpreted as meaning not only legal equality, the elimination of de jure discrimination, but also equality of rights, responsibilities, and opportunities for the participation of women in development, both as beneficiaries and as active agents. *The issue of inequality as it affects the vast majority of women of the world is closely related to the problem of underdevelopment, which exists mainly as a result of unjust economic relations.* The attainment of equality pre-supposed equality of access to resources and the power to participate equally and effectively in their allocation and in decision-making at various levels." [36]

This report differs from the 1975 report in that its first section provides a "historical perspective" on the "roots of inequality of women." It identifies how sexual division of labor, mass poverty, and "general backwardness" of the world are caused by underdevelopment, and are a result of "imperialism, colonialism, neocolonialism, and also of unjust economic relations." Again, this indicates a clear recognition that women's oppression is tied to larger global processes of world order—particularly how economic domination is endemic to any form of inequality. This includes what counts as labor and work, and as the report notes, labor and "work" exclude reproductive labor. One of the major takeaway points of the report includes that "measures for women isolated from the major priorities, strategies, and sectors of development cannot result in any substantial progress toward attaining the goals of the Decade."[37]

By 1985 the report even questions prevailing logic on women and development, specifically relaying "doubt on this over-simplified premise" that "economic growth would automatically benefit women [and] was more widely shared . . . [among states]."[38] This report indicates stratification was actually getting worse and until issues of debt and development were treated as systemic, measures to improve women's lives would be cursory at best. As will be discussed in chapter 5, the belief that economic growth automatically benefits women is now treated as "common sense."

While women's discrimination is tied to unequal global economic order, the implicit solution lurking in these reports is to add women. Women become instruments or means to fixing these larger global issues: "Equality is both a goal and a means . . . for development and peace because national and global inequities perpetuate themselves."[39] For example, the 1980 report notes how states were beginning to recognize women's "potential for problem-solving . . . [and] were beginning to see new possibilities for linking women's advancement to the solution for global problems such as the formulation of a new international development strategy."[40] CEDAW contains the same ideas: "Convinced that the full and complete development of a country, the welfare of the world and the cause of peace require the maximum participation of women on equal terms with men." And in 1985 the report states, "the role of women in development is directly related to the goal of comprehensive social and economic development."[41]

In this narrative, world economic reorganization is no longer a prerequisite for women's advancement; rather women's inclusion is a prerequisite for state development and prosperity. In other words, the script has been flipped. It is "instrumental" because it uses a cost-benefit logic by which women are the tool to achieve goals: they serve a purpose. States should care about discrimination and inclusion, not necessarily because women have rights as human beings, but because states suffer economically, politically, and socially when women are excluded. Thus the impetus for addressing discrimination and promoting inclusion is not necessarily one of justice, rights, or humanity as much as it is about good state practices and "progress." That women become instruments for means to more development, better government, and more peace eventually culminates in the maxim on today's global economy that women are "good governance" and "smart economics" (concepts further developed in later chapters).

Two examples of this instrumental inclusion of women are the treatment of reproductive labor and family planning throughout the reports. Reproductive labor (defined as the unpaid labor related to the "domestic sphere" including child socialization and rearing, emotional care, and household "chores") is understood as a barrier to development and an area where states should provide more resources and legal status. In terms of social barriers, the 1975 report points to the role family dynamics play in limiting women's work options. It calls for the need for more social services and childcare facilities so women may integrate and advance in the workplace. This is further developed in another section on "family in modern society," which outlines a woman's right to choose to enter into and dissolve marriage and challenge sex roles in household labor, and calls for more work flexibilities as important for women to participate in the economy.[42] The message is that sexual divisions of labor limit women's participation in formal economies and this is bad for development. The 1980 report reiterates this link between women's informal labor and development:

> To promote full and equal opportunities and treatment for women in employment, bearing in mind that this requires that both women and men have the possibility to combine paid work with household responsibilities . . . so that women may obtain more highly skilled employment and become integrated into the development of their countries with a view to more rapid and balanced growth.[43]

Note in the above quote that the focus on changing divisions of household labor is important because it impedes women's access to formal employment, which hurts states, not because it is sexist or unjust.

Family planning is also treated as an instrumental issue of "smart economics," not necessarily a woman's right. Family planning is the first area of action in the 1980 report and it states women have a human right to determine their number of children.[44] It explains such a decision impacts a woman's ability to "take advantage of educational and employment opportunities and to participate fully in community life as responsible citizens." Women thus cannot fully participate unless they control their own fertility. While acknowledging women have a right to control their fertility is radical and central to women's emancipation, the implicit message is that fertility matters for state development. When women control their fertility, they can more fully participate in formal economies and thus development. But, since family planning was also connected to population control, this same logic served to justify forced sterilization programs in the name of development.

These "dueling" narratives can co-exist because one narrative alludes to the power of patriarchal and kyriarchical forces without naming it, while the other narrative ignores it. Today's world order relies upon kyriarchy, sexual divisions of labor, and the privileging of masculinities (and other dominant social identities). Kyriarchy, within the context of emerging neoliberal world order, means a world in which nuclear weapons and militarization are the top priority for powerful states and "austerity" is the top priority for developing states with skyrocketing debts. While these ideas of militarization and austerity are part of these reports, there is no link to kyriarchy as a structural force shaping the interactions of states, people, and organizations. But there are continual allusions to patriarchy throughout the analyses. The UN states: "What is now needed is the political will to promote development in such a way that the strategy for the advancement of women seeks first and foremost to *alter the current unequal conditions and structures that continue to define women as secondary persons and give women's issues a low priority*."[45] Here, patriarchy *is* this structure even if not named as such.

Additionally culture, society, and "backwardness" are cited as structural causes of women's oppression. These terms are found throughout the texts, but in the context of how they are used, the more representative term would be "patriarchy." When the UN states "physiological, social, and cultural justification of women's reproductive and productive roles subordinates women," the structure normalizing such justification is patriarchy.[46] But it becomes much easier to blame a single culture or "backwards" state than to implicate the whole world order in women's subjugation. It also deflects policy efforts towards those deemed "backwards" (read: states of the Global South) as deficient in promoting women.

This problem of patriarchy would also help explain some of the other key findings in later reports, including the marginalization of efforts and lack of political will to implement resolutions and conventions on women. As later reports note, there are problems with the degree to which states were actually taking any action. While some progress had been made, leadership at the conference noted there was still a "tendency to regard programs for women as a separate exercise within a given institution or department, too great a reliance on extra budgetary sources to fund such programs, and insufficient co-ordination among them."[47]

It is worth noting here that there were feminists skeptical of the UN World Conferences on Women and saw the state as part of the problem. In 1976, a group of over two thousand women (primarily from the Global North) organized the International Tribunal on Crimes against Women. As political scientist Jutta Joachim notes in her discussion of the tribunal, they worked outside the UN framework and had limited resources and more contentious debates during the process.[48] But they primarily self-identified as a feminist tribunal focused on violence against women. Their narrative was entirely about patriarchal power structures as the culprit for women's oppression. They were willing to name the problem in ways the UN reports could not or did not. Their radical feminist objectives rejected working with governments or business: "As women, we have no allies in individual governments, in the male left or in the male right, in corporate structure . . . or in the population controllers . . . That is why we have to create our own institutions and structures."[49] They called violence "crimes against women," and feminist activists were central in naming and framing violence against women as a human rights issue. But it would still take nearly ten more years for the UN to make the link between women and human rights.[50]

The final point worth emphasizing during this decade is a clear emerging language of "progress," which has a very neoliberal tone. The principles for a new economic order illustrate where the goals are heading: "*Inter alia*, self-reliance, collective self-reliance, the activation of indigenous and materials resources."[51] While these ideas represent developing states' calling for autonomy from colonial and imperial domination, it uses the liberal language of "self" to make such claims. Self-determination is a bedrock of liberal thinking and developing states use such claims because they illustrate the hypocrisy of supposedly liberal developed states engaging in very non-liberal practices, particularly colonial and imperial domination. The word "backwardness," which is found in explanations of women's discrimination, also seems to indicate some "less progressive" states still cling to tradition and the past and this subjugates women. This language of liberal progress also shapes the emphasis on equality of opportunity and anti-discrimination policy throughout all these reports and CEDAW. CEDAW focuses on equality between men and women but equality of opportunity is the emphasis. These ideas get further strengthened via their (re)production in subsequent forums and conventions engaging with women's inclusion.

1985–1994: A Move to Gender

By the 1990s many other UN bodies and groups were adding women and women's rights to their own platforms.[52] It is during this era in which feminist activists shifted strategies to promote women's rights and inclusion as part and parcel of larger human rights agendas. Activist Charlotte Bunch argued in "Women's Rights as Human Rights" that women's rights had been marginalized by the international community as distinct and even trivial: "Failure to see the oppression of women as political also results in the exclusion of sex discrimination and violence against women from the human rights agenda."[53] The title of "women's rights as human rights" thus became the slogan for women activists seeking to include women's rights as part of the Vienna World Conference on Human Rights.[54]

These women activists working in women's rights over the decades were the first to begin using the term "gender violence." This matters because earlier feminist movements (such as the Tribunal), which identified gender as social rather than biological, were grounded in feminist thought in identifying masculinized power as central to women's subjugation. This earlier movement was employing gender as an analytical force to politicize, historicize, and de-essentialize women's exclusion and rights. Gender violence engaged gender as analytical because it explained patterns of violence based on masculine and feminine identities and practices, so men and masculinity were key elements in eradicating said violence.

But as the term "gender" gained traction and moved through global institutions, states, and non-governmental organizations (NGOs), the word became a shortcut for engaging in more critical and nuanced discussions of the power of binaries (and not just gender binaries) in understanding inequalities. As I previously stated, when gender is shortcut, one may acknowledge power without talking about the production of power. Even Bunch's seminal article does not actually define gender, and its meaning in context appears synonymous with female: "However, many violations of women's human rights are distinctly connected to being female—that is, women are discriminated against and abused on the basis of gender." Thus begins the move from "women" to "gender" in which the UN and other IOs begin incorporating women's rights and its terminology without the overtly feminist politics in the process.

This shift from women to gender begins with the World Conference on Human Rights in 1993, which adopted the Vienna Declaration and Platform of Action on Human Rights. Protocol 18 illustrates one of the underlying logics of women's inclusion, which are women's inalienable rights: "The human rights of women . . . are an inalienable, integral and indivisible part of universal human rights." The report emphasizes protection of women, specifically against violence:

> Gender-based violence and all forms of sexual harassment and exploitation, including those resulting from cultural prejudice and international trafficking, are incompatible with the dignity and worth of the human person, and must be eliminated. This can be achieved by legal measures and through national action and international cooperation in such fields as economic and social development, education, safe maternity and health care, and social support.[55]

There is an entire section on "the equal status and human rights of women," which reiterates the dual and dueling narrative on women "as both agents and beneficiaries in the development process." It recalls and includes the same language as previous world reports and CEDAW, though it also frames women's access to health care, family planning, and education as a right. Further, it acknowledges the need for women as decision-makers.

While the language, which primarily focuses on women, is similar to prior programs and conventions, the term "gender-based violence," though not explicitly defined, is used here to mean violence against women as it was in the 1985 report. It replaced "abused" or "battered women" to indicate specific forms of violence. Vienna represents a real turning point in the women's rights movement and there is a clear strengthening of women's inclusion in highlighting the role violence and exclusion play in perpetuating oppression and the need to protect women's inalienable rights and bodies.

The importance of protecting women from violence is further solidi-fied in 1993, when the UN General Assembly passed a Resolution called the Declaration on the Elimination of Violence against Women. This Declaration was the result of women's continued activism after Vienna.[56] Article 1 defines violence against women as "any act of gender-based vi-olence that results in, or is likely to result in, physical, sexual, or psycho-logical harm or suffering to women." Again, one sees where gender and women are used interchangeably. The Declaration goes onto list several forms violence against women may take, including within the family, general community, or at the hands of the state.[57] It emphasizes women's human rights and calls on states to do a better job addressing such vio-lence via laws, education, and resource provisioning. The penultimate article (5) calls on the UN to facilitate states and other organizations to better deal with violence against women. The Declaration picks up where CEDAW leaves off on the issue of violence against women, which as I stated earlier, was not a central focus of CEDAW.

The International Conference on Population and Development, held in 1994, also included provisions on women and many more on gen-der. One of the stated central goals for the resulting *Programme* was "to make family planning universally available by 2015."[58] The *Programme of Action* reads very similar to the previous women's world conference reports, emphasizing many of the same issues such as health care, ed-ucation, violence against women, and political participation. Within the *Programme of Action*, there is an entire section on "gender equal-ity, equity, and empowerment of women," which links sustainable de-velopment to gender equality policies and practices. The first sentence under "basis for action" again reiterates the dual narrative of a feminist structural focus and the instrumentalist one: "The empowerment and autonomy of women and the improvement of their political, social, eco-nomic, and health status is a highly important *end in itself*. In addition, it is essential for the achievement of sustainable development."[59]

During this decade, women's rights and inclusion were clearly being articulated, highlighting the needs to include women as representatives in political positions of power, to recognize their rights in the economy, and women's need of protection from violence. But these normativities are increasingly couched in ideas about women as a means to an end and increasingly use gender as a shortcut rather than a tool for deeper discussion on why women remain subjugated. But it is really the 1995 Beijing Platform where these ideas come together and are articulated in a manner by which states are compelled to respond. It is also the point at which the more feminist narrative of systemic, global oppression begins to lose out to the more instrumental, technocratic narrative of women, in which the shift from women to gender in the language plays a central role.

Beijing: From Women to Gender

The Fourth World Conference on Women in 1995, often referred to as "Beijing," is considered a critical juncture in the development of women's rights and the diffusion of woman-centered policies.[60] It maintains the same goals as previous conferences of equality, development, and peace but declares itself "an agenda for women's empowerment."[61] Although previous women's conferences produced reports highlighting problems women faced and action plans for implementing strategic points, they did not produce the publicity or commitment that Beijing's Platform produced, for a few reasons. The first through the third conferences, beginning in 1975, did not have the same precedent Beijing had, so discussions of women and development were emerging as important arenas for international action but really did not have the same institutional support. In 1975, international organizations and states did not have strong women's sectors or bureaucracies as in 1995.[62] Additionally, by 1995 there was a proliferation of NGOs dealing with women's issues that had not existed in 1975, and so many had not participated in previous conferences.[63] These NGOs served as a formidable force in designing and ultimately ensuring the Platform was a more concrete set of strategies as well as a public and publicized document. That Beijing included non-state actors (albeit in a parallel conference) was essential in making Beijing a globally important referent for women's inclusion. Finally, the issues for action shifted from 1975 to 1995 in key ways as a result of more comprehensive and diverse discourses and research on women, intersectionalities, and even conflict. What is highlighted in this section is the way in which the word "gender" begins to replace "women" in certain contexts, a new development from previous conference reports.

The use of "gender" begins in the mission statement near the beginning of the document, which declares: "The Platform for Action emphasizes that women share common concerns that can be addressed only by working together and in partnership with men towards the common goal of gender equality around the world." The Platform then refers the reader to Annex IV for what the "commonly understood meaning" of gender is: "Gender as used in the Platform for Action was intended to be interpreted and understood as it was in ordinary, generally accepted usage." The Commission on the Status of Women (CSW) put together a contact group to research and prepare a common meaning for the term. The report, however, gives no definition for gender or any reference to other conferences or forums from which they draw their understanding of the term. In other words, gender is not actually defined.

The conference report is commonly referred to as the Platform for Action (PFA). This PFA outlines twelve "critical areas of concern" and subsequent "strategic objectives and actions" for each critical area. Each objective includes a set of actions to be taken by various global actors including governments, IOs, international financial institutions (IFIs), private interests, and NGOs. This makes it distinct in its very clear and targeted call for action among a much larger set of actors than previous conferences set forth. These areas are the same or similar to many of the previous conference reports: poverty; education; health; violence against women; the economy; power and decision-making; institutional mechanisms for advancement of women; human rights; media; environment; and the girl-child.[64]

Beijing is notable and different for several reasons. Political scientist Drude Dahelup emphasizes how important the Beijing Platform and Conference was for the promotion of sex quotas for a few reasons.[65] First, this platform develops new discourses surrounding women's representation, including an explicit recognition of exclusion and a call for "gender balance." It notes in 1995 only 10 percent of legislators are women. While again not explicitly calling for sex quotas (which were still controversial for states to sign onto), it recommended affirmative action policies and a demand that parties examine institutional barriers for women and a specified a target of 30 percent women in government.[66] The subsequent section acknowledges that while most states have adopted national machineries "for the advancement of women," they remain variably effective and empowered and should be strengthened. It also calls for the need to "integrate gender perspectives in legislation, public policies, and programs and projects."[67]

The section on "women and poverty" notes the majority of those in poverty are women and living primarily in developing states. It also cites that poverty rates have actually increased in both developed and developing states (18). The PFA identifies structural causes as the root of poverty, including debt and structural adjustment in a globalizing world, as well as conflict and environmental degradation. The strategies to deal with poverty call on states to address their macroeconomic policies and include a "gender perspective" as well as the "full and equal participation of women." One new development in the Beijing Platform is the addition of sections for what international financial institutions (IFIs) need to be doing. The action items focus primarily on reducing debt for developing states and addressing structural adjustment plans to "minimize their negative effects on vulnerable and disadvantaged groups." It also calls for changing laws for better access for women to credit.

Violence against women is one of the areas for action in the Platform. The section begins by defining it as "any act of gender-based violence that results in . . . physical, sexual, or psychological harm or suffering to women." It then goes on to list a host of forms it may take, including physical and sexual violence, non-spousal violence, and "violence related to exploitation" in the family or community, as well as sexual harassment at work and in educational institutions or violence perpetrated by the state (48–49). It also includes acts of violence in "situations of armed conflict." The section then calls for the need to "enact and/or reinforce" laws and sanctions to punish and redress any violence against women in whatever environment it occurs.

One of the action items calls for "mainstreaming a gender perspective in all policies and programs related to violence against women." It then outlines the need to implement programs and measures that increase understanding of the "causes, consequences, and mechanisms of violence against women" among agents of enforcement and to ensure women are not re-victimized because of "gender-insensitive laws . . . or enforcement practices" (51). Another strategic objective (D.2) appeals for actors to "study the causes and consequences of violence against women and the effectiveness of preventative measures" (54). This compels states to promote research to "collect data and compile statistics" on violence against women and conduct more research into its "causes, nature, seriousness, and consequences."

Crucially, this emphasis on understanding causes and consequences of violence against women is an important shift in the discourse towards technocratic "gender." It is a big shift to recognize states as stakeholders in dealing with violence, but this does so without implicating the state as a perpetrator of, or involved in, violence against women. Feminist scholarship and activism had long articulated how gender and other social identities are a *cause* of violence against women.[68] Patriarchy and gendered social structures privileging masculinity over femininity are one key root of violence, and such ideas were already well developed by 1995. But it is indicative that states, as signatories to the Platform, were more reticent to acknowledge systemic causes of violence like patriarchy (let alone kyriarchy), because the same feminist logic would also implicate state sovereignty, militarization, imperialism, and uneven development in violence against women. So while states may have been willing to identify violence against women as a serious issue, they would not do so in a way that could undermine state authority. This marks an important move from a narrative of world order and systemic violence to a more technocratic data-driven discussion of violence. Within this shift, gender and women are used interchangeably and the more feminist narrative of systemic emancipation begins to disappear.

The Beijing Platform was also significant because it included, for the first time, a section on "women and armed conflict." Now the violence against women framework was being expanded to include "extraordinary" violence during conflict. Importantly however, it is treated as distinct from domestic forms of violence, which has later ramifications (discussed in chapter 6). Sanam Anderlini, a prominent scholar on women's changing roles in security, also identifies Beijing as important in the larger context of women, peace, and conflict: "Beijing and the PFA [Platform for Action] were a turning point—a call to action and an inspiration for many women experiencing violent conflict firsthand."[69] This section represented a shift from the focus on state-level "peace" in previous reports. The discourse shifted to how women experience war rather than why states should make peace. This is also the first women's conference report in which sexual violence and rape is called a weapon of war.[70]

The first "objective" in this section is to increase women's participation in conflict resolution and "protect women living in situations of armed conflict." This includes an action item to "integrate a gender perspective in the resolution of armed conflict . . . and aim for gender balance . . . in all relevant international bodies" (58). It also wants to make sure such bodies provide necessary training so people can "address gender issues properly," such as rape and "other forms of violence against women in armed conflict." But a re-phrasing of these measures indicates (biological) sex or women are what's implied: integrate a *woman's perspective* in resolving conflict; aim for *sex balance* in international bodies; address *women's issues* properly. When sex and woman become synonymous with gender, it depoliticizes what gender is meant to capture, which are the power dynamics of masculinities and femininities in causing and perpetuating violence in the first place.

Objective E.3 identifies the need for non-violent conflict resolution and reduction in human rights abuses. It calls for the incorporation of "gender-sensitive concerns in developing training programs" (61). It also calls on states to "strengthen the role of women and ensure equal representation of women at all decision-making levels" in institutions dealing with conflict. Further, it calls for "protection" of women against rape and gender-based violence. Objective E.4, which is concerned with promoting "women's contribution to fostering a culture of peace," is a bit misleading because it does not call for women to be high-level peacemakers, but primarily advocates for more research on peace and conflict resolution and programs aimed at fostering more peace, all of which should include women. As with the section on violence against women, this section emphasizes the need for more research on conflict as though feminist activists and academics had not cited militarization, imperialism, and masculinities as causes.

More generally, there are a few particular ways in which "gender" is used within the text. Common phrases, which had not appeared in previous reports, include: gender gap, gender disparities, gender equality, gender-sensitive, mainstreaming of gender perspectives, and gender balance. But the meaning of these terms as understood in the ways they are used in the Platform indicates that either "sex" or "women" would better encapsulate the intended meanings and contexts in which "gender" is used: sex gap, sex disparities, sex equality (of numbers), woman-sensitive, and mainstreaming a woman's perspective. While the words "woman" and "women" still appear more frequently, it's unclear what the distinction between women and gender actually means. For example, strategic objective A.4 on "women and poverty" calls for the need to "develop gender-based methodologies and conduct research to address the feminization of poverty," which includes collecting "gender and age-disaggregated data" (25). But without a clear definition of gender or engagement with how gender operates, what makes gender-based methodology or gender-disaggregated data mean something different from sex-aware or sex-disaggregated data?

One repeated term illustrating the problematic use of gender is the phrase "gender gap" or "gender disparity." The section on education calls on governments to "eliminate gender disparities in access to all areas of tertiary education by ensuring women have equal access" or to "close the gender gap" in primary education and illiteracy (28). But the way such phrases are constructed indicates the referents are males and females or the number of girls—not gender understood as socially constructed and pertaining to masculinities and femininities. In many contexts, the word "gender" is about (biological) sex (male/female) awareness and the need to add females, not about the power of masculinity and patriarchy in producing exclusions.

The term "gender-sensitive," which has the potential to perhaps specifically deal with power dynamics, also does not appear to imply such meaning. There are motions for "gender-sensitive" educational systems and health-care training and research (28, 43, 46). The report also includes a strategic objective (C.3), which calls for "gender-sensitive initiatives that address" STDs, HIV/AIDS, and reproductive health (44). But further reading of these actions indicates the meaning is women, meaning neither men nor masculinity are included in the context of these initiatives. A gender-sensitive educational system implies one that ensures women have access to education and gender-sensitive health-care training means it includes classes on women's health. Gender-sensitive initiatives are all centrally focused on better access, education, and resources for women. While worthy endeavors to improve women's access to educational resources and ensure medical training and resources for women's health issues, "sex-sensitive" would still better indicate the meaning for such initiatives.

And finally, "mainstreaming a gender perspective" is used repeatedly throughout the text. In this case, the phrasing can possibly mean more than just women: "mainstreaming a gender perspective into all policies and programs should be promoted so that before decisions are taken, an analysis is made of the effects on women and men, respectively" (58). Because this phrase also includes men, it is possible that to analyze how a policy would affect both men and women and would require analytical gender. However, each time "mainstreaming a gender perspective" appears, it is followed by a strategic objective that calls for including more women. So it would seem one could mainstream a woman's perspective in this same context. Additionally, the use of the word "respectively" after "women and men" would indicate research should be done in the order described, so first on women and then men, as though these analyses would be distinct or separate. In another instance, the Platform states that "women/gender units are important for effective mainstreaming" (122). Here, "women" and "gender" are explicitly used as interchangeable terms.

The point in emphasizing meanings here is that while the Beijing Platform was a critical juncture in the promotion and diffusion of most of the policies discussed in this book, it is also a critical juncture in the emergence of the term "gender" as a substitute and stand-in for "women," biological sex and female. This shift coincides with the strengthening instrumentalist narrative of women as a means to an end. Gender becomes a technocratic shortcut to the complicated discussions of global gendered, racialized, classed, imperialist, and heterosexist hierarchies. But technocratic gender works well within a liberal feminist framework to eradicate discrimination rather than eradicate kyriarchical sociopolitical structures.

Post-2000: Gender Entrenched

Probably the most significant post-Beijing development for women's inclusion is the adoption of United Nations Security Council Resolution 1325 (UNSCR 1325) on Women, Peace, and Security by the United Nations Security Council in 2000.

After Beijing, the United Nations and NGOs focused on the actual implementation of the Beijing Platform, including women and armed conflict. The Commission on the Status of Women was the UN body responsible for overseeing its implementation and the Commission conducted meetings to discuss each "area of action" each year. In 1998 they specifically focused on women and armed conflict, and within the two-week meeting, there was a general consensus that little change or action resulted from the Platform's commitment to women in conflict. A "Women and Armed Conflict Caucus," composed of several NGOs, emerged from this meeting dedicated to operationalizing the proposals.[71] It was at this point this working group decided a Security Council Resolution was the next step, identifying the Security Council as "the power center of the UN, responsible for the maintenance of international peace and security."[72] After months of diligent work and strategic politicking on behalf of the Working Group on Women, Peace, and Security, the United Nations Security Council adopted the Resolution.[73] Felicity Hill, director of the Women's International League for Peace and Freedom (WILPF) and one of the leaders advocating for UNSCR 1325, stated that with the passage of 1325, "the last bastion of gender-free thinking in the UN had fallen."[74] Finally, after half a century, the highest global security apparatus acknowledged how women were directly targeted and affected by war.[75]

UNSCR 1325 calls for women's increased representation in decision-making and the need to recognize and support women's peace initiatives, protect women from gender-based violence, and incorporate a gender perspective into peacekeeping operations—and also mandates that field operations include a "gender component."[76] And while those involved considered it a watershed moment, it was not without some important and gendered limitations.

WILPF identified two themes missing from UNSCR 1325. The first was that there was little discussion of preventing war in the first place and absolutely no discussion or mention of actually ending war itself.[77] Ultimately, to *not* challenge war's legitimacy and apparent normalcy as a political endeavor limits discussions on the role kyriarchy plays in justifying and explaining war. Carol Cohn, a prominent feminist international relations scholar, explains:

> Protecting women *in* war, and insisting that they have an equal right to participate in the processes and negotiations that *end* particular war, both leave *war* itself in place . . . [1325 is not] an intervention that tries either to prevent war, or to contest the legitimacy of the systems that pro-

duce war—that is "to put an end to war". In this sense it fits comfortably into the already extant concepts and discursive practices of the Security Council, where the dominant paradigm holds a world made up of states that "defend" *state* security through *military* means . . . Letting (some) women into decision-making positions seems a small price to pay for leaving the war system essentially undisturbed.[78]

In this sense, the Resolution is about bringing women into security without using a gendered lens to explore the patriarchal and masculinist assumptions, institutions, and practices. In this case that the Resolution is titled Women, Peace, and Security reflects such. Were UNSCR 1325 a resolution on Gender, Peace and Security, a discussion of men and masculinities would also be part of the discussion. Felicity Hill noted how the Resolution focused on "the underrepresentation of women. It did not mention or explain the over-representation of men. It was very far from being a resolution dealing with men and masculinity as causes of women's insecurity."[79] Sandra Whitworth, in her studies of post-1325 peacekeeping, articulated how these UN documents do not deal with issues of militarism or masculinities.[80]

While the Resolution sets forth the means for adding women, not gender, to already existing security practices, institutions, and policies, it still includes the word "gender" many times in which it gets used interchangeably with "women"; for example it calls for adding a "gender component" to field operations but really means to add women to field operations. Subsequent resolutions tied to UNSCR 1325 (UNSCR 1820, 1888, 1889, 1960, 2016, 2122, and 2422) also contain similar ideas such as "gender advisors," "gender mainstreaming," "gender equality," "gender-biased," "gender dimensions," and a "new UN Gender Entity" to help coordinate efforts to deal with sexual violence.[81] The point is, while feminist scholars working on this issue recognize these resolutions are primarily about women and not necessarily gender, even they could not avoid the use of gender as synonymous with women.

Conclusion

Why does it matter that we use gender when we often mean women? Analytical gender can be a useful tool for exploring how the power dynamics of masculinities and femininities have produced the subjugation of many, not just women. It also means having a particular sort of discussion about policies aimed at including more women. Critical feminism would understand the goal of equality to mean dismantling the system of masculinities and femininities and kyriarchy more generally. While women's inclusion is an integral part of this, it is not all of it.

A feminist, analytical concept of gender politicizes, historicizes, and de-essentializes. It politicizes by exploring the dynamics of power in privileging masculinities over femininities and how people (both men and women) are subjugated via gendered divisions of labor, sex-based gender roles, and larger global forces such as states and organizations. Feminist gender also historicizes "how we got here" by focusing on the construction of order and its reliance on gender, including the development of states and economics, and social institutions like families and education. And feminist gender de-essentializes by exposing how there is no stable universal category of "woman" and the construction of gendered binaries are unstable and problematic—how male/female, man/woman has no basis in "nature" nor is it natural but is produced by the historical processes discussed.

This chapter sought to articulate how the development of a dual and dueling narrative on women was central to the emergence of the "gender = women" logic and shaped this norm of women's inclusion and it limits. The first narrative was a somewhat feminist narrative of structural causes of oppression, linking women's subjugation to larger forces of economic order and uneven development in the global system. The second narrative is how women are a means to an end, treating women as instruments for peace, growth, and development and security. These narratives developed over time and eventually the latter narrative became more powerful and with it, a technical treatment of "gender" to mean "women" emerged as the predominant way gender is thought of in the discourse of global governance. Because these documents informed many of the policies subsequently adopted by states (and discussed at length in the next few chapters), activists and politicians also rely on technocratic gender to articulate and argue for add-women policies. More critical discussions of how gender informs world order, and the need to challenge it, are primarily left out of the dialogue—and with it, more radical agendas and policies aimed at deconstructing gendered, raced, classed, heterosexist, and imperialist processes as well.

4

The "Problem" with Women's Representation in Government

Women's inclusion has been promoted via multiple policies and discourses by states and global organizations since the mid-1970s, and the focus on women's inclusion has increased at a steeper and steadier rate since the mid-1990s. Nowhere is this more evident than in efforts to promote women's representation, as efforts to include more women in all branches of government have been pursued in some capacity by most countries. But to end the analysis at the point of understanding why states and organizations promote women's inclusion in government would only tell part of the story.

For example, political scientist Niki Johnson's rich case study work on Uruguayan quotas and female representation illustrate some of these issues.[1] Uruguay adopted a quota law in 2014, but this changed the number of women in office by only 6 percent, from 14.6 to 20 percent. Johnson found that while there is a quota law, it has little impact on putting women into office because informal dynamics of the election process are exclusionary. One issue is, because male party leaders select candidates to run for office, they act as gatekeepers; they choose candidates from their own small factions or networks, which are composed of mostly men. Additionally party leaders claimed there were not any women to put on their lists, despite evidence to the contrary. And finally, party insiders claimed women actually excluded themselves from running, despite women politicians stating there were plenty of women who wanted to run for office.

What this example illustrates is that to understand this "problem" of "gender equality," means digging deeper into "what we know" and focusing on how gender not only matters, but is often reinforced by the very policies meant to challenge it. To do this, this chapter first surveys the literature on what factors account for states promoting more women in government. I will then interrogate these findings by focusing on the five issues key to understanding women's inclusion and how it is not "gender equality." These issues include: 1) the poor implementation of many of these policies and practices, despite mass adoption and diffusion, and the existing pockets of resistance to adoption; 2) the pervasiveness of informal barriers that bounds women's agency; 3) the way in which gendered binaries remain and are even reinforced through these practices; 4) the lack of intersectionality in promoting women or understanding their realities; and 5) the ways in which women's inclusion and efforts to promote women's representation have been co-opted and utilized to reinforce neoliberal world order.

Why States Promote Women's Inclusion in Government

There is extensive research on how women become representatives, particularly on the adoption of quotas to promote women in the legislature and the creation of women's bureaus. Research on women leaders, cabinet ministers, and judges is growing, though only more recently. Factors explaining women's inclusion in all forms of government more generally include institutional design, political shifts, both domestic and global pressure, and contagion among branches of government.

Women's policy bureaus, which are bureaucratic bodies aimed at promoting and protecting women's rights, were the first practice adopted en masse to better promote women's representation in the government. There is a fair amount of variation in the design and power of these agencies and scholars have noted three categories of agencies: those within governments that advise, monitor, and even implement policies; statutory commissions; and consultative bodies.[2] The transnational women's movement propelled the adoption of these agencies while inter-governmental organization relationships with the women's movement also influenced their success.[3] Many of these policy agencies sought out United Nations (UN) support and used policies such as the Convention on the Elimination of All Forms of Discrimination against Women (CEDAW) to reform laws and encourage monitoring.[4] Measuring their effectiveness via the degree to which states responded to these agencies and the degree to which these agencies tried to represent women's interests illuminated some mixed results.[5] Researchers found these agencies were effective at creating alliances and responding to the women's movement by establishing policies the women's movement wanted passed, but not all policies were successfully promoted.[6] Ultimately there did not seem to be specific characteristics of agencies that mattered all the time; they were conditional on particular governments and organizational cultures (in much the same ways quotas are conditional). One consistent finding, however, is that issues of political representation seemed to be the most successful policy pursuits and outputs of these agencies. Issues like abortion and labor were less reliably successful.[7]

There is extensive research on why quotas get adopted—exposing how quota adoption is a complex and highly political process involving both domestic and international actors impelled by women working within and outside of formal political institutions to increase levels of representation.[8] Among domestic explanations, scholars have noted that, although some quotas are adopted because they already embody notions of equality and representation[9], others are adopted because they serve strategic purposes.[10] In other cases it may be a response to internal party conflict.[11] Within states and political parties, women will push for quotas if other parties have them.[12] Political elites do not necessarily have to care about women's inclusion, but can frame their positions within the importance of inclusive democracy and quotas as means to addressing these barriers. These domestic campaigns are often understood as part of transnational informal networks of organizational staff, politicians, scholars, and activists working to promote quotas. Women working within various frameworks of political power—in the UN, in a political party, as an NGO worker, or as a researcher—build networks as a means to disseminate and share experiences about how to get quotas passed.

Scholars focusing on less institutionalized democracies have found an important relationship between quotas and democratic transitions: countries want to design institutions to recognize underprivileged groups within society as a way to legitimate states' emerging democracy.[13] States may also adopt quotas because they are directly encouraged—often by influential international actors—to adopt them.[14] In some cases, post-conflict peace agreements explicitly include gender quotas as part of their peacebuilding and democratization efforts.[15]

Consistently scholars emphasize the international community as essential to identifying why countries adopt quotas because it helps explain not just any single quota, but quotas as a global phenomenon.[16] Transnational emulation is one explanation for adoption, in which transnational movements share adoption ideas internationally, and "tipping" events (such as conferences) provide those trying to implement quotas international momentum to do so.[17] Women's and feminist groups work within and across states to share information on quotas to generate strategies for adoption. This exchange is a key component of transnational emulation, as these feminist and women's groups are often the sources and promoters of quota-related information and experience.[18] The UN has acted as both a direct influence and a "tipping point" catalyst in the promotion of quotas. The Fourth World Conference on the Rights of Women (the Beijing Conference) held in 1995 (and discussed in chapter 3) is cited as a key event in the diffusion of quotas.[19]

Political scientist Mona Lena Krook, in assessing the degree to which quotas work, stresses the importance of situating quotas within a country's candidate-selection process and emphasizes the ways that quotas challenge and work with these processes.[20] She identifies three categories of gendered institutions focused on different features of candidate selection: systemic institutions are related to the formal features of political systems such as electoral systems; practical institutions are the formal and informal practices of political elites; and normative institutions are the formal and informal behaviors that "justify the means and ends of political life."[21] She finds evidence that variation in quota effectiveness, even among different types of quotas, is generated from the ways in which quotas interact and alter these gendered institutions. For example, in Argentina, while there was a proportional representation system (systemic institution), the practical and normative institutions "did not treat 'sex' as a central criteria or category for candidate selection." In other words, sex was not considered a legitimate category for selecting and promoting candidates. But when feminist groups and party members referenced international documents legitimating quotas (normative institution), they were able to pass a legislative quota, which is the practical institution that facilitates candidates getting into office.[22]

There are both domestic and international explanations for why women are promoted in the executive branch. There is a correlation between increases in women in the cabinet and women's increased representation in the legislature, indicating women in parliament have contagion effects in other institutions.[23] Additionally, other research notes women's success as cabinet members may be shaped by the political networks they have access to, particularly in civil society, media, and opposition parties.[24]

How women are recruited into cabinet positions has generated some interesting and important findings. "Generalist" states, in which women cabinet ministers are selected from parliamentary caucuses, have fewer women than "specialist" states where recruitments are selected from outside parliament (more common in presidential systems).[25] This study explains that generalist states have fewer women perhaps because there are fewer women to choose from, and specialist states have more women because the president has more power to appoint them. Evidence from sub-Saharan Africa seems to support this thesis.[26] Larger changes in the number of women in cabinets (as well as in parliament) coincides with the political transitions starting in the early 1990s, in which women embedded themselves as relevant and central.[27]

The type of electoral system also matters. Open-list systems, which are proportional electoral systems where voters can rank candidates, are correlated with more women ministers and the presence of quotas.[28] A study by political scientists Gretchen Bauer and Manon Tremblay supported this finding, as proportional systems had 32.6 percent women cabinet ministers while non-proportional systems had 27.9 percent.[29] Explanations for the overall global increase in women cabinet members cite the importance of international organizations and institutions. The duration of time since a state ratified CEDAW is also a key factor in explaining world leaders' propensity and pressure to include women, something over which they have greater control.[30] Though in some regions, such as Sub-Saharan Africa and Western Europe, women cabinet ministers existed before CEDAW was even discussed.[31]

There are clear regional trends; for instance, women are better represented in Europe than in Arab states.[32] Yet, within regions, serious disparities remain, bringing into question a contagion effect.[33] For example, sub-Saharan Africa has a higher-than-global-average of women in cabinets, but the data are skewed at both ends with some countries, like South Africa and Nigeria with levels around 40 percent and Djibouti and Sierra Leone at less than 7 percent.[34] Thirty-four countries had a Minister of Women's Affairs, which was a woman in all cases but

Zambia.[35] In Latin America, today's women cabinet ministers serve about the same amount of time as male cabinet members, which was not the case in the 1990s.[36] Many scholars have noted women historically hold fewer cabinet appointments and when they do, they are often relegated to feminized offices associated with lower status, an issue with these policies, among others, that I will focus on in later sections.[37]

Women are more likely to become national leaders in parliamentary systems and more likely to be prime ministers than presidents, which is likely because women can "bypass a potentially biased general public and be chosen by the party."[38] According to political scientists Farida Jalalzai and Mona Lena Krook, parliamentary systems are also built on skills of collaboration so often considered more feminine. Presidential systems, on the other hand, work independently of legislatures, so are considered more masculine because leaders are expected to act quick and decisive. Women leaders are first political "outsiders" before rising to executive office and only gain office after a political "flux" of some type, such as political transition, domestic scandals, or major political party defeat.[39] As in other offices, there is a correlation and often a direct link between higher levels of women in one branch of government with the executive branch. And the greater the supply of "eligible" women (defined as those with previous political experience such as serving in the legislature) means the greater likelihood of having a female executive.[40]

Political parties are another factor impacting the promotion of women executives. In general, leftist parties are more likely to select women leaders, though this is not universal.[41] Political parties do appear more likely to choose women leaders during political upheavals and major social unrest.

There are two major factors in explaining higher numbers of women in courts: the number of seats and how the seats are appointed. In terms of how women become judges, it has been shown that the more seats there are on the bench, the more women judges.[42] It also matters how judges are selected, so states that use exams and merit systems have more women than those relying on political appointment.[43] These courts tend to deal with administrative and procedural issues rather than constitutional issues, so are also considered less prestigious because they have less influence within states. How justices are selected also matters for women's presence in office: 43 percent are selected to the court by presidential appointment and when the selection process is based on merit systems, women are more likely to become judges.[44]

Finally, for most of these policies that seek to add women, certain characteristics of the women themselves matter, sometimes referred to as "supply-side" factors. Levels of education, employment, access to financial resources, and connections to those already in power also matter in predicting higher levels of women in parliament, as judges and national leaders.[45]

Understanding Poor Implementation of Women's Representation

Despite the fact that scholars now know about the conditions under which women are more likely to be promoted in office, the global average of women in government remains quite low and varied. These low global averages indicate widespread variation in both adoption and implementation of women's inclusion, as certain states appear to pursue and implement such practices better than others. So while the policies and practices have global reach, they do not necessarily have universal support or implementation. Among most of these practices, the results and explanations for variation in implementation are similar. This is perhaps not surprising because all of these policies are highly correlated and interrelated.

One major factor in understanding women's representation is that the presence of women begets more women. A woman-centered policy/practice (like a quota or women's bureau) or greater numbers of women in one institution will impact the likelihood of more women's representation in other institutions. Increases in women in cabinets, parliaments, and the executive and judiciary sectors are all correlated in some way.[46] States that have a woman national leader, higher levels of women in parliament, and a women's ministry are usually more likely to also promote women cabinet ministers.[47] While there is correlation here, theories of causation do not consistently point in one direction or the other; rather, these policies are mutually reinforcing. In other words, if a state is resistant to one practice, it is likely to be resistant to many of them. Also, if a state has few women in one branch of government, it is likely to have low numbers of women in other branches.

Institutional design matters greatly in both adoption of policies and practices, and implementation.[48] While many explanations are conditional (on a host of contextual variables), there are a few common characteristics among these policies that result in adoption and better implementation. One important aspect is electoral system design.

How women are recruited into cabinet positions shapes women's access to cabinets. Parliamentary systems usually promote cabinet ministers from within their parliamentary caucuses, so women selected for cabinet positions are already part of government. In most presidential systems, cabinet ministers are selected from outside government, so appointed women may not already be part of government.[49] Studies find fewer women in the cabinet in generalist models and a higher number of women in specialist models (because the president has more power to appoint).[50] Women are also more likely to become national leaders in parliamentary systems and more likely to be prime ministers over president.[51] Judges also follow this trend, as 43 percent are selected to the court by presidential appointment. Coalition-based governments, in which cabinets are generated from multiple parties, may promote fewer women.[52] This also seems to hold in sub-Saharan Africa, where coalitions based on politicized ethnic groups tend to have fewer women.[53] Open-list systems are correlated with more women ministers and the adoption of sex quotas.[54] Another study supported this finding, as proportional systems had 32.6 percent women cabinet ministers while nonproportional systems had 27.9 percent.[55]

More recent studies have found women are more likely to be national leaders in dual executive systems with more dispersed authority holding the weaker position of authority, and women directly elected usually hold "nominal positions" (historically, this is only thirteen of fifty-five national leaders).[56] Women historically hold fewer cabinet appointments and when they do, they are often relegated to "feminized" offices associated with lower status.[57]

Political party orientation also matters. Left-leaning parties are more likely to elect women executives, though this is not universally the case.[58] They are also more likely to send women to parliament and promote women to cabinets.[59]

Global explanations, including the adoption of international policy initiatives on women, also matter for many of these practices.[60] The time since the ratification of CEDAW helps in explaining world leaders' propensity for, and pressure to include, women in cabinets, something over which they have greater control.[61] In terms of sub-Saharan Africa, women first emerged in cabinets around 1975 at the same time as the UN Decade for Women.[62]

Political "flux" also matters, either in the form of political crisis or democratic transitions, as institutional changes may offer women windows of opportunity to enter the system and change the rules. Many female national leaders have emerged due to death of spouses/parents and poor political maneuvering on the part of those in power.[63] Larger changes in the number of women in cabinets (as well as in parliament) coincide with the political transitions starting in the early 1990s, where women activists capitalized on political transitions. Quotas also emerge in post-conflict situations.[64] Democratic transitions remain an important explanation in the promotion of all of these policies, though the effects may not be immediate; in the case of women in parliament or congresses, it may take a while for democracy to have an impact.[65] This effect can be strengthened by a strong women's movement.[66] The adoption of women's policy agencies, sex quotas, and women in executive positions became an important tenant for international aid and development.[67] International financial institutions identify women as key actors in promoting strong democratic governance.[68]

Informal Barriers and Bounded Agency in Women's Representation

While there are key institutional factors that shape women's inclusion, including type of electoral system and political party, levels of procedural recruitment, and phases of political transition, altering these has not resulted in significant global change. What change has occurred has been very uneven. Additionally, these changes in law or procedures do not necessarily translate into practice: there is substantial evidence that the adoption of a sex quota does not guarantee increases in women's representation.[69] Indeed, newly adopted quotas are more likely to be resisted than complied with.[70] A deeper look into *why* these explanations matter begins to illustrate the ways in which gender informs institutions, which can be only partly remedied by women's inclusion.

The policies and practices aimed at increasing women's inclusion often target discrimination, and in the case of quotas and policy bureaus, can actually change the rules. But despite this, sexism and kyriarchy remain, bounding the degree to which these anti-discrimination policies and practices are effective. In other words, changing the rules does not necessarily change the practices, beliefs, or ideologies of those who create, promote, and maintain the rules.

If one delves into the above discussion about what factors affect the adoption and implementation of women's representation, and thus inclusion, it is evident informal rules and beliefs matter in shaping women's access to and participation in government. Generally women have better access to positions of power if: 1) the office or position is less competitive and of lower prestige and power; 2) women are more insulated from the popular vote; 3) women are better qualified and connected than their male counterparts; 4) other powerful women are already present; and 5) the (kyriarchical) status quo is ripe for disruption. None of these phenomena are codified in law or procedural documents, but instead result from expectations about power and gender among both men and women. And all of these factors may ultimately bind the degree to which women can successfully navigate male-dominated institutions.

First, when the office is less competitive, it is more likely to include women, and this holds for all branches of government. Systems that have more total seats (in parliament, courts, or cabinets), promote group over individual competition (like parliamentary systems and parties), and already have women in government positions, tend to have more women holding political office overall. This all translates to less competitive rules, and the existing presence of women in government positions means more women are likely to secure a place in government. Less competitive institutions include those with more seats and or lower levels of prestige. In cross-national studies of national courts, the more seats, the more women judges.[71] These courts tend to deal with administrative and procedural issues rather than constitutional issues, and so are considered less prestigious because they have less influence within states. As women occupy lower procedural administrative courts rather than constitutional courts, they have less influence over policy. One survey of women judges in the European Union indicated women believed unfair criteria depressed their participation.[72]

As previously stated, women are more likely to become a prime minister than a president, which is a lower prestige office in many cases. And in dual-chamber legislative systems, the more prestigious chamber usually has fewer seats, which translates to fewer women. While women's inclusion matters, it also means men's exclusion, and this appears to be easier to agree to when costs of men's exclusion (in numbers and power) is lower. Indeed, international pressure to promote women in office seems to have affected only lower-prestige cabinet appointments for women.[73] Interviews with women cabinet ministers call their own appointments "window-dressing" without "real power."[74] So, how does it happen that the promotion of women to the most elite positions in states, result in them feeling that they do not have the same political power as their male counterparts?

More recent work focuses on backlash against efforts to include more women.[75] Pressure to adopt quotas may promote a male backlash against such policy changes, resulting in resistance to change. This can include challenging the legality of quotas, which have been overturned by governing bodies in Russia, France, and more recently, Kenya.[76] In such cases, without a strong transnational feminist presence, a quota is likely to fail, as illustrated in the case of Chile, which continued to reject a quota: "Men would not be disposed to being replaced by women."[77] In a study of "gender parity" in cabinets, leaders may face resistance from their own parties. Political scientists Susan Franceschet and Gwynn Thomas found that if a leader is weak and imposes parity on her or his own party, it is less likely to be accepted.[78] Ultimately it is because men fear a loss of their own access to political office *to women* through increased competition that they may try to thwart women's inclusion.

Candidate selection processes matter greatly, whether women are in office or not. A cross-national study finds that when democratic structures are weak (like in transitioning states), informal political structures (like client networks) may shape women's access to power.[79] In studies of both Canada and Uruguay, the (biological) sex of the party gatekeeper—who recruits candidates to run for public office—is correlated with whether or not women are chosen to run for parliament.[80] In the Canadian study, the authors posit that informal signaling and implicit sex preferences affect whether women run. A Central American female legislator reiterates this: "In order for women to be elected to Parliament, the political parties have the responsibility of trusting in women, encouraging them, and putting them forward in constituencies where they can be certain of electoral success."[81] In parliamentary systems (where party leaders become prime ministers), few women hold leadership positions in major parties and so they are not part of the pipeline to national executive office.[82] Thus gatekeepers have to want to promote women.

Another informal strategy in applying quotas is to include women candidates on more than one list (for higher and lower parliamentary houses), so if they win in both races, the men can secure another position in at least one of the offices.[83] That men can shape if and how women seek office is not necessarily caused by the structures of these institutions, but by, again, social and cultural issues about the value of women. There is not necessarily anything inherently unequal about how these institutions are designed, but the people within these institutions bring with them gendered beliefs and stereotypes, resulting in women's limited access and hampering women's agency in challenging it.

Another issue here is that women are better off when they are insulated from the voting public. When the public votes, women are less likely to win. As there are more women cabinet members when appointed by the president, most explanations find it is important because women can then "bypass a potentially biased general public and be chosen by the party."[84] In other words, when an executive has control over appointment, women have a better chance of inclusion than if such decisions were left to a vote.[85] Political leaders may also appoint more women to distinguish themselves from their own party.[86]

Additionally, other research has shown that the presence of more women in government does not necessarily change public attitudes about women in government.[87] If women continue to lose popular votes and require elites to put and keep them in office, then the issue becomes more about the public and their opinions or beliefs: why they choose not to vote for women or why they think women are less qualified.

Politically elite women are much more likely to become representatives. Again, there are not usually specific rules on *who* can run for office or be appointed, but *who* a woman is matters greatly. There is quite a bit of evidence that women heads of government often have family connections that account for political success.[88] And more well-connected women may be able to better navigate male-dominated political networks to become legislators as well.[89] More recent work found that "no woman holding dominant executive power in Latin America or Asia had ever come to power without familial connections."[90] Indeed 30 percent of women leaders had familial ties to former or current executives.[91] In some countries with quotas, like Argentina and India, male elites will nominate their wives and daughters for office to guarantee their own seats.[92] So leaders find ways to follow the letter but not the spirit of these laws. While it is important that women are getting access to the highest political offices, their tenures are bounded by gendered expectations about women's roles in public life. This limits their agency to make changes for women and men alike, particularly when they are treated as appendages of a man's regime.

Related to this last issue is how women's inclusion in one branch of government begets women's inclusion in other branches. In many studies, the presence of many women, or a quota or women's ministry, is a strong predictor of more women in another office.[93] Explanations tend to focus on women prioritizing the inclusion of other women, or "breaking the glass ceiling," but this indicates that some form of social and political pressure among women elites may play a significant role in getting more women included, thus the onus is on women to help other women. However, more recent research found that female parliamentary leadership is actually correlated with fewer women cabinet ministers and women in less prestigious ministries. This may be because women leaders do not reap any public benefit from appointing more women to office while their male counterparts do.[94]

Gender Still Matters in Women's Representation

Because these issues of low numbers are consistent across branches of government, and because these practices are all part of women's inclusion, the reason for a lack of significant increases across these policies is the same: "adding women" does not deal with all the ways institutions are gendered. A gendered institution is one in which the formal structures and informal dynamics reinforce gender differences.[95] While some women have benefited from efforts to increase the number of women in government, a central structural cause of inequality—the perpetuation of a gendered binary of masculinities over femininities—persists, result-ing in women's bounded agency. An apt analogy is that women have been added to the "game," but the rules of the game have otherwise remained the same. Thus, only a small portion of what shapes women's agency and political power has been addressed. This hinders women's likelihood to succeed on their own terms and reinforces the very pro-cesses that excluded women in the first place because the rest of the sexist, masculinist rules remain. This status quo is one built on dichot-omous understandings of sex and gender and its perpetuation within these policies results in these troubling numbers and data of women's inclusion.

While scholars have noted how woman-centered policies may exacer-bate gender difference, others have argued such policies, such as quotas, "serve to re-gender politics away from the masculine norm, and thus legitimize the idea that women are a politically relevant collective."[96] But, as highlighted in this section, women remain important *as women*. Masculinity still matters greatly in explaining why men dominate politi-cal institutions and femininity still matters in explaining why women are over-represented in certain political areas, especially family and health. When one delves into explanations for women's representation, such as institutional designs, political change, and informal dynamics, gender is one of the only analytical forces that can actually explain why such variables or explanations exist. Women are thus expected to either act like women or more like men. But this leaves gender binaries in place and women are left having to navigate them.

In most places women are over-represented in "feminine ministries" or portfolios related to home, family, and "care," such as culture, educa-tion, and children. Additionally women are also underrepresented in "masculine ministries," such as defense, finance, and foreign affairs.[97] Women ministers will also face a tougher challenge moving to more masculine domains once in the cabinet. These findings are consistent in Canada and Arab states as well.[98] While there has been some change over time and these patterns do not universally hold across all minis-tries, this reinforces what is women's domain versus men's domain and thus, binary gender is left intact. Gender determines what roles women and men do and should play in government.

Similar patterns are found in national leadership. Scholars have noted in Latin America the idea of "marianismo," in which women's identities are derived from their male relatives, means women are expected to fulfill the agenda of these men and gain political advantage by aligning with their male relative's platform.[99] In other words, women are considered for leadership as extensions of already existing male political leadership, which also appears to be the case in some Arab states.[100] In Asia, many women leaders were daughters of male founders of states, and acted as "symbols of their fathers or husbands."[101]

One general theme underlying many of these conditions has to do with the *gendered sociopolitical capital* men and women need to get into office. Sociopolitical capital encapsulates how women and men are assigned masculinized and feminized attributes that may either help or hinder access to political power. This capital can take the form of networks and power brokers, but also assumptions, beliefs, and stereotypes. This capital is sociopolitical because it is based on socially constructed ideas about gender, but it is political because it produces differential effects on men and women and is thus about power. Political scientist Elin Bjarnegård's research on the over-representation of men in parliaments explicitly examines this sort of capital. She found that clientelist political systems favor men's access to candidate selection, especially in states with weak democratic institutions. This clientelism was best explained by men's "homosocial capital," in which men sought out other men to build powerful networks based on strategic positioning and contacts.[102] This was also the case in research on Uruguay.[103]

Another study of homosocial capital found women parliamentarians have fewer resources to provide important client services to their constituents because their patronage networks are weaker, though states with more women or with quotas have better results than states without quotas.[104] In a study of women and parliament in North Africa, women were less likely to benefit from clientelist networks, in part because women are more excluded from public life and have fewer resources from which to draw on for help.[105]

A major component of this capital, besides that such networks are reserved for men, is that it includes how men consider one another "more alike and more predictable." Said differently, men prefer other men in their power networks, not only because they are more likely to occupy positions of power and connectivity, but because they also occupy masculinity: this is what makes them "alike and predictable." Men's homosocial capital can be understood as masculine capital and it is the "currency with which parliamentary seats can be bought in certain political contexts."[106]

This masculine sociopolitical capital extends to the public as well. Several studies indicate the public prefers male representatives because societies associate public office and leadership success with masculinity, not femininity.[107] Surveys of the public in the United States found the public had more confidence in men to handle issues such as foreign policy.[108] Further, respondents who considered war, security, or terrorism to be the biggest issues facing the U.S. were more likely to say a man would do a better job in dealing with these issues as President.[109] In a cross-national study predicting women's representation in legislatures, cultural values about women mattered more than any other explanation—countries that generally agreed "men are better in politics" had fewer women in office.[110] Sociopolitical capital is also evident in ideas about women's leadership. One particular term used in many of analyses of public perception, and even scholarly research on women in office, is the idea of "competency." Competency, as a leadership quality, should be understood as a masculinized virtue. This is because leaders are assumed to be competent by virtue of having achieved office, a male-dominated but also masculine space. In a study of Arab states, stereotypes about women's political capabilities limit their willingness to run and discount their value once in office. Women are considered weak, poor decision-makers, and generally incompetent.[111] As this is a gendered idea, the public is more likely to assume male leaders already have competency because they are much more likely to occupy masculinized spaces. Women, on the other hand, have to work harder to achieve perceived competency because it is not a given for "femininity" to include "competency" or even "leader."

Women may garner greater masculinized sociopolitical capital by having more experience and education than their male peers. This is why it is so important women have some political experience prior to higher offices, so they are more easily deemed "competent."[112] Higher education also really matters because in some cases women cannot then be accused of lack of knowledge about politics.[113] In Latin America, women need to be better qualified in order to switch to more prestigious cabinets.[114] In explaining how women become nominated for cabinets, it is women's status among elites that determines whether women get nominated, not institutional factors or larger forces of social equality at work.[115] Women's "status" is gendered in that it is directly tied to perceptions and connections that women make in masculine institutions. Because men form networks primarily among themselves, women have to embody traits valued in a masculinized environment. Women's competency is produced through more experience and education; they do not just have it by virtue of their sex or gender. An American study found that while a woman senator's perceived likability rating was not affected by prior attitudes about women, the perception of her competency was, indicating likability may be tied to traditional gender roles, while the perception of competency is tied to leadership and thus masculinity.[116]

One of the implicit assumptions in adding women is that they will act for women, bringing a different set of interests and approaches than their male colleagues.[117] There is quite a bit of evidence to indicate that this actually happens to the benefit of women, but this also means women are seen as different from men, and this difference is then the justification for why they are needed in government.[118] This is troubling for a few reasons in that it reinforces gender binaries and difference, but also forestalls important discussions about expectations for male representatives and masculinities. Without critical discussion about *why* we rely on women to represent women, men are not called upon to answer for why they apparently so poorly represent 50 percent of their constituents or why women cannot represent men. And anytime such differences are assumed, it becomes easier to justify women's presence in "feminine" and feminized aspects of government as a logical extension of difference. This can also mean women who are in office bear a responsibility their male colleagues may not, which may shape a woman's tenure and leadership experiences in ways they do not want or did not anticipate. This may impact their ability to climb the political ladder or achieve leadership positions within political parties and government more generally. It is a political "double bind," in that women in office must act for other women while participating in a political system that arguably does not work or act for women on its own.

Women leaders have to walk a fine line of balancing feminine and masculine characteristics in order to be effective.[119] While the inclusion of women in public office clearly matters and is important, it should be problematized in how women are expected to act to be successful. While these policies have had success for some women, they remain very elitist. Even for those women who find power, these practices create a bounded agency in which women do what they can but continue to be reminded their sex matters. Gretchen Bauer and Manon Tremblay, in their overview of women's access to the executive branch, sum it all up: "Gender roles seriously limit female participation in governments."[120]

Poor Intersectionality in Representation

Women are not a single group, but they embody and are understood through "a collection of categories," meaning women are impacted by other social identities like race, class, sexuality, and geography.[121] These identities intersect in ways that complicate both policies and discourses aimed at women's inclusion that treat women as a universal and single category. This matters in representation because who represents whom may impact the distribution of resources in a state as well as shape the legitimacy of those acting as representatives.[122] Theories on representation have shifted focus from "just get the women in" to "it's not enough just to represent this marginalized group."[123] Scholars argue that by focusing on specific groups, other subgroups are ignored, which undermines the legitimacy of representatives and representative institutions more generally. What is really important, as many scholars claim, is how much a group can hold its representatives accountable for supporting their views and policies.[124] Political theorist Suzanne Dovi adds to the theory by stating that there should be two criteria for descriptive representatives: 1) the group and the representative must mutually recognize one another and what role is being played in the representation; and 2) representatives should represent "dispossessed subgroups," or those within a group who are even still more marginalized (for example, being a woman is an important group identity, but to ignore that class plays an important factor within the group would be negligent).[125] If women do not engage the diversity of women's identities or experiences in advocating on behalf of other women (and in situating themselves), then the impact of the presence of women is little different from the status quo.

In this sense, one must ask: Which women are actually included as representatives in government? As discussed in the previous section, women have to find a way to counter a sociopolitical capital deficit by having "more" of important political resources than their male peers, such as education, status, and access to those in power. But this capital is not just shaped by gender, it is also informed by class, race, and sexuality. Most women in the world will not have access to these necessary resources to even entertain the idea of public office, so the pool of women who become political officials is quite small nearly everywhere in the world.

Studies on women executives and cabinet ministers found women's status as "elites" was more important than their biological sex in opening doors of political power.[126] Elite status includes higher levels of education and experience, but also political connections. Women cabinet ministers are significantly more qualified than their male colleagues.[127] This includes higher levels of education and more professional experience in international organizations and the private sector. Many women ministers were considered "specialists" in their field.[128] Other research finds the presence of elite women in one branch of government will directly impact more women in cabinets and in more prestigious ministries.[129] This is not the case, however, when there is a woman prime minister.[130] Other local studies have found women's success as cabinet members may be shaped by the political networks they have access to, particularly in civil society, media, and opposition parties.[131] Women must have the time and resources to make such connections in the first place; this often means being located in urban capitals to participate, so geography also matters. To even entertain the possibility of running for public office becomes a monumental task when one is expected to have more of already scarce resources (money, time, connections) to even compete. The number of women in countries who can do this is quite small. If this is the case, then is representation in government really the best metric of gender equality when so few can meet such standards?

While empirical studies on race and representation at the global level remain limited, the existing research indicates women of color are substantially underrepresented among representatives and that sex quotas and ethnic quotas tend to benefit (ethnic) majority women and ethnic minority men.[132] In a cross-national study conducted by political scientist Melanie Hughes, while majority men (defined as the racial/ethnic/religious majority in a given state) were 39 percent of the population, they held 72 percent of seats in the average legislature.[133] Hughes also found minority women, on average 11 percent of the general population, held only 2 percent of legislative seats compared with 15 percent of seats held by majority women; and this already low number is dragged down by the fact that one-quarter of states included no minority women at all. Minority women held more seats as compared to majority women in Latin America, Africa, and the West but on average "minority women are represented at only 16.9 percent of their population share."[134] What this indicates is, not only are the women being added to government wealthier and more educated, they are also more likely to be from the ethic/racial majority.

Another recent study by political scientist Karen Bird focuses on states with both sex and "ethnic" quotas—do such states better include ethnic minority women?[135] She posits these systems of inclusion frequently operate independently of one another, often to the detriment of ethnic minority women, so these women are not better represented. Bird also finds that when ethnic quotas have existed for a while, the likelihood of adopting a sex quota is much harder. She notes that how institutions are combined matters deeply because when they are not "nested," these quotas can actually "augment the idea that *men* are the most appropriate representatives of ethnic minorities, and that *non-minorities* are the most appropriate representatives of women." A case study in Bolivia on this very issue indicates within-group dynamics and the formulation of a common "political strategy."[136] Research on India also finds that women are being nominated at the cost of the "least powerful male politicians." While minority women are elected at higher rates than ethnic-majority women, this has come at the expense of minority men, who had benefitted from ethnic quotas.[137] These studies highlight how political unity is not simply given but requires people with multiple identities to find shared meaning and ideas to project an agenda. Gender, as well as class, race, and geography, is never guaranteed to produce this.

Women as "Good Governance" in Neoliberal Order

The final issue, which represents the culmination of the previous four, is how women's representation, and thus women's inclusion, has become a tool of neoliberal order. One must look to the global system in which these policies are pursued, which means linking women's representation to liberal democracy and neoliberal economic order within which women's inclusion is promoted. Women's representation has become fairly widespread in part because women's representation works within a neoliberal governance mentality that privileges equality of opportunity and rationality. All of these efforts to promote women's inclusion via representation have been lauded by global organizations, and are even considered measures of "gender equality." But these are often promoted by organizations to make states more efficient and effective, not to fundamentally change the status quo or advocate for the re-distribution of material resources.[138] This greater effectiveness and efficiency women's presence may bring is then linked to economic growth, development, foreign investment, and foreign aid.

As states pursue neoliberal democracy that privileges individualism, anti-discrimination, equal rights, and free markets, women have worked within this context by pushing for the removal of legal obstacles limiting their rights and opportunities.[139] Efforts to include more women in government—via dedicated bureaucratic agencies, quotas, and informal efforts to create sex parity—are consistent with a culture of non-intervention in the economy, a key feature of neoliberalism. Mona Lena Krook examines the complications that quotas present for feminists, noting that given the global neoliberalism in which they are situated, may contribute to a problematic separation between political empowerment and social and economic empowerment: "Quotas and neoliberalism are . . . often partners in the pursuit of a new world order."[140] This same logic extends to women's bureaus and efforts to promote more women in cabinets and judicial systems. The promotion of both democratic regimes and women's access to public office go hand-in-hand: being and becoming democratic buoys the importance of representation as part and parcel of democracy, especially for women. Indeed, more women in government is an indication of democratic and democratizing institutions.[141]

But why are states and global organizations so keen to promote women's representation and inclusion in government? Why are women considered a strategy of good governance? By delving into documents on why representation matters, it becomes evident global power brokers promote women because of essentialized ideas about the value women bring to male-dominated institutions. These essentialized ideas cite women as more honest, selfless, trustworthy, peaceful, and better spenders in states. Women in government are also cited as having major ripple effects for society at large, so women's presence begets more women in the economy, and thus changes societal views on women more generally. It is worth digging into these claims to consider how ideas essentializing women reinforces gender binaries and obscures the trade-offs women's representation actually encompass.

The World Bank perpetuates gender binaries in its promotion of women's representation and inclusion as a strategy of good governance. A seminal World Bank publication in 2001, *Engendering Development*, promoted women's access to public office, explaining that women are less corruptible and "are more community-oriented and selfless than men." The report then goes onto cite several studies that find women to be generally less likely to take bribes, and women in business are less likely to pay bribes to government officials. It also finds that "corruption falls as the proportion of parliamentary seats held by women rises."[142] There is no discussion as to why women are less corrupt following these findings; being a woman is enough to qualify her for an allotted role in government. Selflessness and community-orientation may be understood by those in power to be part of a woman's nature. Said differently, it does not matter where a woman comes from or what she stands for, her natural inclinations towards honesty make her a good anti-corruption actor. Additionally, such discussions reverberate the realities of public-private dichotomies in which women's roles as "homemakers" are historically justified using the same logic of selflessness and caring. So while it is now considered prudent to include women in the public sphere, it still is based upon the dichotomization of difference in which "private sphere" qualities are considered important for better government.

The other component of governance cited within the text is how "exclusion narrows perspectives." The discussion identifies how women bring to government different perspectives and increased legitimacy; it cites surveys with women politicians who identify the representation of women, as well as other "parts of society," to be part of their governmental role. The section then identifies how discrimination and exclusion promote "distrust and resentment, which influences the larger social climate and jeopardizes development prospects." Another way to read it is that more diverse representation reduces the risk of dissent from historically excluded groups. Underlying this discussion is how women in government are seen to generate more trust among citizens. The prevailing logic follows that those who have more trust, in part because they believe their interests are represented, are more willing to work with their government to promote their interests rather than using potentially "destabilizing" mechanisms of dissent. Women in government then, provide more social stability and social stability is part of good governance.

While this report from 2001 is somewhat dated, the World Bank has doubled-down on women's representation and its value for governance. While in 2001 there were not explicit calls for quotas, by 2013, quotas are treated like a panacea for many state social ills. *Women, Business, and the Law 2014: Removing Restrictions to Enhance Gender Equality* reinforces the links between women's representation and stronger governments and economies. The report explicitly identifies legal quotas as an important aspect to promoting women's greater economic opportunities. The report states women's increased representation may translate into "more equitable representation of women's interests." The same study correlates women's representation in parliament with greater social spending and greater labor force participation. It also states quotas "might help allocate women's talents more efficiently," and these talents may then change attitudes and social norms, leading more girls to get better educations and to spend less time on domestic chores.[143] Again, this list of the public benefits of women's representation and inclusion is not accompanied by discussions of why it takes women in office to promote more social welfare and stronger states. It also ignores the issue of why men's representation has accomplished so little on behalf of women.

An additional issue arises, in that often these policies are not adopted out of democratic ideals and practices but for strategic purposes. The motivation among IOs, political elites, and feminist activists for including more women may stem from different assumptions and goals. Indeed political elites use women's inclusion as a strategy to garner power and votes, and the World Bank promotes inclusion because of essentialized views on women as "politically pure."[144] For example, when the world robustly responded to the recommendation from the first UN Women's Conference to create national women's agencies, feminist scholars noted the apparent "bureaucratization of feminism." The interests of governments and feminist activists aligned in a tense way, and feminists were weary of what Judith Squires refers to as "co-optation and depoliticization."[145] States supported the policy for many reasons, including not wanting to be seen as illegitimate.[146] This depoliticization of feminist pursuits via the institutionalization of add-women policies in government was troubling because governments and IOs began supporting these policies for more tactical purposes, not necessarily because issues of social justice mattered. Rather, women became proxies for equality, democracy, stability, justice, and peace. Women's representation and inclusion are increasingly an essential component of an efficient and effective world order.

Strategically, these discussions are good for women's claims to the right to be part of government because it identifies how women apparently fill roles men have not fulfilled. In addition, it opens a space for the public/private dichotomy to be taken seriously and addressed by policy-makers by encouraging discussions as to why women are more selfless. The logical leaps that quotas can somehow lead to girls spending less time on domestic chores is troubling in that it takes shortcuts in explaining exactly how quotas, as an effort to promote gender equality, should have such transformative changes, offering very little evidence to support these claims. If these discussions are derived from the belief that women are inherently/naturally more honest, caring, and driven by selflessness, then other "natural" claims may also be justified, claims that reinforce women's differences as part of the justification of their oppression. All of these policies of adding women—while promoting women as adding distinct views and interests—can also limit their political power by justifying that differences in power are derived from natural differences between men and women, rather than socially constructed, hierarchical dichotomies.

As some of these policies and practices become more "effective," it is important to think about what they are now more effective *at*. National quotas are more effective at getting women into parliaments; but that quotas are needed implicitly means without them women would be excluded even more than they already are. In this sense, a quota may be thought of as an indicator of women's inequality, not gender equality. What this means is that to have a quota may indicate a state's willingness to address women's exclusion, but to simply have the policy should not be a measure for equality, which is often implied in research. Additionally, while quotas seem more effective at getting women into office, there is less known cross-nationally about their impact.[147]

This leads to the important issue that liberal democracy and democratic institutions are inherently gendered. By extension, then, feminists see them as undemocratic because despite offering greater opportunities for women to participate they still do little to guarantee large political benefits.[148] Why do feminists think institutions, such as legislatures or democracy, are gendered? Because if they were gender-neutral, we would see equal numbers of men and women in equal positions of power, and nowhere is this the case (though a few states, like Rwanada, have achieved sex parity or better in parliament, no state has sex parity in all branches of government). As Virginia Sapiro states, "politics itself has gender."[149] The expectations that those in power in democracies will not or cannot advocate on behalf of a broad coalition of different groups (an underlying assumption of descriptive representation) makes one wonder if liberal democracy should be a pinnacle model for states. Efforts to include more women may serve to placate or cover up broad exclusion and domination unless the institutions within democracies are addressed as gendered and problematic.

These efforts to put more women in government may never really fix the problem of inequality. What I mean is, if a political system favors a few to act for many, and this is usually based on masculinities and male domination, then an emphasis on "who represents who" may not be as important as why institutions meant to be equal are so unequal. As Elin Bjarnegård's work on male over-representation found, informal dynamics matter greatly in understanding when democracy produces women's representation. One of these "informal" institutions is clientelism, or "the exchange of personal favors for political support." There is a range clientelism may take but such practices are *endemic* to democracy since power brokers are always trying to secure votes to win. Clientelism then may represent only one of several "informal" institutions of democracy that impact composition of institutions in ways that will consistently have impacts on whether women are included. If these informal dynamics always matter, then a focus on formal institutions and their composition can only deal with one aspect of exclusion, leaving perhaps countless other ways liberal democracies systematically exclude women.

In the larger scheme of women in this world, women's representation has very little *direct* impact on women's inclusion more generally because it emphasizes an aspect of inclusion that is inherently unequal: very few people, especially women, will *ever* hold office. Yet it is a cornerstone of any "gender equality" measure and platform, in part because of the long logical leaps and causal connections made between women's representation and improved government, governance, and society. As institutions such as political offices are gendered, efforts to improve women's representation do little to alter more than the composition of institutions, leaving gendered cultures and individuals in place.[150] In this sense, women's representation may actually reinforce the status quo of masculinist power structures.[151] The pool of possible candidates for office may get larger, but it is still an elite process that itself may not change—the inclusion is still quite exclusionary.

An additional issue is how this emphasis (some may even call it obsession) on representation as a key aspect of gender equality has found more traction in global politics over other issues such as abortion and poverty.[152] This matters because in neoliberal world order, predominantly men in a predominantly kyriarchical global system define how gender equality/women's inclusion gets envisioned. Women's formal representation is privileged over redistribution of resources and reproductive justice, and the policies promoted by global organizations and adopted by states reflect such power dynamics.

Conclusion

As states continue to promote the norm of women's inclusion, the global shift has been rather amazing. At this moment, more women are in public office than ever before and the gains continue. States continue to adopt quotas and add women to cabinets and benches and even as national leaders. The Global South continues to promote women in ways the Global North, particularly the United States, should notice and learn from. Women have been able to shape their states' policies and represent other women in ways not seen in modern history. But a look at the similarities among these policies and practices indicates that while they matter, they are rife with gender bias that bind movement towards genuine equality rather than just inclusion. By promoting these policies without critical discussions about why they are not having more universal and significant impacts on the numbers and power of women in office, we shift the focus from asking, "how can we change the overall institution?" to "look, women are a part of the institution."

All of the issues discussed in this chapter can change and a future of continued systematic exclusion is not inevitable. For example, continued research and discussions about the informal dynamics of democracy and democratization will go a long way towards dealing with how gender roles and dynamics shape formal institutions.[153] Perhaps even a reimaging of alternative forms of government could spark ideas about how to systematically address informal institutions. Additionally, acknowledging which women are being included as part of these efforts will also foster greater discussion about the complexities of women's identities—and that other measures to address marginalized identities should be part and parcel of quotas and parity and any future meaning of "gender equality." Finally, coupling efforts to promote women's representation with specific measures to allocate material resources to marginalized groups would help frame representation as part of the efforts to promote equality, rather than as a synonym for equality or simply, the end game of it.

5

The "Problem" with Recognizing Women's Economic Rights

In the 2012 *World Bank Development Report,* President Robert Zoellick writes, "Gender equality is a core development objective in its own right. But *gender equality is also smart economics.*"[1] This echoes the Bank's 2006 "Gender Action Plan" titled *Gender Equality as Smart Economics.* Indeed, Hillary Clinton and Michelle Bachelet have made similar comments about gender as part of an equation of "smart economics" and it's become a sort of rally cry for promoting women in growth and development strategies.[2] But why are women smart economics? The 2012 report continues: "Greater gender equality can enhance productivity, improve development outcomes for the next generation, and make institutions more representative."[3] This chapter dissects this logic of "gender equality as smart economics," including the policies adopted to enact such logic and the limits of treating gender as a variable in economic productivity. It also questions the degree to which ensuring women have better access to employment, land, and credit really counts as "progress" in a global system built upon the exploitation of people and in particular women.

Women's inclusion, as outlined in previous chapters, is not limited to women's representation in government. Indeed, even states have prioritized how to better recognize women and include them in their economies. Recognition of women's economic rights often receives less attention in global politics (and the study of global politics) than women's representation in government or the protection of women from violence. But the growing emphasis on the links between women's "economic empowerment" and state economic growth and development has been a cornerstone of both developed and developing states. The idea is that working, owning property, and having access to credit greatly benefits women, their families, and their state. Based on this logic, there have been a growing number of states passing laws to improve women's access to property, credit, and employment.

But even with such developments, the news is still not very good. The same World Bank report notes "excess relative mortality of girls and women" as well as other disparities such as segregation in types of economic activities, wage gaps, different care work responsibilities, gaps in assets, and "constraints to women's agency in both the private and public spheres."[4] The types of work women find, even though they are now in the labor force in much larger numbers, has changed very little. The International Labour Organization's (ILO) latest report on women's employment is even bleaker, noting "gender gaps in the labor market have worsened," and women are again facing higher unemployment rates and more economic vulnerability than men globally, even though these numbers had been diminishing prior to the 2008 global economic crisis.[5] In other words: women still account for the majority of the world's poor and economically vulnerable and still have control over fewer resources.

Given the resources—both economic and human—dedicated to promoting economic growth and development, why aren't more women better off? Why hasn't women's increased inclusion in economic policies and the labor force translated to significantly lower levels of economic inequalities of women nearly anywhere in the world? And why are trends reversing in some cases? To guide the study of the global push to increase these rights, I engage the catchy slogan, popular at the World Bank and elsewhere—"gender equality is smart economics," which outlines what women's inclusion means in the context of growth and development, what it means for economic policy, and why such policies are not, in fact, promoting gender equality.

In the context of economics, gender equality is the absence of "gender gaps." In most contexts, gender means "sex" and the gap is either a number or increased access to a resource. The other major component in calculating gender-equality-as-smart-economics is ensuring "access" to resources—both material and symbolic. Access often means changing legal codes so they are less discriminatory, ensuring "equal opportunity." This includes ensuring women have access to decision-making positions to better allocate such resources.

The chapter begins with a discussion of the research on the conditions under which states promote women's economic rights. It then explores the five major issues with women's inclusion as they apply in this area of policy. It culminates with a critical and "gendered" analysis of women as smart economics. This includes a brief discussion of microfinance, the "productivity trap," the constant global economic crises, and how the recognition of women's economic rights has actually produced women's economic *insecurity* as part of neoliberal world order.

Why Do Political Actors Promote Women's Economic Rights?

While women's inclusion remains powerful at a global level, the impact is primarily seen within states. Understanding how states are influenced to change legal codes regarding women informs our understanding for how add-women efforts are normalized via policy adoption. In this case, states recognize women's economic rights under particular conditions, especially when there is political flux—including changing political institutions and legal codes. These rights also change under pressure from the global women's movement.

Democratizing political institutions is the first major factor that has led to increased recognition of women's economic rights. The phrase "democratizing political institutions" is meant to cover the variety of ways in which scholars identify some type of democratic institutional change as important for states that are recognizing women's economic rights. This includes changing legal systems, secularization, and "flux" of some variety. Indeed, work on women's economic rights, such as that of Shawna Sweeney, finds "democracy" correlates with higher levels of economic rights. Essentially, Sweeney argues that democratic institutions, in this case constraints and competition for chief executive and political participation, are important because women can be a "more important constituency" via political participation and representation.[6] Other scholars note additional democratic and democratizing political institutions that play a large role in economic growth, including an increasing importance for civil legal systems, more women in parliament, and expanded citizenship rights.[7]

Within this context, one of the major factors in explaining why states choose to promote women's economic rights has to do with changing legal systems. Much of the research on women's changing economic rights focuses on how an increased push for civil law over family and customary legal systems has meant more changes in women's access to property, inheritance, and employment. In the World Bank's assessment of women's economic rights, *Women's Legal Rights over 50 Years: Progress, Stagnation, or Regression,* the authors cite the importance of different legal systems in explaining when and how states revised women's economic rights.[8] For instance, in 1960, Eastern Europe had more economic rights for women than any other region, in part because the Socialist Revolution in 1917 diminished the church and made marriage a civil status, granting women equal status in property rights. The report notes that systems based on the Napoleonic or German civil codes gave women more property rights though limited women's employment and asset control. Common law systems in the United Kingdom and former British colonies gave women more autonomy to work but limited their assets and inheritance. The report identifies "hybrid systems," which combine civil and customary or family laws appeared to limit women's economic rights the most, appearing primarily in southern Africa. Ultimately, historical legal codes had long-term ramifications for women's economic rights.

Another factor coinciding with changing legal systems, is the importance of political secularization, or the degree to which the state operates separate from religion.[9] Because most religious institutions are male-dominated and patriarchal, particularly fundamentalist versions, the subordination of women's economic rights may be decided in religious dogma and practice. Where this is also part of the state apparatus, women have fewer outlets with which to challenge their exclusion. This matters particularly because customary and family law often coincide with religious traditions, so places where the rule of law is shaped by religion, customary practices of women as property or in need of male "protection" persist, further discussed in later sections.

As is the case with women's representation, political "flux" of some sort can also matter. Flux can include peaceful transitions, or conflict and regime change. Changes in constitutions after conflict resulted in new laws in Kenya in 2010 and political transitions in Fiji in 1970 and Spain in 1978 (authors note this can also lead to a regression in rights, like in Yemen in 1994).[10] In Nepal, women's land tenure developed during its civil conflict because they demanded more rights as a new constitution was being developed.[11]

The other major sect of factors, which are the same as in the case of promoting representation and protection, have to do with the recognition of women's rights in public life—including ratification of CEDAW and the number of women in parliament. As is the case with the other policies, the ratification of CEDAW is correlated with states' propensity to positively change laws regarding economic rights. One study found CEDAW ratification had an effect within five years of ratifying, particularly in states with weak rule of law.[12] This may be because CEDAW explicitly focuses on anti-discrimination and economic rights are an obvious issue to address. The presence of more women in government is also associated with better economic rights for women. When the percentage of women in parliament is above 25 percent, support for property rights for married women and reduced laws regarding permissions is stronger.[13]

Poor Implementation of Women's Economic Rights

While women's inclusion in the economic realm has improved, there is a long way to go both in policy and economic outcomes. As discussed in previous chapters, if changes require women's activism and democratizing political institutions, then the adoption of such rights are conditional, not universal, and these conditions are often gendered. Generally, while women are participating in greater numbers in the economy nearly everywhere, their "productivity" and earnings remain much lower than men nearly everywhere. In all regions of the world, women still do more unpaid work than men.[14] And when combining both productive and reproductive labor, women everywhere work more than men.[15]

Among women who are employed, lower salaries, lower-wage work, and less reliable forms of employment are common. As the ILO states: "The overrepresentation of women in low-wage jobs seems to be a universal characteristic of labor markets."[16] In developing regions, roughly 75 percent of women's employment is in informal work.[17] And overrepresentation of women in low-wage and informal work translates to less pay and pensions later in life, even in developed countries.[18]

Despite these facts, there is resistance to adoption of policies to recognize women's economic rights. At least eighty states do not legislate equal pay for equal work.[19] South Asia and the Middle East and North Africa (MENA) have done little to change constraints on women's property rights and have even introduced some new ones.[20] Even when there are legal rights for women and girls, there are a variety of arrangements that disproportionately and negatively impact their access to, use of, or control over property.[21] In Nepal, land is still passed from father to son unless daughters remain unmarried past the age of thirty-four years; overall only 10 percent of Nepalese land holdings belong to women.[22] Even where land rights may be communal, women still find themselves excluded from the same use as men.[23] Additionally, rights may exist in writing only, so while there may be equal land tenure rights in many states, women are not landowners.[24] Nearly 25 percent of states in one World Bank study still did not recognize women as heads of household.[25] Consistently women own less land than men, and often the ownership gap is quite large.[26] In one study in sub-Saharan Africa women accounted for, on average, 24 percent of landholders.[27] A study of wills in Mexico found assets were transferred to spouses 39 percent of the time, to sons 29 percent of the time, and daughters 9 percent of the time.[28]

The World Bank's 2012 *Development Report* titled "Gender Equality and Development" finds similar issues in land access and businesses. A study of sixteen developing states found female-headed households had smaller land holdings in fifteen of those states, and other studies corroborate such findings nearly all over the world. In Latin America, men account for 70 to 90 percent of farm owners. Woman-owned and -managed businesses are less likely to get loans than men's businesses and women are less likely to apply for credit and have greater credit constraints.[29] A European Commission study found one of the main challenges for prospective female entrepreneurs was access to financing.[30]

In many states, women are still legally excluded from certain forms of employment. One study found seventy-seven countries restrict what sort of work women can do.[31] Globally, there are very few women who work in mining, construction, or heavy industry factory work. In one cross-national study, over 50 percent of states restrict women from doing the same jobs as men and many of these are in high-paid industries.[32] For example, in Russia women are formally excluded from 456 jobs, including agricultural truck driver, train conductor, deckhand, plumber (if working with sewer systems), and furnace cleaner. In some developing regions, over 75 percent of women's employment is informal and thus not protected by state laws.[33]

In general women's economic rights lag behind men's nearly everywhere. This is in terms of outcomes but also with regard to policy implementation. The next section looks at what issues continue to mar
implementation. The goal is to elucidate why, despite significant efforts
to promote women's inclusion in economic activities by improving their
rights and focusing development initiatives on women, serious economic inequalities and insecurities persist for women.

Informal Barriers and Women's Bounded Agency in Exercising Economic Rights

Informal barriers to women's full economic rights and participation are
subtle yet widespread. While the conditions under which states promote
women's economic rights include increasingly democratized and secular political institutions, regime changes, and transnational pressure,
these do not fully elucidate the condition of women's economic rights.
Even when states are or become more democratic, stable, and connected
to the global women's rights movement, this seems to have little effect
on women's access to the "goods" a state economy provides, like high-
paying jobs, credit, and property. Underneath changing institutions and
international pressure are informal barriers that bound women's agency
to fully realize and access these resources. These informal barriers are
evidenced in work segregation, vulnerable and lower-paying work con-
figurations, customary laws, and sex bias.

The first informal (though sometimes also formal) barrier, which res-
onates all over the world, is sex-based work sector segregation, or what
the World Bank calls "employment segregation by gender." While often
there are no formal laws prohibiting women from certain jobs (and con-
versely encouraging their participation in others), women's labor is over-
represented in service and agriculture while men dominate "industry"
and manufacturing.[34] These differences hold across levels of economic
development, in which women work in "communal services" such as
education, health, and social services.[35] In advanced economies women's
employment in industry has decreased by 50 percent, and 85 percent
of women are now found in services, mostly health and education.[36]
Globally women account for 63 percent of clerical and support staff and
only 33 percent of managers.[37] Sector segregation has actually grown, so

women are increasingly over-represented in service sectors, accounting for one-half of women's employment globally.[38]

Women are still more likely to experience more vulnerable forms of employment—those low or non-waged jobs, such as those found in the informal economy. In sub-Saharan Africa, 70 percent of women working do so in vulnerable employment (compared to 51 percent of men).[39] These are usually lower-wage sectors, such as selling goods or working informally as domestic help. This helps explain the global wage gap for women, which today averages 24 percent.[40] There are not specific rules necessarily blocking women from working in certain industries (though as previously discussed in some cases there are). But there are patterns of behavior pushing and pulling women into certain sectors and men into others. Informally one's skills and vocational training, gendered expectations about who does what sort of labor, and cultural pressures create these forces driving women and men into different jobs. Women's higher service employment rates may also be due to their more "flexible" time schedules. Women whose primary responsibilities are to maintain a household and children may still want or need to work in the productive economy. Service work may be more conducive to these schedules. But again, these are not formal issues but informal gendered practices shaping women's decisions. Women's bounded agency in the face of differential time constraints and needs ultimately impacts what sort of work is available and allowed. Female entrepreneurs are more likely to do such work out of "necessity" rather than "opportunity" and female enterprises are more likely to be home-based and much smaller than those owned by men.[41]

Even within agricultural production there are informal barriers, such as what sorts of crops one produces. Crops are sexed, in that men tend to produce and control cash/commercial crops, while women engage in much more subsistence farming.[42] Women also earn less from farm output when crops are sold.[43] Emphasis on cash crops away from subsistence farming was a key development strategy in the 1960s and '70s, and changed the value of land. This also favored men's production, exacerbating women's poverty in two ways: 1) women do not get resources they need to produce food, and 2) land is privileged for economic productivity, which then goes to men who produce cash crops. These patterns, discovered in the 1970s, did not inform structural adjustment of international aid—further limiting women's access to necessary resources to control and produce on land.[44] The privileging of cash farms over subsistence farms still remains, along with patterns of distributing necessary farm goods, such as fertilizers. Changing property laws and emphasis on cash crops increases value of land, making it more appealing for men to keep land for their own cash crops or sell it, which actually displaces women.[45]

Another one of the major informal barriers to women's economic rights has to do with the degree to which states privilege customary/ family law over civil/statutory legal codes. Because civil legal codes are often associated with more economic rights for women, customary policies become an important and sexed "loophole" for traditional property provisioning.[46] There are a growing number of states recognizing customary laws without including or enforcing anti-discrimination policies as part of it. As noted in one of the seminal studies on women's economic rights, "there has been a clear regression with respect to the constitutional exemption from equality and non-discrimination provisions for customary laws and religious laws—more countries in sub-Saharan Africa, Middle East and North Africa, and South Asia carry these constitutional exemptions in 2010 than 1960."[47] One in four countries in this study still did not allow women to be a legal head of household. For example, in 1988, Bolivia introduced a law requiring women have their husband's permission to work. It was challenged and found unconstitutional in 2003 but has yet to be amended and is still in effect.[48] In other studies in sub-Saharan Africa, women did not know there were statutory laws giving them land rights. Additionally in some cases even when women had the titles to land, power dynamics within the family and communities negatively impacted women's access to this land.[49] In South Africa, even when women were aware of their land rights (still guaranteed under customary law by the South African Bill of Rights equality clause), they were often "thwarted by traditional leaders who insisted that land be acquired through men."[50] In researcher Thuto Thipe's work on women's land rights under the Traditional Courts Bill, she found women's claims to land were often subject to the informal, gendered beliefs of traditional leaders. Thipe quotes South African landholder Nikeziwe Dlamini, who wrote about her own experience with land rights:

When I was twenty-one years old, I went to a local traditional leader to ask if I could be allocated land to establish a home for my two children. I was sent away and not allocated land in my own right as a woman. I was advised to look for a male representative. My property is now registered under my sister's spouse's name. This worries me a lot because I fear that should anything happen to me, my children would not have a home of their own and might be forcibly evicted. Most traditional councils expect women to be represented by their male relatives. Imagine you are forcibly evicted from your marital home and expected to be represented by the same marital male representatives and having your land registered under the name of the very same male relatives who evicted you from your home. What does that mean? They could still come back and evict you. Because the property will still be registered under their name.[51]

Along the same lines, many states have marital property laws that, on the surface appear "gender-neutral" but in practice tend to hurt women more. A recent study of these laws finds most states condition property ownership so that either all property (assets) remains separate depending on whose name they are in, or all property has partial sharing in which only those assets acquired while married are controlled by both parties.[52] But while this does not seem like it should be worse for women, in practice it is. The spouse who starts with less does not accumulate future assets at the same rate; the spouse with fewer assets is almost always a woman. Additionally most of the states that recognized property as separate do not "count" nonmonetary labor (such as caring and reproductive labor). This means women's unpaid contributions to a family do not garner any allocation of tangible household assets in the future or in divorce. In India 60 percent of women, compared to 30 percent of men, have no assets to their names.[53]

The final barrier has to do with subtle sex bias among employers, which affects women everywhere. Studies consistently find preference for male employees, even if women have exactly the same credentials.[54] A study found science faculty at universities, both male and female, are also more likely to select men for their labs and offer them higher salaries.[55] Another U.S. study of law students found both men and women associated judges with men and housework with women, indicating implicit bias (though students also appeared cognizant of such biases and attempted to avoid them in decision-making).[56] Seventy percent of women and men across thirty-four countries viewed science "as more male than female."[57] These effects are compounded by racial and ethnic discrimination as well.[58] Formally, often women and men are equally qualified for work, but when industries are dominated by men who have implicit biases to work with other men, then women again lose out.

Gender Matters in Women's Economic Rights

To understand why women work in certain industries, are systematically paid less, and own less property, inheritance, and credit, one must critically engage gender, not as a shortcut for women's subordination, but as an analytical tool to make sense of these trends. Gender matters in understanding why labor is so often sex-segregated: when certain jobs exclude women, they often do so primarily based on assumptions about masculinities and femininities. As the UN Women 2015 report states: "The labor market [and] stereotypes about suitable occupations for women and men serve to maintain the existing gender division of labor. Young women and men who move into occupations that are associated with the opposite sex risk disparagement or ridicule."[59]

For example, women are discouraged (and sometimes formally excluded) out of certain work based upon ideas about what is "harmful" towards women. This may include both physical and moral harm. For example, Bolivia's labor law specifies women cannot work in "occupations that harm their morality and good customs," but this is then determined by employers.[60] Women are often restricted from working at night, which may have to do with assumptions about when women are needed in home life, but it could also have to do with ideas about protecting women from the vulnerabilities of nighttime.[61] The idea women are more vulnerable to predation and violence (particularly sexual violence) at night is based on paternalistic and antiquated ideas about women's weakness, virtue, and femininity. Additionally, since "women's work" is usually valued and paid less, men do not seek out such jobs.

Heteronormative familial structures and ideas informed by gender and sexuality also shape women's economic rights: "The mechanisms excluding women from land rights have been legal, cultural, structural and institutional. They are interrelated and have as their basis patriarchal ideologies embedded in the constructions of masculinity and femininity and the 'proper' gender division of labor."[62] Some of these specific gendered practices include: economic assumptions about families as unitary entities and headed by men; assumptions about marriage relationships; assumptions of male heads of household; gendered divisions of labor within families; and the centrality of women's reproduction in understanding most economic forces.

The pervasive assumption of a male-headed nuclear family unit, treated as a single entity, still shapes how we think about families in economic discourses. There are two assumptions worth interrogating here: the male head of household and the unitary family. Economic models and many governments assume families act as unitary actors (household as an individual), in which it is assumed families pool all resources and income. They also tend to assume each household has a traditional father-mother organization where the man is head of household. This is problematic for two very gendered reasons. The first is the reality that many households are not run by men.

Research has shown there are many female heads of households for many reasons, particularly outmigration.[63] Women then may use land and find employment and be "productive" even though the household is still considered male. Sex bias persists in policies and allocations of resources based on the pervasive breadwinner/homemaker binary in which "the male head of household is thus seen as the legitimate claimant" in land claims.[64] Women still derive their status in relation to men in most parts of the world.[65] Because men are assumed as head of household then property land rights remain male-dominated.[66] The other gendered assumption is that households pool resources, despite that research indicates men and women allocate household resources differently.[67] Such an assumption does not take into account household gender roles and how these inform resource allocation.

There has been a lot of change in thinking about these assumptions and recognition that there are many women heads of household, and members of families make decisions differently. But this has actually led to another issue in which it is now accepted as "common knowledge" that women will spend on families and men will not.[68] This "gender control over household resources" assumption that women will invest their economic assets in their children persists.[69] Women are cited as more likely to buy mosquito bed nets for children while men were more likely to buy for themselves, citing that as the breadwinner, an adult male believed he was more entitled to such protection.[70] This is echoed in the 2015 UN Women Report, which links women's access to land and productive resources to food security and "livelihood sustainability for the whole household."[71]

But what this does is focuses the world's development agencies on how to get more resources to women rather than asking why men do not feel the same needs to support their children as women do. And this is critical: when gender is a shortcut for women, we focus on better inclusion of women to the detriment of men and their household roles. Changing this discourse would require debunking the "fact" of gendered resource allocation by focusing on the pervasive gender binary of breadwinner/homemaker that underlies this "fact" of women's family priorities. Here is how gender created and perpetuates this scenario: historically (and presently), it was (and often is) assumed the breadwinner shared appropriate resources of his work with his family, though resources still belong to him. Since women do not "earn" in this scenario, they have no ownership over earned resources—they are stewards of it and thus assumed to behave differently. Men, as owners of their resources, have discretion over how much wives may allocate and how much men may keep. For example, in Nepal, women may make claims to the land only if men do not fill their breadwinner responsibilities.[72] But it is important to realize there is nothing innate or biological in this and there is no reason men should not be expected to allocate the same resources to their children that their wives would. It is worth interrogating further why some men do not treat children as a priority for resources over themselves.

An associated issue is the ways in which marriage assumptions and practices inform the recognition of economic rights. Unmarried women's property and inheritance rights were recognized before married women's rights.[73] This is because this land could be kept in the family. Studies in sub-Saharan Africa found families did not want to give young unwed daughters or widows land because they may (re)marry and the property could then be used by another man's family.[74] According to one group working in Kenya with young AIDS widows, inheritance was often contested by in-laws despite being guaranteed by law.[75]

Many couples worldwide are not legally married; if national laws specify land rights based on legal marriage, then women may not be covered by such laws.[76] Poverty plays an important role here since marriages can be cost-prohibitive for a variety of cultural and legal reasons. It also means marriage laws that do not recognize polygamous marriage would put certain wives at a major inheritance disadvantage. Heteronormative marriage laws also restrict economic rights and assets for same-sex couples.

A focus group in Uganda illustrated another interesting belief that may shape land claims. Participants specified lawfully married men and women who did not have children did not have the same land rights, as these were related to expectations about inheritance. Women and men believed that since children inherited land, women did not themselves have a claim to it except as a mother guarding inheritance.[77] While legally these women have rights to the land, their communities' beliefs, as well as their own, shape the degree to which women would even make claims.

The final and perhaps most obvious gendered binary has to do with time allocation for reproductive labor in the household. There are not laws requiring women to do more housework and child-rearing but *everywhere* in the world women do. And because women have less discretionary time, they have less time to engage in wage-based employment.[78] In no country, developed or developing, do men contribute more reproductive labor than women, and in no country do women work more than men in so-called productive labor.[79] On average women do two-and-a-half times more unpaid labor (childcare and housework) than men.[80] Even with increases in education and income for women, things still do not change very much. In a study of five wealthy European states, over 40 percent of women work part time because of family responsibilities.[81] The United Nations, in their study on women's labor, specifically identifies how gender matters in understanding work differences: "*Perhaps* it is more acceptable for women to adopt masculine behavior, such as working for pay, than it is for men to adopt feminine behavior, such as doing housework and care work" (218; my emphasis). What is being articulated here is that because we live in cultures that value masculine over feminine, it is more acceptable for women to engage in masculinized endeavors, like paid work, than for men to engage in feminized endeavors, such as reproductive and caring labor. This is especially true in neoliberal capitalism where markets only value what has actual monetary worth. Caring for one's own children or maintaining a household does not generate tangible market income so this necessary labor is not "valued."

The need to combine paid and unpaid labor usually translates to less job mobility and advancement for women. And flexible work, which is supposed to allow women to combine productive and reproductive labor tends to be lower paid labor as well. I further focus on this issue in the next section, but the point remains: our social organization and heteronormative families fundamentally shape women's access to and understandings of their economic rights.

Intersectionality in Women's Economic Rights?

As with most cases, intersectional analyses paint a starkly raced and classed world for women's economic rights. Additionally, women's economic rights are directly impacted by geography and heterosexuality, further marginalizing those in the Global South and those who may not subscribe to a "traditional" heteronormative family arrangement. In general, poor women have very few economic rights, despite being specifically and consistently recognized in international conventions, protocols, and reports (see chapter 3). Development organizations continue to point to the "most vulnerable" women who disproportionately bear the brunt of global economic forces, including crisis.[82] The most vulnerable refers to poor, rural women who bear additional burdens because their complex identities situate them in the most marginalized positions in the global system, their feminized identities compounded by one another.

The first work on women and development, in the 1970s by economist Ester Boserup, focused on rural women and how removed they remained from development resources.[83] This work laid the groundwork for thinking about intersectional issues in development in which being a woman is difficult, being poor even more difficult and living in rural areas further exacerbates both sex and class in important ways. But for these "most vulnerable women," not much has changed, as access to material resources remains limited.

Poverty begets poverty, so poor women, who are often racial minorities, have less access to all of these resources economic rights should guarantee and so they remain poor. But, because these resources are gendered and raced, those most needing such resources and rights have the least access to them.[84] In Latin America, there are more women among the regions' poorest, and woman-headed households have increased since the 1990s despite overall declining poverty rates.[85] Additionally in forty-one out of seventy-five countries, in one study conducted by UN Women, women are more likely than men to live in the poorest households.[86] Furthermore, poor women (and men) are less likely to marry because of cost, which affects their access to credit, pensions, and property. In Latin America, indigenous women, whose livelihoods depend on land access, are impacted by global demand for natural resources. They often lack access to securing the land they have used for generations.[87]

This gendered and classed poverty culminates into poverty rates among the elderly. In the European Union, the poverty rate of elderly women is 37 percent higher than that of men.[88] As women get older they are still more likely to be poorer than their male peers. This is, in part, because women are: 1) less likely to even have a pension; 2) more likely to have lower lifetime earnings due to receiving lower-paying, more part-time and informal work, which translates into much lower pensions, and; 3) more likely to interrupt work for childcare, and contribute more personal income to family needs, resulting in less discretionary income to re-invest in retirement.[89]

The next section explores the effects of women's economic rights on intersectional identities by focusing on microfinance, an effort to "help" the most vulnerable women in the world, which ultimately relies upon and reinforces gendered, classed, racialized, and geographical binaries.

Women as Smart Neoliberal Economics?

These economic rights policies and practices are cited by international organizations as important for several reasons and have served to motivate and justify states' adopting changes in women's access to productive economic resources. These reasons often rely on the logic of consequences, in that recognizing women's economic rights and contributions matters because it enables them to be more "productive" in the economy, which has benefits for women but also for states and their economies.[90] Said differently, women in the economy should be seen as "progress" and an indicator of a "progressive" state. As the latest *Progress of the World's Women* report from UN Women states: "Some see in women a largely untapped market of consumers, while others speak about the opportunity of 'unleashing the economic power and potential of women' as a means to solve the lingering problems caused by the global financial crisis and stalled growth."[91] The report adds that women's participation can "enhance the competitiveness of export industries." According to the Food and Agricultural Organization, "promoting gender equality is not only good for women; it is also good for agricultural development."[92] It would seem, then, that women are the key to the world's economic success.

With greater economic rights women can start a business by having physical space to operate; access to credit (by leveraging property); and more ensured income. Economic rights also have social/welfare benefits: ensuring better food security; providing a social safety net; ensuring physical and social mobility of women and families; securing prosperity of future generations; promoting better access to political processes; and ensuring greater environmental and social justice.[93] Ultimately, the logic goes, when women can work, they can "maintain an adequate standard of living" and be treated "with respect and dignity"—both of which are "crucial to advancing gender equality."[94]

The causal arrow between women (gender) and growth and development points both ways: economic growth and development are good for women,[95] and women are good for economic growth and development.[96] One popular theory, articulated by Claudia Goldin in 1995 and supported by others, argued a reciprocal relationship between women and growth.[97] She stated it is a U-shaped relationship in which early development jobs are primarily created for men, and female labor participation declines. But as development continues and men move into white-collar jobs, women's formal economic participation increases. Others argue it depends on for whom "market opportunities" are being created. If it is for women then growth ensues, but if it is for men then growth and stability are actually reversed.[98] But generally economists and leaders have long promoted the idea of women's development—via education, health, and access to wealth and property—greatly benefitting state development processes, and economic rights have become central as a poverty reduction strategy.[99]

The first reason cited by various economic institutions and researchers is that women's increased economic rights (in property and employment) and education will make them more "productive."[100] What I mean by productive is, women will have a greater ability to participate in "formal" economic activities, including increased agrarian productivity as well as increased participation in other labor sectors. This line of thinking reaches the "logical" conclusion that, "women's employment is essential in the fight against poverty."[101] The World Bank's 2012 report on gender and development argues limited economic rights constrain women's entrepreneurship because it means women have less collateral for loans.[102] Other work notes how when women have to ask for permission to work or have non-autonomous mobility, they are less attractive as employees in the formal sector. Furthermore, when women have economic rights they have social safety nets during economic crises and are better able to leave violent relationships.[103]

There is strong evidence about the importance in recognizing women's economic rights. Economist Bina Agarwal, in her long career of studying women's land rights in India, cites how women's increased access to property (and specifically land) improves "efficiency" in land use. She finds that women may have better production on land due to better access to credit, different choices in crop production, a wider pool of collective knowledge and talent, and better bargaining positions in demanding government resources.[104] In Ethiopia, where family laws were reformed in 2000, researchers have found that female participation in the labor force increased in more "productive sectors."[105] One study found by improving women's property rights in Burkina Faso and reallocating land and fertilizer from men to women, agricultural production increased by 6 percent without any more resources.[106] Another study found securing land titles freed up women in Peru to participate in the formal labor market because they no longer had to physically guard their property.[107]

Women's inclusion and the recognition of economic rights illustrates the pervasiveness of the "common sense" that adding women produces globally. This is evident through a discussion of three "effects" of gender = women in the context of neoliberal governance and world order. While this is by no means an exhaustive study of the effects, these three issues are illustrative of the logic of consequences in promoting women as smart economics in a system that relies on gendered binaries to function. The purpose is to illustrate how engaging analytical gender means (re)assessing certain economic processes as central to perpetuating women's subordination (and many men as well). The first is the treatment of microcredit as an empowering practice for poor women. The second is the persistent focus on changing men and women's roles in the global economy rather than focusing on changing the economy (and its gendered values). And the third is the centrality of crisis to the global economic order and its disproportionate effect on feminized and marginalized groups.

Gendered Microfinance

The first "effect" of this gender = women narrative and the importance of intersectional analyses is illustrated by the trade-offs in the promotion of microcredit as a panacea for poor women in developing (and increasingly developed) states. Global financial institutions and development organizations have promoted microcredit as a central strategy for poverty reduction and women's empowerment. Indeed, the United Nations declared 2005 the "International Year of Microcredit."[108] It began in the 1990s and the World Bank promoted it "to show the more human side of development" in a system focused on economic growth.[109] In a 2007 study, over 150 million people used rotating savings and credit associations (ROSCAs); 83 percent were women.[110] The idea is to generate small loans for people, particularly women, so they may have much needed capital to start businesses. The idea is to alleviate poverty by providing small loans in the name of "self-help."[111] It grew out of the economic rights push, especially during the international conferences discussed in chapter 3, in which states agreed that poor women should have access and rights to credit, savings, and insurance.[112] This strategy became an almost universally lauded approach to poverty reduction for two reasons: 1) because it (sort of) acknowledges access to credit as a problem for women, the poor, and those in rural areas and; 2) because it brought those dispossessed into the economy by encouraging entrepreneurship and self-employment.[113] While primarily located in the Global South, microcredit has also emerged in the Global North. This includes the United States where it emerged in response to reduced social services, though it has "been adopted as a form of empowerment that is heavily racialized and feminized."[114]

The types of microfinance enterprises varies greatly, from community savings associations to private commercial banks, but the basic idea is loans are backed by a group of borrowers rather than an individual borrower. This means collateral is generated through relationships and trust within a group, "as the individual would lose their reputation if they defaulted."[115] Traditional ROSCAs do not require management, while more organized versions may require more institutionalization to generate interest and further income. There are different theoretical paradigms underlying models of microfinance, and they promote different discourses about how microcredit works. Microfinance also has different assumptions about women's role in such programs.[116] As one author puts it: ROSCAs all have the same goal but a different understanding of the means to meet such a goal.[117] Regardless of the model and assumptions for microcredit programs, they all serve more women than men. The "guru" of microcredit, Muhammed Yunus (who founded the Grameen Bank in Bangladesh and won a Nobel Peace Prize in 2006) explains why the bank's customers are 96 percent women:

> From the beginning, I had complained about the banking system on two grounds. One complaint was that the banking system was denying financial services to the poor people through certain rules it had set up. The second allegation was that the banking system also was not treating women fairly. If you look at the gender composition of all the borrowers of all the banks in Bangladesh, not even 1 percent of the borrowers happen to be women. I said this is a very gender-biased organization. So when I began, I wanted to make sure half the borrowers in my program are women so that they are even. I did that. It was not easy because women themselves didn't think that they should borrow money. I had to do a lot of convincing. I encouraged them to believe that they can borrow money and make money. Part of that effort was to overcome fears—cultural fears—and the fact that they had never had any experience with business and so on. *Soon we saw that money going to women brought much more*

benefit to the family than money going to the men. So we changed our policy and gave a high priority to women. As a result, now 96 percent of our four million borrowers in Grameen Bank are women.[118]

Women are the primary target for microfinance in the South and North and the money usually supports home-based work enterprises, meant to breaks cycles of dependency on the state and poverty.[119] The United Nations, among others, lauds the use of microfinance in empowering women and ending women's poverty by facilitating women's participation in "the mainstream economic and political processes of society."[120]

However the actual degree to which microfinance reduces poverty and empowers women has been challenged by both large-N and case study work.[121] There is a prolific research agenda exposing the limits and even dangers of these projects. There has been backlash all over the world, noting predatory lending practices, such as high interest rates and strict repayment structures.[122] India has seen high numbers of suicides and bankruptcy in certain areas due to problems with loan repayment, and even the Grameen Bank is under investigation.[123] There are also "no-pay" movements in Central America and India.[124] Even the World Bank has recently changed their tone on microcredit, noting, "it is not clear how much microfinances has increased access to formal financial services . . . or whether, given the small size of the loans, it has lifted constraints for women who want to borrow slightly larger amounts."[125]

But the whole system of microfinance relies upon and perpetuates gendered binaries, and illustrates the larger logic of many anti-poverty endeavors. This is evident in assumptions about the loans—including why women make for good debtors and how loans will be used. Microfinance targets women *because they are women,* relying on gender roles in family and community to explain why women will make for better debtors. First, there is an assumption that women will use the money to, in some way, benefit their families, reflecting their more caring nature. Also, women's "social capital" means they are more trusting community members and are better at mobilizing a community's resources. Local customs and practices may essentialize gender and ethnicity in assuming community relationships as inherently beneficial without recognizing the disproportionate burden placed on women to maintain community ties and practices.[126] More nefarious studies found micro-credit staff preferred women because they were perceived as "more conscientious and docile clients" who devote more time to group activities, which decreases program costs.[127]

Assumptions about how such loans will be used are also gendered. The theory underlying microcredit is financiers will support entrepreneurship so women can start or enhance a business. They can then generate income that will then be used to pay back the loan and there are many cases of this happening. But there are also many cases of women using loans, often via profit-driven banks, to build houses, pay for health care, and subsidize poor farming outputs due to drought.[128] These women then take on additional loans to pay off what they already have, resulting in greater debt that may result in land forfeiture. This is gendered in a total lack of understanding about poor women's needs in the current global economy. While long-term financial stability for women and families is the goal for global development institutions, women, especially poor women, may have more immediate and fundamental needs such as food security and shelter. Predatory for-profit banks that do not insist on a business plan for lending, and are motivated by interest-based profits, would not necessarily care what the money is for or how it will be repaid, leaving women in a bind. In India, bankers made sure in instances of default loans and loan recovery that women felt responsible for their husbands' loans not even made through micro-lending.[129]

Ultimately these processes by which women are drawn into financial services industries is part of a larger process of "restructuring of state-society relations" in which market solutions replace public support.[130] It often formalizes financial relationships between credit and banking institutions and communities of poor women.[131] This means women get drawn into global markets in ways they may not fully understand or over which they may not have much control. Additionally, this control is increasingly handed over to "experts" and technocrats, whereby neoliberal "expertise," in which women may not sufficiently participate, replaces democratic decision-making.

As scholars Christine Keating, Claire Rasmussen, and Pooja Rishi note in their 2010 article, this requires a change in ideology whereby microfinance is about self-help and part of "a politics of responsibilization in which social problems such as poverty and unemployment are increasingly seen as the consequence of individual failures."[132] This means obscuring the reality that credit means debt and debt carries risk. This preference for poor people (particularly women) to take on debt, rather than states to ensure a social safety net that includes basic income, social transfers, and access to assets, is the preferred market model in which individuals rely on private capital rather than public support. In emphasizing how women now have this service available, which has continually been emphasized as a good way to promote their economic rights, they are brought into the global market via one of its least stable institutions, which are credit markets. Indeed, certain microfinance banks now trade in global financial markets. Microfinance is uncritically seen as a strategy for women's empowerment and gender equality by various financial entities. But the onus is on women, *because they are women*, to participate and absorb the burden of risk for families and economic forces in their communities by using credit systems over which they may not have much control. But those promoting these loans fail to see how they rely upon gender binaries to function and how microfinance does little to deal with structural poverty and inequality that perpetuates women's economic insecurities (and many others) in the first place.

The "Productivity Trap"

The second way in which the global focus on women's inclusion and its "gender = women" narrative in economic rights has had significant effects is the very way we talk about how to include women in economic activity. It is encapsulated by this idea of women and gender equality as "smart economics." The World Bank, in its 2006 report, wrote: "Forget China, India, and the internet: economic growth is driven by women."[133] The central point, which has long been a key aspect of liberal feminist work, is that women should have the same access to the economy as men do. Recognizing women's needs and perspectives in employment, credit, and property remain the central ways to better ensure women's full economic participation. Anti-discrimination policies sought and seek to better ensure women could make their own wages, own their homes and land, and start businesses.

While it matters that women have access to tangible resources, this recognition has also shaped discourses surrounding women's inequality in wages and poverty more generally. What I mean is that mainstream discussions about how to "help" women economically focus on making improvements to women's productivity and access to financial inputs. The focus is on how to lessen sector segregation and bias in hiring women. The focus is on how to enable women to more actively and productively contribute to economic activities. The focus, however, is not on what counts as productivity in the first place and how we value labor in this world.

The "productivity trap" is a popular economic term meant to capture the degree to which women get caught in a cycle of low-paying and more vulnerable employment because of "gendered" constraints on time and poor access to necessary resources such as land, credit, and markets. This focus on productivity is central to economic discourses on "gender differences in labor markets."[134] The World Bank's 2012 "Development Report" dedicated an entire section to this issue, which it argues affects women everywhere. They define the productivity trap as "persistent employment segregation by gender traps women in low-productivity, low-paying jobs" related to "time use, poor access to land and credit, and limited access to certain markets." They then argue it requires interventions that "lift time constraints, increase access to productive inputs among women, and correct market and institutional failures."[135] Other reports highlight similar issues even though they may not call it the same thing (see UN Women 2015c, for example). It is entirely about "eliminating barriers" to women's full participation in more productive economic activities. It is about increasing women's inclusion and recognizing women's rights to economic activities. The World Bank report cites that eliminating discrimination against women managers and workers could increase overall productivity per worker from 25 to 40 percent depending on types of labor and degree of exclusion; additionally, increased productivity can increase women's agency via control over household resources.[136]

It is worth noting this report represents a continuing and improved awareness on behalf of economists, international organizations, and mainstream academics about how types of labor and time restraints are gendered. The analyses on time management clearly represent some engagement with "caring work" and how women disproportionately do such work. They note how subsidized childcare, better infrastructure (transportation, water, electricity), and part-time work can help women to be more productive (though they note there is a wage penalty for many part-time jobs). They also recognize that "social norms about gender roles" shape how families view women's work, their mobility, family formation, women's agency, and violence.[137] This includes a study on "gender and economic choice" and found the definition of a "good man" has "evolved" to include some degree of family care; however the definition of a "good woman" is described primarily via domestic tasks and has changed very little. These studies are important in providing further evidence for what feminists have long argued regarding the barriers created by gender roles. These analyses do engage an element of analytical gender in identifying how these gender roles are constructed and thus can change. But the bottom line in this productivity trap logic is flawed: because women do not have time to increase productivity and thus their income, men need to use some of their time (presumably discretionary time) to assist in caring and reproductive labor, which then frees up women's time for paid work. But the "social norms" that prevent such scenarios, and how markets and market logic may hurt women, are not the focus here. Smart economics means changing rules so women can work in the productive economy, own assets, and participate in markets. Gender equality means more women in instances where women remain underrepresented and with less "voice."

When one digs into the economistic language and ideas deeper in the report, their engagement with a feminist and analytical conceptualization of gender starts to fall apart. The report identifies how "individual preferences" regarding women's roles as caretakers shape their decisions and choices for work.[138] In other words, women work in lower-paying and informal work, in part, because they prefer it or prefer their reproductive roles. But this idea of "individual preferences," a common phrase in economics to indicate individual-level decision-making, is treated as though preferences exist outside of our social environment and kyriarchical structures. As I have argued, women have agency and make individual choices, but these decisions are still bound by sociopolitical and cultural restraints. One does not make a decision in a "gender vacuum," where identities based on sex, race, class, sexuality, or geography do not inform what types of resources and jobs are available. One does not make a decision about work outside of the already gendered economy in which one operates.

Additionally I would offer an alternative understanding of the "productivity trap" than one in which women are stuck in low-paying work that perpetuates poverty. Rather, I would argue that states, economists, and the development community are stuck in a productivity trap, whereby their understanding of women's access to economic resources is stuck in an idea that the goal is for women to be more productive in formal economic activities. There is apparently no other possibility besides greater formal economic participation for women's improved economic status. In this sense, productivity *is* the trap for our ways of thinking in engaging global economic activity. *In other words, the trap is not the inability to be productive but what experts count as productive in today's economy.* The narrative of the World Bank report (and others) is how to make women into better workers, not about what we value as work.[139] The goal of this neoliberal market economy is not to de-gender the economy, just re-allocate sex-based distributions between productive and reproductive hours. There is no critiquing the global economic logic of what gets valued, but how to shape behaviors of men and women to better participate in this logic. This is actually endemic to liberal market economics in which capitalism assesses value to that which is paid as productive. As scholars have noted, "classic liberal economic theories have presumed a very low value associated with women's labor."[140] We do not value reproductive labor as productive—unless it is done for someone else and for wages.

While clearly it is an improvement that reproductive work is even called work or labor, it is still widely accepted that it does not "count" as productive work. But until this sort of labor has more actual value, why would men change their attitudes towards it? There is little rational reason for men to do more free work and possibly less paid work and/or have less discretionary time. But according to the implied assumption of how women get more time to be productive, this is the calculus offered.

Ultimately, changing the roles of women and men in the economy without changing what we monetarily value in the global economy, which relies upon gendered logics, will not emancipate women or men.

Classification of work and labor is embedded in masculinities and femininities: paid/unpaid, skilled/unskilled, productive/reproductive means we value men and women differently. Since the global economic system needs someone to do unpaid, reproductive work in order to keep human civilization going, gender, as well as race, class and geography, become default categories for assigning who does this undervalued and unpaid work. Scholars note the feminization of labor and work, in which certain groups are rendered vulnerable by their typically feminized (read informal, lower-paying and service-based) jobs, such as migrant communities, who fill a gendered economic need where women may not.[141] It would require a massive shift in thinking about what counts as work and how we distributed resources based on this new calculus to actually promote gender equality rather than women's inclusion.

One of the other issues feminists have pointed out is the degree to which changing property rights is even beneficial to women. One can understand this movement to promote women's property rights as a move to privatize, individualize, and commodify land, as market-oriented systems would prefer. But community structures may benefit women more and one must ask: Whose interests are served in potentially privatizing land?

One important way in which this calculus is manifested is how this sexed economy begins in the womb, evidenced in a strong global preference for male children, which is tied to access to economic productivity and mobility. Female infanticide is tied to economic systems in which inheritance and access to employment mean greater value for men because economies are designed to reward men as economic units. Estimates are that in East Asia there are 134 million "missing women" due to sex selective births, infanticide, and higher survival rates for boys under five than girls in the 1990s.[142] The system has done very little to challenge this—men really are more economically "productive" nearly everywhere and while it is obviously gendered and socially constructed, changing the calculation means fundamentally shifting the value of work, not just women's role in it.

A System in Constant Crisis

The final effect, central to capitalism, is its predilection for a gendered cycle of crisis, austerity, and vulnerabilities.[143] This is most recently evidenced by the global economic crisis beginning in 2008/2009, which affects people still today. Recent data and reports outline the lingering effects of the economic crisis. The latest reports from the International Labour Organization and the United Nations Human Development Report have noted the effects on women of this current economic crisis. The 2012 ILO report, *Global Employment Trends for Women*, explained how the stimulus approach for economies of 2009 was replaced by austerity policies in 2011/2012, which led to a "double dip in GDP growth in some countries." The 29 million net jobs lost by women during the global economic crisis have not been recovered. The International Monetary Fund's (IMF) downgrade of global GDP growth for 2013, from 3.8 to 3.6 percent, led the ILO to estimate that an additional 2.5 million jobs for women could be lost in 2013. The ILO report continues, "The crisis appears to have worsened gender gaps in unemployment across all regions."[144] Finally, it reversed employment growth rates of women and they estimate it will not recover until 2017. The 2014 United Nations Human Development Report, *Sustaining Human Progress: Reducing Vulnerabilities and Building Resilience*, echoed the ILO's findings. The report notes women as a particularly vulnerable group (along with children, the elderly, migrants, and minorities) to economic and climate change shocks. One study cites they found economic downturns increased female infant mortality fivefold and the Human Development Report notes that the current crisis "has resulted in an estimated 30,000–50,000 additional infant deaths in sub-Saharan Africa, mostly among the poor and overwhelmingly female."[145]

But neither global economic crises nor their gendered effects are new. Global political economic (GPE) scholars have noted how crisis is endemic to capitalism, based on structural contradictions between individual and collective interests via unequal exchange of labor, goods, and services.[146] The quest for monopolization generates polarization of reward hidden by a false binary between the economic and the political.[147] Indeed, as James Mittelman recently noted, "capitalism without crisis is an oxymoron."[148] Feminist GPE scholars have also identified the gendered nature of both capitalism and crisis, which relies upon, perpetuates, and normalizes gendered, racialized, classed, and geographical inequalities and ways of thinking.[149]

As economic crises are not new, neither is the gendered response, which in the last forty years has come to favor "austerity." Structural adjustment plans (SAPs) were the World Bank's short-run strategy to deal with economic decline and external shocks to promote long-run economic growth.[150] In response to debt crises in the 1980s, neoliberal economists identified governmental interference in the market as the cause.[151] The idea was that adjusting the governance structures in developing states would signal investors to these developing states' commitment to capitalism because SAP policies promoted low inflation, devalued exchange rates to increase competition, and reduced government spending. These export-oriented policies were supposed to "enhance private capital in support of expanding international trade."[152]

The results of such measures, however, were catastrophic for many women, as women were the most likely to depend on social services that supported their roles in providing reproductive labor in the household.[153] Health and education resources provided by the state were severely cut, leaving women's health needs unfulfilled and pushing girls out of the education pipeline. Feminist scholars identified how the rise of informal economies (such as home-based and sex work) resulted from the "Global South" shift from productive to service economies.[154] Even the United Nations Development Programme (UNDP) and UNICEF criticized the policies.[155] Many women were not able to reap the apparent benefits of structural adjustment and thus disproportionately bore the austerity measures through increased labor in informal economies and instability in formal labor.[156] Ultimately feminist and critical scholars consider these policies "biased against women in conception, implementation, and valuation."[157] The World Bank is willing to acknowledge that SAPs were in some ways "harmful" to gender equality, citing how job reallocation, nontradable sectors (like subsistence agriculture), and girls' education were negatively impacted, but it still claims that women's status and equality, overall, improved as a result of SAPs.[158]

One of the important illustrations of crisis and vulnerabilities is the centrality of informal work (vulnerable employments) to the global economic system. The ILO found in 2012, globally over 50 percent of employed women were working in some type of vulnerable work (it is worth noting men's rates of vulnerable work were only 2 percent lower).[159] In Africa only 40 percent of men and 33 percent of women engaged in salaried or wage employment on a regular basis, indicating a large informal economy and weak market institutions.[160] Rates were also higher for women in Middle Eastern and North African states and negative in European states. Economist Lourdes Beneria situated informal work as illustrative of the "low road" of development, where pursuits of increased capital lead to mixed results for global women. She identified the "vicious circle of poverty and powerlessness" that resulted in the realization that informal economies *are not epiphenomenal*, but are best understood as resulting from neoliberal policies and pursuits of capital that rely on hierarchies of oppression and are justified by lower consumer prices.[161] What is key here is *vulnerable/informal work is central to global capitalist trends*. Measures to encourage more women into formal work are shaped by: 1) crisis that increases and exacerbate levels of vulnerable work among women and other feminized groups; and, 2) the need for feminized labor to produce cheap goods, which is endemic to global economics. In this sense, gendered economic crisis is a cornerstone of capitalist processes.

Climate change, which changes the value of land and labor, remains another key crisis in the global economy and is also illustrative of the gendered nature of economic growth and development. The UN noted how climate changes is a risk to the entire planet but some are more subject to losses than others.[162] Those "others" are women. A 2012 Brookings Institute Report noted women are a greater risk for natural hazards than men, particularly poor women in poor countries because disasters exacerbate already existing discrimination and inequality and can lead to new forms of vulnerabilities. Women account for 75 percent of those displaced by disasters and 70 to 80 percent of those in need of emergency assistance post-disaster.[163] Women and other marginalized groups face barriers to recovering from disasters because of fewer resources and assets.[164] When arable land diminishes due to drought and flooding, the value of land changes and land-grabbing practices emerge (within communities and on a scale from global corporations), usually to the determinant of women's land rights.[165]

Overall, the economic strategies promoted under the guise of "women as smart economics" produces some troubling trends for women. In a neoliberal world system entrenched in market-oriented capitalist ideas, marginalized labor is a necessity and women provide a large source of such labor. Gendered beliefs about women and their community ties, their "preferences" for caring and reproductive labor, and their abilities to weather crises are central to making a global market system work for those in power. Unless the entire system is critiqued with a gendered lens, small changes to promote women's economic rights will only have small effects, perhaps helping some women to better participate in the economy. But to help some women is a long way from securing full gender equality.

Conclusion

As development institutions continue to promote women as smart economics, they do so in an essentialist and simplistic manner.[166] While women do need access to more resources, including income and property, they also need an economic system not built and reliant upon gendered labor patterns and the subordination of so many groups, including women. Diane Elson, in her assessment of the World Bank's 2006 Development Report, *Equity and Development,* found that even though the World Bank had changed its discourse, indicating an apparent "post–Washington Consensus," the focus of development remained the same.[167] This was to emphasize equality of opportunity, not outcomes. She cited how economic policies were about the distribution of "assets, access to markets, and political voice—not on the distribution of income." And this equality of opportunity is the crux of liberal feminism and thus women's inclusion more generally, so should not be surprising. This represents a hegemonic way of thinking about global economics: eliminate barriers to opportunities and everyone should prevail. But gender (race, class, sexuality, and imperialism) operate at so many levels that removing legal barriers does not necessarily trickle down or up to other levels where gender operates. Ultimately, a system is in place that relies upon gender binaries and logics rather than challenging it.

It is also worth noting the continuing economic crises and preference for "austerity." Greece had to decide to eliminate social spending or exit the European Union. While the economic hegemons may no longer use the terms "structural adjustment," the ideas of austerity and emphasis on inflation over social spending remains the platform for economic growth models for both developed and developing states.

A new calculus of the productivity trap that recognizes reproductive labor could include policies to ensure a basic income. A universal basic income is defined as "an unconditional social transfer set at a level that assures every citizen subsistence."[168] Promoting a basic income, either within states or universally, would mean a recognition of how the rearing of children and family maintenance, central to the creation of future workers, is critical to the productive economy and productive labor.

Growing economic inequality at the global scale has more recently gained traction in mainstream media with a focus on this "crisis of structural inequalities" in which the global elite get wealthier, while the "global majority" struggles to find work and secure income.[169] But while we're perhaps ready to talk about income inequalities, we still have a far way to go to understand how those inequalities are informed by gender and other complex identities.

6

The "Problem" with Protecting Women from Violence

One of the most important and central agendas within the transnational women's movement has been around the issue of violence against women. Violence against women and women's security more generally are an important aspect of women's inclusion. It represents the degree to which women have been added to security discourses and practices, indicating the formalization of the protection of women from direct violence within and between states. While perhaps not quite as obvious as including women in formal government institutions or economies, protection and security remain a central institution of people, states, and organizations. And importantly, protection is a central aspect of women's inclusion—and is more readily obvious in the degree to which violence against women protocols have permeated larger discourses and practices of security at all levels. This includes the more recognizable policies adopted by states to protect women, like anti-rape and sexual harassment laws. But it also includes the increasingly important anti-violence against women movement that has emerged in response to global conflicts, often referred to as the Women, Peace, and Security (WPS) framework. This movement is embodied in United Nations Security Council Resolution 1325 (UNSCR 1325), which identifies how women are both targeted during conflict and ignored in efforts to end it. This may be one of the most important areas of "progress" of women's inclusion: the "outing" of violence directed at women and the changing of resources and knowledge surrounding it.

There have been major improvements as a result of this movement to end violence against women: the very idea that women are targets of certain forms of violence and *naming it* (domestic violence, sexual violence) is in itself paramount.[1] The creation of battered women's shelters for women to leave violent partners is a vital, tangible result of this movement. In some cases, researchers find that after these movements take hold, an "increase" in violence against women is often due to more reporting, since the issue is not as hidden as before. The ability to prosecute violent partners and rapists is clearly an important change in most countries' domestic legal systems. Many work places have protocols for sexual harassment and zero-tolerance policies for it, allowing women to work in safer environments.

Women working for peace are better organized and now have an international framework upon which to make their claims and unite. There is evidence of changing values about women and violence, that it is becoming less tolerated or acceptable. The value of these policies should not be underestimated and conditions are markedly improved for many women in the world as a result of these policies. According to women's rights activist and researcher Purna Sen:

> Prior to the successes of the women's movement against violence, in many countries women would not seek protection from, or redress for, violence suffered at the hands of men known to them. Agencies with mandates to uphold the peace and enforce the rule of law (lawyers, the police, and the criminal justice system) would not take such reports seriously and women were often blamed for the violence they suffered.[2]

Despite this "progress," however, violence against women remains a *global epidemic*. While organizations such as the European Union or UN Women consistently identify lack of data on prevalence and enforcement, the World Health Organization (WHO) produced its own report, which paints a distressing picture of the degree to which all women's lives are shaped by violence on a daily basis.[3] According to the most recent global study of violence against women produced by the World Health Organization in 2013, one in three women *worldwide* experience intimate partner violence during their lifetimes—and this average is fairly consistent across regions. And this violence against women is not isolated to the "private sphere" or households, it has also become an increasingly visible issue in situations of war and conflict where it is also at epidemic levels. During conflicts in Bosnia, Rwanda, and Sierra Leone, sexual violence was epidemic, and this appears to be continuing and is documented in every active conflict today; in Syria, women cited fear of rape as the number one reason for fleeing.[4]

So why do women still have to deal with epidemic levels of violence despite so many states passing laws to address it? Why do violence against women policies and practices only seem to get adopted and implemented if both local and transnational feminist movements and women in government make it happen? Or if powerful actors impose it on states? This chapter explores the "problem" with violence against women policies and practices, which illustrates how gender remains a central explanation for this epidemic. As is the case with other aspects of women's inclusion that I have discussed in this book, these policies primarily focus on women, not gender per se. And, as in other chapters, part of the problem is how women and gender are used synonymously in discussions of violence under the rubric of *gender-based violence*. Because violence against women practices treat "gender-as-women," violence gets treated in ways that do not adequately deal with how gender (the socially constituted and hierarchical structures and behaviors organized via practices of masculinities and femininities) *causes* violence. Often political actors are centrally focused on dealing with violence against women without also centrally focusing on men and issues of masculinity and femininity (in addition to class, race, and sexuality).

Another issue relevant here is how violence against women centrally focuses on issues of direct, personal violence. While trying to end violence to women's and girls' bodies is urgent, the neoliberal world order in which this has happened has silenced issues of structural violence and important links between structural and direct forms of violence. Direct violence "most often means male violence against women, ranging from battering and burning to sexual harassment, assault, mutilation . . . and torture."[5] Physical harm is direct, such as sexual assault and domestic abuse. Structural violence includes kyriarchical structures as well as the socioeconomic forces shaping people's ability to live. Structural violence may include policies and practices promoted by states, military, and police, and it also can be committed through systemic oppression of minorities or limiting access for groups to certain goods (such as clean water or education). It can be related to limited access to decision-making structures, such as states, but also to post-conflict negotiations, and disarmament programs, as well as a lack of decision-making authority in formal political structures. Structural violence is often excluded from discourses on protecting women, obscuring how direct and structural violence are interdependent, in that the inequalities of structural processes (like limited access to formal power structures) shape how direct violence operates and is expressed.[6] The pervasive and gendered beliefs and myths underlying policy adoption and implementation indicate that changing laws or increasing women's access to protective laws and services does not adequately address violence as a gendered institution. Because these links are obscured, neoliberal world order—which privileges individuality, market economies, and rationality—remains unquestioned. What "counts" as violence against women remains narrowly focused on symptoms rather than causes of such violence, including neoliberal economic globalization.

This chapter focuses on both the violence women experience and the policies meant to end it. The chapter identifies poor implementation and how the underlying beliefs that violence against women is a women's issue and a private affair complicate the success of these policies and do not adequately destabilize gender binaries. Because neoliberal world order is perpetuated through masculinized violence, violence against women policies that treat "gender" to mean "women" ends up complicit in the liberal world status quo. This is because violence becomes a way to actually reinforce gender roles as a product of globalization and the feminization of labor.

Why States Combat Violence against Women

What accounts for the diffusion of violence against women policies and adoption among states and in peace processes? Explanations for the adoption and diffusion of violence against women policy all tend to find similar explanations/variables and these cluster on institutional, dynamic factors. The movement to end violence against women is motivated in part by the costs of such violence to individual women, communities, and even economies more generally. Most obviously are the physical, emotional, and psychological effects on women who directly experience violence that centrally motivate addressing violence against women via policy outputs. From death, injury, and disease to mental health issues and fear-based control, the costs to women's bodily integrity are a daily reality for far too many women. Effects in communities also include ostracization, particularly if women have been trafficked.[7] Few are repatriated "because of limited chances of rescue and significant costs of transport to home communities."[8]

Economic costs of violence against women in the U.S. are estimated at over 12 billion dollars; this includes lost productivity, health care costs, and missed work.[9] Trafficked women in forced servitude reduce salaries among other poor women and when employers know this, the work environment for non-trafficked women may become oppressive and abusive.[10] The economic costs for women are often more direct. One Canadian survey found one-third of women who had been sexually harassed reported their jobs had been affected by it, and these women may feel forced to leave their jobs.[11]

In terms of explanations for why states adopt violence against women policies, the first factor consistently cited is an active feminist or women's movement.[12] Political scientists Mala Htun and Laurel Weldon conclude that "women organizing to advance women's status have defined the very concept of violence against women, raised awareness, and put the issue on national and global policy agendas."[13] Additionally, Weldon's work on violence against women legislation in democratic states found an autonomous feminist movement a necessary condition for articulating violence against women as a "public problem rather than a private affair."[14] Their autonomy allowed such organizations to hold governments accountable. While much of the earlier feminist work in the 1970s and 1980s was focused on creating more services for victims, they had not yet advocated for state solutions, which they began doing more systematically in the 1990s.[15]

An active women's or feminist movement also matters for promoting women's anti-violence policies during peace processes. Based on case studies of "successful" peace processes (according to their attention to women in the agreements), active women's movements appear particularly important for creating an "*agenda*" for what women want in peace processes and "*access*" to the process. These cases included Guatemala, Burundi, the Democratic Republic of Congo, Darfur (in Sudan), and Uganda. Among these five more inclusive cases, all included a women's movement that spelled out demands and also had some sort of access to the peace process.[16]

For example, in Guatemala, women were organized and participated as part of the "civil society sector." They created general demands regarding development and repatriation and reintegration; criminalization of sexual harassment and domestic violence; expansion of women's citizenship rights and political participation; protection for indigenous women and general indigenous rights; and increased access for women to credit, housing, land, and education.[17] Provisions relating to all these topics are included in one or more of the actual peace agreements, indicating the clear success the women's sector had in making their voices heard as part of the peace process. In Burundi, women had observer status to the negotiations and were able to use this to get all "nineteen negotiating parties to accept the need for women's involvement in the peace process."[18] Each of these parties then sent two delegates each to the All-Party Burundi Women's Peace Conference that forged their women's agenda.[19]

The next key variable in explaining violence against women legislation and women's inclusion is the presence of women's bureaus or "policy agencies." These agencies correct for "gender bias" in institutions by shifting focus and priorities beyond men.[20] These agencies translate feminist activism into policy output; this is the case in both stable and emerging democracies.[21] However, in the absence of a strong feminist movement, women's policy machineries do not advocate for violence against women policies, so their importance is conditional on an active and independent feminist movement.

There are parallels between women's inclusion in state-level policies of violence against women and women's inclusion in peace processes— particularly in how women's success in promoting their agenda appears contingent on *advocacy* among those in power. Similar to the function of a women's policy bureau, women advocating for peace need someone in power who understand women's inclusion as part of their mandate and priorities. In the same way policy machineries can advocate for violence against women legislation, parties to peace processes can also advocate for the women's agenda to be part and parcel of the overall peace process.[22] In Guatemala, women's rights activist Luz Méndez, who was part of the rebel negotiating commission, stated she learned from El Salvador's failure to address women's issues, and consciously made it an issue in the commission.[23] Additionally, during the initial Darfur peace process, the African Union (AU) had women as mediators (their delegation to Darfur included women) and promoted women's security in peace processes. Additionally UNIFEM, the predecessor organization of UN Women, was able to work directly with the AU to promote the Darfurian women's agenda.

Another factor in explaining the promotion of women's security via the adoption of violence against women policies is "imposition" of some form. Imposition represents explanations in which certain states wield resources (material and symbolic) to encourage policy adoption among other states. In the European Union, sexual harassment initiatives diffused among states because the EU provided support to do so, and when Greece and Portugal did not comply, more binding mandates were adopted.[24] Within the EU, countries who acceded later (after 2004) were to be held to higher standards and more scrutiny than earlier states, in part because violence against women issues are more prominent in later accession processes.[25] Later member states were under more pressure from the EU to pass and implement violence against women laws. The EU also made available financial incentives via the Daphne Project, which funded programs focused on violence against women, including promoting new legislation.[26]

Another form of imposition can be money. In the former Soviet Union, U.S. NGOs and the United States Agency for International Development (USAID) supplied grant money to former Soviet states to foster the growth of crisis centers. This, in turn, fostered a growing expertise on dealing with domestic violence and publicizing the problem (though political scientist Janet Elise Johnson notes it also limited organizations in certain contexts because of the power dynamics of donors, states, and recipients).[27] In Kosovo, the UN Mission "coerced" the government into passing legislation, so violence against women policy was externally imposed, while in Slovenia and Croatia states were influenced by "social pressures" to enforce new policies.[28]

This imposition has also happened during peace processes. In the Democratic Republic of Congo (DRC), UNIFEM worked with women to increase their participation in the process and then made sure these women knew what sort of reforms would be discussed and beneficial to women.[29] In Uganda, UNIFEM supported women's efforts to create a peace caravan that traveled from the DRC to Uganda.[30] In Burundi, UNIFEM worked with Women for Peace to train women in leadership and sponsored the All-Party Conference.[31] During the last round of negotiations in Darfur, a Gender Experts Support Team, invited by UNIFEM, Canada, Norway and Finland, actually participated in the peace negotiations after having met with women's groups to form an agenda.[32] During Darfur's negotiations, neither party really cared about women's issues, but the African Union and UNIFEM made sure to advocate for women's issues and that they be included.

Another theme emerging from the studies of violence against women policy adoption and diffusion is how changing attitudes among the public may shift acceptance, and thus enforcement, of such policies. In this sense attitudes are both a cause and effect of new violence against women laws. When states enact legislation, people are less likely to think domestic violence is justifiable and women are more likely to report violence they experience.[33] Additionally, when women are more exposed to the "global script" that violence against women is a human rights violation (via policy adoption, media outreach, and development programs), the more likely they are to reject intimate partner violence; this pattern can happen as quickly as within five years.[34] This could also be understood as "acculturation" in which actors internalize global norms against violence against women, which fosters better implementation of new laws.[35]

The diffusion of all such policies is also tied to a transnational feminist movement that linked local and global movements with powerful institutions.[36] These movements have mattered in the adoption of all women's inclusion policies discussed in this book. Local actors learning and sharing transnationally shaped the emergence of global ideas that violence against women should be stopped. Ratification of CEDAW and the Beijing Platform also matter for adoption of violence against women practices.[37] Regional conventions also matter in strengthening local movements.[38]

Sexual harassment policies, which are often adopted as part of employment laws, are also affected by how they are framed. Most states have harassment policies which are included as part of "equality and sex discrimination laws" or labor laws, while a scant few include sexual harassment as criminal or human rights law.[39] This is most likely tied to CEDAW, which outlines harassment as an issue of discrimination. Recent work on sexual harassment in the European Union found it rarely mentioned and when it was, the language was "gender-neutral" and framed in the context of equality issues of rights and employment rather than as a women's rights issue.[40]

Implementing and Enforcing Violence against Women Policy

The first issue to address in making sense of why such policies are not working is poor implementation. Consistently, large-N reports and case studies indicate that the data on violence against women and its pervasiveness are often unsystematic but also lacking. Additionally, these policies are also poorly implemented because of lax enforcement and poor resource allocation to address violence against women.[41] Another key issue is the lack of data on implementation and the pervasiveness of violence.[42]

In Poland, there was a lack of clarity about the laws and political will to change the laws.[43] This seems consistent across post–Soviet states and in Latin America where there is either marginal or minimal implementation.[44] According to the latest UN Women Report, "the implementation of these legal provisions is rarely supported by adequate investments in services, in capacity building of service providers and in the public campaigns needed to effectively prevent violence against women." Resources also matter in explaining adoption and implementation. In post–Soviet states, "most domestic violence organizations . . . have been almost solely supported by grants from foreign donors."[45] Were such resources not provided, these policies may not have been adopted in the ways they have.

In terms of trafficking laws, the United Nations cites that even though convictions are increasing, it has not been proportionate to awareness.[46] While many states have adopted trafficking protocols, 40 percent had not yet had a single conviction of these laws. Thus, one could argue this international protocol had an effect on the diffusion of anti-trafficking policies but that actual implementation has been much slower. The United Nations Office on Drugs and Crime's 2009 report on trafficking also indicated regional variations in laws and convictions. Many African states, but also "high income states," had no or partial anti-trafficking legislation, and convictions were primarily concentrated in a few regions—South and Central Asia, Eastern and Western Europe. North and Central America and southern Africa had the fewest anti-trafficking laws, though it is worth noting the metric was "at least ten convictions per year."[47] The disappointing implementation of violence against women represented in UNSCR 1325 extends to peace processes as well. Nearly one-half since 1990 made no mention of women's inclusion at all.[48] In 2011, only two of nine agreements included provisions for women (Somalia and Yemen) and of the fourteen UN negotiations in 2011, only four included any women negotiators.[49]

Informal Barriers in Addressing Violence

The main problems discussed throughout this book help us understand the issues with violence against women legislation and implementation. Informal barriers are a key aspect for why violence persists and policies do not always work. One major "informal" barrier has to do with a "leaky justice" pipeline in dealing with violence against women. What this means is, justice remains elusive as reporting and prosecuting violence directed at women works its way through the justice system, resulting in low prosecution rates. The UN Women report titled, *In Pursuit of Justice*, notes:

> While law is intended to be a neutral set of rules to govern society, in all countries of the world, laws tend to reflect and reinforce the privilege and the interests of the powerful, whether on the basis of economic class, ethnicity, race, religion, or gender. Justice systems also reflect these power imbalances.[50]

The report also found underreporting and attrition with regard to rape cases to be another significant issue. In one study out of South Africa, only 17 percent of reported rape cases went to trial, and of all reported assaults, only 4 percent resulted in convictions. These numbers were only slightly higher among Western European states. The UN also found that "across fifty-seven counties, on average 10 percent of women say they have experienced sexual assault, but of these only 11 percent reported it" and this is consistent across all regions.[51]

The laws outlining how to report crimes against women are explicit, but women report in a justice pipeline run predominantly by (racialized majority) men nearly everywhere in the world. Institutions are gendered and justice systems do not exist separately from those who work in these institutions. When these individuals bring their own ideas about violence and justice with them, this may impact the degree to which any justice system can work for women (or anyone else for that matter). This barrier illustrates how changing rules and removing discriminatory practices may not eradicate violence against women in the way feminist activists want. If we go back to explanations for inclusion—feminist activism, women's policy machineries, imposition, and transnational movements—an important caveat emerges: changing the rules does not necessarily change the beliefs/stereotypes and ideologies of those who create/promote/enforce the rules.

The second informal barrier has to do with who challenges violence. There is a consistent finding that violence against women is not an issue unless feminists make it one.[52] It takes women specifically focused on violence to begin the process of violence against women policy adoption. This is despite the fact that there are absolutely no legal or formal barriers for men or men's groups (or any other non-sex-based group) to also advocate for violence against women policies and changes. This becomes an issue for two reasons. The first and most obvious is that in places where feminist organization is difficult, lower levels of violence against women awareness, policy adoption, and criminalization will persist. As many scholars and activists have noted, no place in the world is without violence against women, so if feminists cannot be autonomous and organized to demand change, women are excluded from domestic security discourses and practices. For example, some states have very little violence against women policy outputs. According to the UN Women's global database on violence against women, around twenty states—primarily Middle Eastern and post-conflict states in sub-Saharan Africa—have violence against women legislation focusing on only one area (primarily domestic violence) or none at all. Some of these states do not have particularly strong feminist movements; in others, many of these groups are stifled in their participation by Islamic regimes that may see such legislation as pro-Western (such as Saudi Arabia, Sudan, United Arab Emirates, and Yemen).

The autonomy of such a movement matters because governments may co-opt violence against women policies for other means. Ukraine, for example, had strong violence against women policies. However the adoption of these policies "displaced" women's groups, so the women's movements lost leverage and the policies ended up being adopted without implementation.[53] In Moldova and Armenia, these movements were not autonomous from the state, which helps explain their poor domestic violence policies.[54]

The same is true for peace processes and women's inclusion. When women do not have access to the process and an agenda, peace processes do not include women's security concerns. In El Salvador, while women's groups certainly made demands for reform and justice throughout the war, these did not coalesce into a unified set of demands until *after* the accords.[55] One female commander involved in negotiations, Lorena Peña affirmed that "the special problems of women were simply not discussed during the negotiations."[56]

The second, related issue, which may shape both adoption and implementation, is the strength of women's policy machinery to promote violence against women policies in government.[57] The point here is that weak agencies that directly focus on domestic violence policy and output would have little authority to promote change. In Ukraine, while there was a policy agency, which helped explain the adoption of violence against women policies, it was usurped for political purposes, rendering it ineffective in implementing policies.[58] In Argentina, the National Women's Council had few resources and leadership conflicts with the President so it was a weak institution, leaving the violence against women movement without a necessary government ally.[59]

A lack of "advocacy" also matters in explaining exclusive peace processes. For example, in El Salvador, while the military had been at least 30 percent women (and maybe up to 40 percent), there was no advocacy for women's security among the guerilla leaders by the time peace negotiations happened.[60] This included the female commanders who did not prioritize women's issues and even saw them as a distraction from their revolution.[61]

Violence against women policies are not adopted, diffused, or implemented without global "influence." I use the term "influence" to cover the range of ways global forces impact a state's propensity for adopting violence against women policy. It includes: the impact of global agreements like CEDAW or the Beijing Platform; material resources provided from foreign sources for states to implement violence against women policies; and social "pressure" on states to change their behavior. While most states have ratified CEDAW, Iran, Somalia, Sudan, South Sudan and the United States have not. Most of these are states I previously listed as having poor violence against women policy records.[62] Building upon Mala Htun and Laurel Weldon's argument that withdrawing reservations about CEDAW may signal a stronger commitment to violence against women legislation, states that do not withdraw reservations would have weaker policies.

These global agreements are connected to social "pressure" and presumably, when there is less pressure, like the absence of regional agreements, states are less likely to adopt policies. This includes post–Soviet states, which did not adopt policies based on regional pressures.[63] The United States may also be a strong case here in not ratifying treaties because of an idea that the U.S. considers itself outside the purview of pressure to do what other states do. In regards to the Middle East, a recent treaty includes several states with lower violence against women indexes and policy outputs, but there are not any regional agreements on violence against women as there are in Europe, Latin America, or sub-Saharan Africa.[64] Based on some of these findings, promoting feminist activism and ensuring better implementation should decrease violence. But if we dig deeper into why these policies are poorly implemented and why feminist activism is a necessary condition for women's inclusion in security via violence against women policies, what emerges is the problem of "gender."

Gender Matters in Understanding Pervasive Violence against Women

Because binary gender underlies the naming, logic, and implementation in all violence against women practices, activists have similar complaints about the outcomes of violence-related policies. Due to the fact that violence against women policy is poorly implemented, violence remains a central problem for many women. In fact, violence appears to actually be on the rise in some places, even when considering a rise in reporting and awareness as a contributing factor. This indicates states are not doing enough to actually eradicate violence. If one delves into explanations of inclusion, exclusion, and persistent violence, the dynamics of gender and how they shape institutions emerge as the consistent and underlying theme. Laurel Weldon and Mala Htun have argued that violence against women policy "challenges, rather than reinforces, established gender roles in most places . . . Addressing violence against women requires challenging male privilege in sexual matters and social norms of male domination."[65] At some level this is true; publicizing violence against women does begin to elucidate male domination of women. But I would also argue the way violence against women and gender-based violence are framed and politicized also actually reinforces gender roles. This begins with what we call such violence and the pervasive gendered myths that remain part of the discourse on violence against women.

If one looks up the term *gender-based violence* on the internet, what one finds is explicit *violence against women* discussions—from the World Health Organization, USAID, Women's Refugee Commission, and International Justice Mission, just to name a few. And this linking between gender-based violence and violence against women elucidates the limits of violence against women policies and practices that centrally focus on women, not gender. It is another case of "gender = women." This aspect of women's inclusion was a vital intervention, and tremendous progress in terms of resources and awareness has happened as a result of this movement. But when gender-based violence and violence against women are treated as equivalents, it obscures the dynamics of masculinities and femininities as the *cause* of violence.

The term "gender-based violence" *could* correctly describe violence perpetrated out of hegemonic and toxic masculinist identities, but that is not the focus of these policies, or even the concept itself. Because it is used interchangeably with violence against women, which situates women as passive recipients of violence, analyses and policies are aimed at women and improving their resources for dealing with violence. These policies are not about challenging masculinity and its relationship to violence. Since most violence is perpetrated by men—against both women *and* men—why not focus on *male-perpetrated violence*? How would policy objectives shift if the focus were on stopping men from being so violent in the first place rather than helping women cope from receiving such violence?[66] While in theory efforts to criminalize domestic and sexual violence should prevent violence by deterring it through fear of punishment, this does little to change the culture in which masculinity and violence go hand-in-hand.

Using the term "male-perpetrated violence" still leaves much to be desired if we take gender to be relational (and the reality that women also perpetuate violence).[67] *Masculinized violence* would better link violence to the binary thinking and attitudes that privilege anger, order, control, rationality, and dominance that underlies most violence. This would be more inclusive of directing discourse and policy outputs towards larger discussions of who perpetrates violence against whom and what is being challenged or maintained through acts of violence. It may make violence against women a men's issue (rather than just a women's issue).

Focusing on masculinized violence would also open the space for dealing with violence against women as also very heteronormative. Assumptions about family structures and nuclear families inform violence against women policies. This means they may not recognize or criminalize violence within same-sex relationships or possibly inter-generational violence. The language of violence against women also obscures the role heterosexism plays in defining masculinity nearly everywhere in the world. Masculinity is often defined by and maintained through heterosexuality because masculinity is defined through virility, dominance, and conformity. "Masculine" men are assumed to prefer women and to reject the feminine, so homosexuality is seen as a disruption to this order of human behavior. This is particularly relevant for parsing out why promoting feminist activism will not be enough to change violence against women.

Three very gendered ways of thinking permeate violence against women approaches. These ways of thinking also help us understand why violence persists and why the onus is on feminist activists to make changes. Violence against women is still considered a "women's issue," a "private affair" and a "woman's fault." All of these beliefs are based upon and problematically reinforce gender binaries. These informal biases matter in shaping formal and informal practices, particularly implementation of violence against women legislation. These myths, based on traditional gender roles, obscure the reality that, "men use violence against women to preserve their privileged role of power; that is, women are expected to obey and respect their husbands or partners."[68] Such myths shape the "justice pipeline" in dealing with violence from the beliefs about what constitutes violence against women and what causes it—from reporting such violence to sending offenders to prison for violating violence against women laws.

What does it mean that something is a women's issue? More generally it is this idea that because it affects women, women should deal with it. When something is a women's issue, it implicitly negates that it is also a men's issue or something men need to address. In other words, violence *affecting* women is the focus. Again, as a central premise of this book is that gender is relational, when the relationship between masculinities and femininities and men and women is obscured, gender and gender roles are not challenged. In Australia, a national survey noted an increase in "diminished responsibility" for perpetrators of domestic violence (read: men's violence against women-partners) in which sexual violence and general violence is excused away by focusing on angry outbursts or women "asking for it." Additionally, men were more likely to think that domestic violence is perpetrated equally by men and women.[69] These are noticeable changes (since 1995) in which the narrative of violence is still centered on women and appears to be shifting even more responsibility or blame for violence from men to women, reinforcing the idea that this is a women's issue.

Perhaps if we called it masculinized violence, it would be considered, at minimum, a men's issue or really a "gender" issue. This gets realized in the emphasis being on feminists to get everyone else to listen and respond to *their* issue. While feminists may prioritize and publicize it, broader institutions such as governments and organizations do not. In fact they do not have to because it *is* a women's issue—so women will deal with masculinized violence by generating policies and support to then pressure those broader institutions to create change. But this leaves governments and individuals off the hook for dealing with the complicated reasons why violence is epidemic. And, as the research has shown, without women's policy advocates in government, policy adoption and implementation are not likely to happen.

The second detrimental way of thinking is the pervasive myth that violence against women is a "private" affair or not really violence. This is manifested in what "counts" as violence; often what happens in the private sphere (within the family) does not "count" as violence. For example, one World Values Survey found that in seventeen out of forty-one countries, more than one-quarter of people think it is justifiable for a man to beat his wife. Two-thirds of states that have domestic violence laws do not actually criminalize rape within marriage; this is in part because of "traditional" patriarchal values, as many consider sex within marriage a "right" of any husband.[70] A consistent pattern among attitudes is how violence against women comes into conflict with "traditional" (read: entrenched) cultural norms resulting in poor adoption rates or implementation. In an Australian national survey on violence against women, while most respondents to a national survey classified physical and sexual violence as domestic violence, one-quarter still thought non-physical forms of violence were not domestic violence, and there was actually a decline in the number of people who thought slapping or pushing a partner as a very serious form of violence (from 64 to 53 percent).[71] This means nearly half of Australians think causing harm via slapping or pushing a female partner is not a serious issue.

As UN Women spells out in their report, *In Pursuit of Justice*, it begins with discriminatory laws (which are meant to be addressed by many of the policies adopted by states).[72] For example, many states have still not criminalized rape in marriage or grant many rights within the family. This goes back to beliefs about violence as a private affair: historically, the report states, "legal jurisdiction has been divided between public and private matters, leaving the private sphere of the family 'outside justice.'"[73]

The other persistent belief/myth is that violence against women is somehow women's own faults, also known as "victim-blaming" (this is acutely the case in sexual violence). In both Scottish and Australian surveys, the myth that rape is a result of men being unable to control their sexual needs still remains pervasive and the most likely explanation for such violence. Indeed, victim-blaming also remains a strong issue in which women "ask for it" through their dress and drinking.[74] Even where policies exist and women are using them to stop violence, "victim-blaming" remains a major issue in which the violence in the home is still considered a private issue among police who are failing to enforce the law.[75]

The rise of "violence against women" as an institution also appears to have created a backlash against women's rights. In Tajikistan, a resurgence of "traditional" values, particularly kinship networks focusing on "protecting" women, has shaped the discourse on violence against women by reinforcing patriarchal ideas about violence in the family, so forced pregnancy and beatings are not considered violence by family members.[76] In Slovenia and Russia, right-wing parties argued against domestic violence policies as somehow eroding traditional families by linking women's empowerment with increase in women's violence: the policies were believed to be anti-family, anti-fertility, and anti-marriage.[77] Both Mozambique and Sri Lanka had bills in the legislature to allow/require rapists to marry their victims and similar laws have been proposed or were only recently overturned after protest (as in the cases of Malawi, Pakistan, and Morocco).[78]

These same myths apply to conflict and post-conflict situations as well.[79] Violence explicitly directed at women is tied to ideas that women ask for it, are somehow complicit in it, or it is not really violence. However, in conflict and post-conflict settings, there is an additional belief surrounding masculinized violence with profound effects. Violence against women is considered an inevitable, yet less important part of conflict. When someone uses the phrases like the "spoils of war," often to include "raping and pillaging," they treat violence against women as though it simply happens during conflict, void of agency or the explicit acts of (primarily) men. But, when violence against women is treated as inevitable, yet less important in understanding war and violence, it renders such types of violence outside the purview of what to study and understand during conflict. In this sense it was not until the 2000s that security actors began to address violence against women as a central phenomena upon which to focus analyses and resources. Ultimately there is nothing inevitable about mass rape or the explicit targeting of women, but beliefs about it as a side effect of war render it such.

The treatment of violence against women as a women's issue and the myths of violence as a private affair matter because they shape people's beliefs and actions. If security officials—be it police officers, lawyers and judges, politicians, or conflict mediators—consider violence against women a problem for women to deal with, or believe women are somehow complicit in their own victimization, at minimum poor implementation will continue. I would thus argue these pervasive, gendered ways of thinking continue to underlie the problem of violence and subsequently do not seem to be challenging gender roles as much as one would hope. In the beginning of this section I quoted Laurel Weldon and Mala Htun who argued violence against women "challenges, rather than reinforces, established gender roles in most places" and that "addressing violence against women requires challenging male privilege in sexual matters and social norms of male domination."[80] But it is possible to challenge male domination and privilege while simultaneously reinforcing gender roles and binaries because the focus of these policies is not centered on gender, but women. To say something *"challenges rather than reinforces"* sets up a false dichotomy that such processes cannot exist or happen simultaneously.

But policies can simultaneously challenge and reinforce binaries, especially if sex, gender, and women are treated as the same. This paradox is endemic to add-women/add-gender approaches that *do* challenge male domination by exposing how women are excluded, but without exposing the masculinized logic upon which we are organized and operate. As liberal feminism identifies discrimination in laws and access as the cause of women's oppression, addressing male domination should be sufficient for eradicating violence. But as violence persists and even increases despite changes to laws and access, we have to move beyond discussions of sex to those of gender, something liberal feminism and liberal feminist policies do not encourage. One can identify male domination of institutions as a problem and adding women as a remedy without necessarily destabilizing gender binaries in answering what *causes* male domination in the first place. Adding women to exclusionary institutions does not entirely destabilize gender binaries because gender is the relational, mutually constituted process of masculinities and femininities and this is not yet part of the dominant discourse on violence against women (though as I point out in the next section, it is part of the feminist discourse surrounding violence against women). And I make this argument because of the liberal world context in which such discourses and activities happen.

An Intersectional Lens on Violence against Women

As I mentioned earlier in this book, intersectionality is an important concept in understanding gender and gender equality, and this is especially true with regards to the issue of violence against women. Kimberlé Crenshaw, the first to use the term, initially developed the idea of intersectionality in the context of the study of violence against women of color: she explored how domestic abuse and rape are "frequently the product of intersecting patterns of racism and sexism, though often not represented in discourses of either feminism or antiracism."[81] In her experiences working in battered women's shelters in the United States, she noted most of the women there were under and unemployed and poor. She writes:

> Many women of color, for example, are burdened by poverty, childcare responsibilities, and the lack of job skills. These burdens, largely the consequence of gender and class oppression, are then compounded by the racially discriminatory employment and housing practices women of color often face.

Crenshaw goes on to illustrate the complexities of violence against women. She notes prior to 1990, the marriage fraud act stated women and men must be married two years to apply for permanent resident status. This resulted in many immigrant women staying with abusive husbands for fear of losing their immigration status. The U.S. Congress changed the law in 1990 to exempt battered women, but the conditions for the waiver required "proof" of abuse from police, medical personnel, and social services, which were difficult for many women to obtain. There were also cultural barriers to discussions of violence against women and men often controlled women by controlling their legal status.

While Crenshaw's examples appeared dated, in reality these same issues persist.[82] More recent work continues to illustrate how violence against women policies and practices often emerge from a white, middle class, and Western experience.[83] This intersectional work challenges the often-universalist assumption underlying women's violence that domestic violence affects everyone equally and that all women are equally susceptible to such violence. While violence against women is universal in the sense that no country is immune from it, certain women are more susceptible to such violence and unable to leave it because of the dynamics and stress, poverty, and racism play as causes of violence more generally.

Case study work emphasizes how policies aimed at assisting women who experience violence may end up further marginalizing them. For example, in South Korea, NGOs seeking to help migrant sex workers tried to make women "innocent victims" of trafficking, which actually made it more difficult to promote HIV/AIDS programs for them. In anti-trafficking programs in Cambodia, scholars found efforts to help Vietnamese women in sex work "may inadvertently compound their risk of violence, debt, and isolation from health services."[84]

Issues of intersectionality remain problematic for development of violence against women policies. Political scientists Celeste Montoya and Lise Agustin explore the issue of "culturization" in which the EU emphasizes "cultural" forms of violence for certain groups of women (read: non-Western) generating a false binary between "European gender equality and anti-violence" to violent "others."[85] These "others" are then held to higher standards and the violence against women policies are less about protecting women than creating and reinforcing dichotomies between states as "insiders and outsiders." In this sense, violence against women gets co-opted as a strategy to enforce difference through apparent "good governance" strategies. And this is especially the case for the impact of class and wealth on violence.

A Neoliberal Feminist Status Quo

The neoliberal world order in which these policies and practices exist remains central to understanding the trade-offs of women's inclusion via policies aimed at protecting women. The first issue is the lack of engagement with intersectional praxis and how violence is not just gendered but raced, classed, and ultimately structural. Within this a paradox emerges in which economic practices *have* challenged gender binaries via globalization and the feminization of labor, but violence is actually used to reinforce gender in response to these shifts. In other words, another reason why violence against women is increasing is because global processes generate more vulnerable and informal work patterns (in essence, feminized work patterns); men find other means to re-assert their masculinity and violence is one way to do so.

The violence against women/"good governance" nexus relies upon problematic assumptions of gender (as women), and the role economics has in ending it. The underlying message among certain IOs, such as the World Bank, is violence against women is bad economics—and while true, this reinforces the rationalist, neoliberal emphasis on citizens as economic units, not people. For example a recent press release about a World Bank report on women states:

> The need for systemic responses by governments and the international community to prevent and address violence against women is urgent and long overdue. Progress on this front would support efforts to *reduce poverty and boost shared prosperity*. . . . This underscores that the loss due to domestic violence is a significant *drain on an economy's resources*. Violence against women and girls is a global epidemic, with devastating consequences for individuals, communities, societies, and economies. Addressing this challenge head-on promises to significantly *advance our efforts to end extreme poverty and increase prosperity for all*.[86]

States are given an economic imperative for dealing with violence, rather than a moral or justice-based motivation. This line of thinking does not necessarily require discussion of causes of such violence. And because discussions about cause are not happening, the pervasive assumption that women's economic empowerment will *decrease* violence against women remains unchallenged, despite evidence that women's economic empowerment may actually *increase* violence against women.

Economic inequalities within families and within societies are directly tied to the levels of violence women experience daily and during conflict. One UN study of thirty countries found in eighteen more than half of women reported having little say in household decision-making. The lowest ranking country was still 25 percent, meaning in all households at least one-quarter of women felt they had little decision-making power in their homes.[87] Class and economic inequalities are a major factor in linking masculinities to violence: so when women make economic and political gains, violence actually increases as men fear they are losing their dominance due to women's empowerment.[88] As women everywhere have become more active in the paid and unpaid workforce, men's roles as "breadwinner" or "provider" has been disrupted and this "breadwinner masculinity"—resulting in lost entitlements—may result in increased violence against women.[89]

Neoliberal globalization, which has resulted in the increase of "feminized" labor (temporary, migratory, unskilled, and service) means women are in higher demand for certain types of work. This is especially the case in developing states where export-growth oriented economies have challenged the "gendered divisions of labor and resources."[90] And while this has resulted in some women having more autonomy, this is not universally the case. This challenge to gender divisions, while de-stabilizing gender, has also resulted in a backlash against women and increased levels of violence rather than decreased levels of violence—contrary to the narrative linking women's increased autonomy and employment with greater empowerment.[91] Again this counter-narrative, while being exposed by feminist activists and academics, is not the same narrative of the World Bank, IMF, or even the United Nations. Without a more central discussion of how inequalities breed violence and an intersectional focus on violence as sexed, classed, raced, and imperialist, these processes remain outside dialogues on how to deal with violence against women—to the detriment of women.

This "governance" approach has also permeated how we think about and deal with violence against women during and after conflict. Political scientist Jacqui True calls it a "securitization" of violence against women, in which IOs, in creating international frameworks to deal with violence against women, emphasize violence as a security issue rather than a political economy issue.[92] But as with representation and recognition, the protection of women in conflict has been co-opted in some problematic ways throughout the global security industrial complex. For one, it may obscure the structural inequalities that cause conflict and gendered violence in the first place. In the last five years, the majority of peace agreements including woman-centered provisions have focused primarily on protection from sexual violence, begging the question why sexual violence is privileged over other types of violence, security, and inclusion.[93] Both Mali and the Democratic Republic of Congo's (DRC) latest peace processes included the need to stop, investigate, or prosecute sexual violence as a war crime without specifying women or gender in the text. Given the slate of resolutions specifically targeting sexual violence in conflict (UNSCR 1820 (in 2008), 1960 (in 2010) and 2106 (in 2013)), it is perhaps not surprising that states with conflict are explicitly recognizing this. Perhaps no reference to women or gender is an important development, representing an increased awareness that sexual violence also affects men and boys, though this is most likely not the case.

This central focus on sexual violence in conflict is also potentially troubling because it may represent a fetishization of sexual violence in which it has become *the primary issue* of negotiating women's security to the detriment of other issues central to women's lives. According to political scientists Maria Baaz and Maria Stern, this global focus on sexual violence has produced a "commercialization of rape," particularly in the DRC, where rape narratives and issues are used to solicit aid and attention from the international community.[94] However, they note this increased attention and resources are not usually accompanied by a more critical discussion of the colonizing and racialized narrative produced by such measures. Moreover the treatment of rape as a war crime also treats sexual violence in conflict as an exceptional form of violence, rather than endemic to the daily life of many women (men and children) before, during, and after conflict.[95]

Finally, references to sexual violence need not specify women or gender because "women" is already implied. Given how sexual violence is categorized by international documents and practices in explicit documents centrally about women, this obscures more complex discussions about why sexual violence occurs and to whom. As subsequent resolutions on sexual violence are all linked to UNSCR 1325, they are implicitly focused on women because 1325 is the Women, Peace, and Security framework; the framework is noticeably not named Gender, Peace, and Security.[96] This ultimately could mean discourses and resources allocated for women's protection are funneled primarily to sexual violence and protection during peace processes, further marginalizing *all* the ways women experience insecurity. It also means resources to address the sexual violence of men and boys remains outside the purview of "protection."

UN Women has come up with some "best practices" to deal with ending violence against women. These include: comprehensive legal and administrative activities (constitutional, civil, and criminal laws); laws that must cover all women and girls; efforts to "ensure no custom, tradition, or religious tenet may be used to justify violence against women and girls"; funding to implement legislation; the collection of data on prevalence of violence against women and impact of policies to address it.[97] While all these practices are important and would surely help in promoting better implementation and maybe even reporting of violence, these primarily focus on *managing* violence against women, not *eradicating* it. "Best practices" for eradicating violence would require challenging the power of gender, which underlies logics and strategies of violence. Even calling it "gender-based violence" while meaning "violence against women" obscures who perpetrates violence and we miss out on the dynamic of violence in relation to preserving masculine/feminine dichotomies.

There are "hints" of the possibility to bring in feminist gender and masculinities, where the report calls for challenging customs and traditions, but in further reading, the actual focus is on "forced or child marriage and female genital mutilation," and again, "creating legislative measures," but what about masculinities as the tradition underlying violence more generally?

Conclusion

While masculinized domination and power are at the root of this kind of violence, this conversation may be obscured by focusing primarily on protecting women to the deficit of why men are so violent. Conversations about violence against women have shifted to thinking more about the role of men, particularly among feminists, and even among leaders. Australia's former Prime Minister Kevin Rudd stated in 2008: "On their own, all the laws in the world can't stop violence against women unless there is a genuine change in the way that . . . men think."[98] But this has yet to broadly inform reevaluation of how we approach masculinized violence through changing laws and rules and more importantly, our belief systems. Ultimately because this has been an add-women, liberal feminist approach, it has also done little to challenge the liberal world order in which we operate, which again illustrates how liberal feminism may actually reinforce rather than challenge the very processes subjugating women and perpetuating violence.

While positive developments have happened with regards to increased criminalization of violence and there is a clear pattern of more states adopting more legislation to address more types of violence against women, some reports find violence against women is actually increasing. By digging into what we know about the conditions under which violence against women policies are pursued (autonomous feminist movements, women's bureaus, imposition, changing attitudes, and transnational activism), what emerges are the informal barriers and binary logics that shape poor implementation. A leaky justice pipeline and the need for autonomous feminist movements shape policy effectiveness, and ultimately this affects whether women will make their private violence public. Three beliefs/myths underlie these barriers: violence against women is a women's issue, a private affair or not violence, or the fault of women. These inform the men and women who ultimately shape the justice systems and policy outputs dealing with violence. Finally, neoliberal globalization and governance play a key role in perpetuating gender roles and thinking that shapes violence, particularly a lack of awareness of how intersectional identities and structures shape violence, and the use of violence to reinforce gender in response to the feminization of male labor and markets. Ultimately, eradicating violence against women will require a radical shift in discourse on the nature of violence and gender—in which the focus is on the relational dynamics between global neoliberal patriarchal structures and people, men and women alike.

Beyond Add-Women Politics

A popular phrase in our current public discourse in the twenty-first century is the "Century of Women." Hillary Clinton, Michelle Bachelet, Tom Brokaw, Nicholas Kristof, and Sheryl WuDunn have all made claims in some way to this effect.[1] While usually this phrase compares women's oppression to other forms of historical and structural violence, such as slavery and totalitarianism, it is also compared to the Industrial Age and the "American Century," alluding to the role women play in promoting global progress. This phrase embodies the problems of "gender equality" as a global norm. While many want women's rights and agency to increase in the twenty-first century in ways it has yet to do, this will not happen if the focus is simply on adding more women and calling it gender. While women's inclusion is an important global norm, it does not link the domination of women with larger forces of structural domination, including between different groups of women, nor does it necessarily deconstruct gender order. Nearly twenty years into the twenty-first century and similar discourses from the 1970s remain, and while one may now substitute gender for women when talking about equality and empowerment, the logic of how to do it has actually changed very little. While more radical conversations were happening in the 1970s about causes of women's subjugation, those have been co-opted and replaced by technical gender (women) and gender as a shortcut—effectively obscuring kyriarchy and the power of gender in perpetuating violence, exclusion, and poverty.

The year 2017 marks an important benchmark in this campaign to promote women. It has been over forty years since the first International Women's Conference, more than twenty years since Beijing, and fifteen years since the adoption of UNSCR 1325. To think about how much has changed for women since 1975 is nothing short of remarkable. States are actively promoting women in government; they are criminalizing violence and promoting women's economic rights. It has required countless hours, serious organization, and a concerted effort to change states' relationships to women. It also took tenacity and a willingness to deal with the often-violent backlash that accompanied this push against male dominance.

But there is still a long way to go and hopefully this book is seen as a call for changing the dialogue to focus less on women and more on the dynamics of gender in shaping women's experiences as well as men's. It is about no longer taking the "gender shortcut," but rather critically engaging how polices may challenge male domination without necessarily challenging masculinity. It is about moving the discourse beyond what works for women to also focus on the implications for the policy choices being made in the name of "women." Let this be a call for challenging the meaning of "gender equality" to encapsulate more than it currently does, and to clarify women's inclusion as part of, but not equivalent to gender equality, and never power-neutral.

The Politics of Women's Inclusion

This book began by exploring a paradox: states continue to promote women's inclusion via policies affecting every aspect of women's lives—their inclusion in decision-making, their inclusion in economic activity, and their everyday existence as safe citizens in public and private life. Thanks to women's activism, over nearly two-thirds of states have some sort of sex quota for promoting more women in parliament; nearly the same number have criminalized sexual assault and domestic violence. Many states have also replaced statutes in which women's access to employment, credit, and property required male consent. But the paradox is that, despite such a concerted assault on male dominance and discrimination, women's exclusion, experiences of violence, and access to good jobs and income are rather depressing. The central explanation for this paradox is that these policies aim to "add women" while calling it gender, which is not enough to challenge kyriarchy and its system of privileging masculinities (and other dominant identities) over femininities and thus generally men over women. Central to this paradox is the idea of gender equality, which has become the keyword for all of these efforts to promote women.

It is necessary though not sufficient to increase women's representation in government, to recognize women's economic rights, and to protect women from violence. It is necessary because the world needs: 1) actual women in institutions where they have historically been excluded; 2) legal systems and states institutions to consider women when designing and implementing projects and policies; and 3) states to care about women and to do something about it. But it is not sufficient to get to the root cause of exclusion, poverty, and insecurity, which is a kyriarchical system that perpetuates binary thinking about a host of powerful social identifiers such as gender, race, class, sexuality, and geography. Kyriarchy runs deep and it shapes how we look at the world and how we interact with one another. While adding women may challenge this to a degree, one can include women and still maintain belief systems that women are different, inferior, incompetent, incapable, and undeserving. And this is manifested in the problems all of these practices and policies exhibit.

In order to illustrate the power of gender and kyriarchy in producing this paradox of women's inclusion, I used analytical gender to expose five issues all these policies and practices exhibit. The first, most obvious trend is poor implementation. There is a long way to go in even following through with what is "on the books," let alone the resistance of some states still to adopt some of these policies. States may have quotas, and property and domestic violence laws, but just because they write the rule does not necessarily mean the political will to enforce it exists. And if enforcement does not include resources, the rules become window-dressing for states and officials to participate in the self-congratulatory practice of caring about "gender." And there seemed to be a lot of this.

This led to a discussion of the second (interrelated) issue, which is women's bounded agency as a result of informal barriers and beliefs. In the context of women in government, this was evident in how women are more concentrated in less prestigious and less competitive offices and when they are more insulated from a voting public. In women's economic rights, customary laws tend to work against women's claims for land and women continue to be pushed and pulled into certain work sectors: those lower-paying and more vulnerable. And implementation of violence against women policies are marred by a "leaky justice pipeline" and an entrenched belief that violence against women is a women's issue (so it is on women to deal with it). The point is, despite formal rules being in place to actively promote greater women's inclusion, informal beliefs and practices—sometimes including conflicting rules and ideas and sometimes conflicting people—who also have genders and gendered ways of thinking, continue to shape political will and implementation.

The third issue was the persistent gendered binaries informing these policies and barriers. These gendered binaries construct logics whereby men/women come to be associated with particular masculine/feminine characteristics. In the context of women's representation, the perception that women need to be competent is entirely gendered and based on masculinized assumptions about leadership. Additionally, certain executive offices over time are feminized, leading women to become concentrated in particular ministries such as family, women, and health. In the push to promote women's economic rights, assumptions about family and marriage inform access to land and credit. In some states women can still not legally be heads of household and the most recent push for development unquestionably accepts that women and men allocate households resources differently—it has become a "fact," rendering more critical analyses of why spending patterns are gendered moot. And in efforts to protect women, violence is still treated by many as a "private affair" based on this public/private divide informing what is considered in the domain of regulation and what is not.

The fourth issue is the ways policies that add women do not adequately ask "which women" are being added. What is systematically obvious throughout these analyses is the fact that poor women of color remain disproportionately limited in access to political power, economic resources, and efforts to end violence. It is elite women who make it to office, while rural women all over the world continue to fight to get land for subsistence farming; these categories of women live in different realities. And as labor remains feminized via global neoliberal processes of accumulation, this places a disproportionate burden on poor families, and means violence gets used to reinforce gender at all levels of development. We simply cannot only focus on women as a singular category in which helping one helps all. Class permeates issues of access and inclusion everywhere in the world and race and ethnicity create "haves" and "have nots" when resources are limited. And the Global North continues to reap the benefits of a large underclass of poor, racialized, and marginalized Global South women and men.

The final, and perhaps the most important, issue is the ways in which adding women in the context of a neoliberal world order actually perpetuates subjugation and gendered binaries. In other words, the ways we promote women's inclusion may not sufficiently challenge the very processes that oppress women and others in the first place. And in calling this all "gender equality," we are not having these conversations. Consistently women's inclusion is part of a narrative of good governance, but it relies upon essentialized views of women as more honest, community-oriented, and selfless. The other narrative is how adding women is smart economics; investing in women produces economic growth and human capital so states can harness more productivity from its citizens. Within this context, violence against women in conflict has been securitized and even fetishized, where sexual violence has become the central focus for peacebuilding agencies to the detriment of other potential basic and immediate needs of women. In this way it has produced a narrow discourse of victimhood for women in conflict. It is also evidenced in the gendered practices of microfinance that targets women, sometimes with predatory lending, because of assumptions about women as honest and reliable.

The result is a hegemonic discourse in which gender and women get used interchangeably and we miss the political and analytical value feminist gender gives us to critically interrogate women's positions in this world and why there is persistent resistance to even women's inclusion.

Who Is Good at Women's Inclusion?

One key point emerging from many of these policies and practices is that the Global North is not better at promoting women's inclusion than other regions, which is often assumed to be the case. Developing states and the Global South more generally are making faster transitions and are adopting policies and practices of women's inclusion at much faster rates than their northern counterparts. While Scandinavian countries more or less set the bar for promoting women's inclusion in all of these issue areas, Latin America has also done exceptionally well in promoting representation, recognition, and protection.

In terms of promoting women in governments, Norway, Sweden, and Finland were among the first to have some form of sex quota in the early 1970s, and among the first to mandate parity in cabinets in the early 1990s.[2] But after the 1990s, Latin America and sub-Saharan Africa challenged this leadership by implementing stronger policies. Indeed, the first prime minister and dual female executive leadership was in Sri Lanka; and Asia more generally has a long history of active women in the executive (though not so in other branches).[3] Latin America leads the way in adopting legislative sex quotas.[4] The region sits above the global average for women cabinet ministers (18 percent versus 12 percent global average), and women tend to hold more higher-prestige ministries.[5] Sub-Saharan Africa has more reserved seat quotas, and certain southern African states rank among the highest percent of women in government.

One of the key "non-findings" among many of these policies and practices is there's no correlation between adoption of add-women policies and levels of economic development.[6] These policies and practices appear across a range of states. This belief that women's leadership is probably correlated with or caused by economic development gets to the root of assumptions about the relationship between these policies and what it means to be a modern or "progressive" state.[7] But a look at the trajectories of these policies casts doubt on a west/east and north/south diffusion of core, "learned" states sharing with the "learning" periphery. Political scientist Ann Towns's work on policy agencies and quotas deals with the ranking of states according to these policies and how they actually often follow a "bottom-up" trajectory. This means the Global South promotes the policies rather than just accepts them, as is common wisdom, which dictates that such progressive policies come from the "more developed" and "equal" North.[8]

Towns identifies how women's policy agencies emerged from "lesser" advanced states in terms of women's equality, including from the communist East over the capitalist West.[9] Communist states wanted to emphasize women were better off under socialism than capitalism— suggesting that the communist states were more progressive in terms of women's empowerment and thus, did not need the same sort of machinery to promote women (who were already represented within socialist parties). The North was also challenged from developing states, which identified modernization and development as a central cause of women's oppression because it created inequalities and ignored women's roles in traditional economic household practices.

While Western Europe has had the most female national leaders, Eastern Europe, Latin America, and sub-Saharan Africa are not far behind. If you look at combined totals from the Global North and Global South, the Global South has had more female leaders.[10] Sub-Saharan African states have an average of 20 percent women cabinet members, above the global average.[11] Additionally, women in unified parliamentary systems and directly elected by popular vote are found primarily in Latin America and parts of Asia; these women tend to have more executive power than their counterparts in dual executive European systems.[12]

A look at the promotion of economic rights follows similar patterns. In one study of economic rights, OECD states started with more inequalities than Eastern or Central Europe and both regions have eliminated sexist policies on the books almost entirely, while Latin America has very few remaining.[13] Sub-Saharan Africa had the most constraints on women's economic rights but has also reformed the most, again showing much quicker improvements than even OECD states. The World Bank noted how changes in women's birth rates took one hundred years to decline from six to three children in the U.S., but thirty-five years in India and twenty in Iran. It also took the United States forty years to increase girls' primary education levels to 88 percent, a feat that took Morocco only ten years. Generally the report notes "improvements that took one hundred years in wealthier countries took just forty years in some low and middle-income countries. Change has been accelerating."[14]

Violence against women policies do not appear to be tied to level of economic growth or democracy, either. Laural Weldon and Mala Htun's 2013 article, which uses their "Index of Government Response to Violence against Women," illustrated how Latin America scored higher in responding to violence against women than most European states by the 1990s and very few countries had much on the books prior to that. The authors find wealth and length of democratic governance do not account for government responses. Another study they published in 2012 found wealth did not predict when women would organize to combat violence and democracy had a minor effect, so women may organize in democratic and less democratic states.[15]

The Middle East and North Africa (MENA) region lags the most in promoting women's inclusion most generally. This includes fewer quotas and women in government, fewer economic rights for women, and fewer violence against women laws than anywhere else. While there are Middle Eastern states promoting women's inclusion (e.g., Israel, Lebanon, Jordan), this region also represents the oil monarchies of the world, which are strongly Islamic and generally restrict both human and women's rights at greater levels. Some regions are better in promoting one area of inclusion over others. For example, Eastern Europe adopted economic rights much earlier than most places but lagged and continues to lag on violence against women legislation and response.

Clearly states adopting these policies in the last few decades do so in a different global climate than their predecessors. The adoption of women's inclusion policies creates a positive feedback loop by which this norm's power grows and further encourages other states to bandwagon. But this narrative is not one in which the West does it first and the rest catch-up, even though this is often implied in norm diffusion models of these policies. Rather, Eastern European states and Latin America have their own long histories of promoting women, despite not being so well known (at least among English-speaking countries). Eastern European states did so in the name of socialism and Latin American women have long organized in the face of repressive military regimes. So the patterns of adoption, while indicating steady inclines, do not adequately illustrate the variation in such inclines and the ways in which norms diffuse because of reasons other than income and imposition. I emphasize the leadership of the Global South because perhaps, in searching for new policy ideas that could be promoting gender equality, we ought to look beyond the "usual suspects" of the Global North for policy innovations.

Backlash

Another key theme worth addressing is the violent backlash in response to efforts to promote women's inclusion, which I argue is endemic, not epiphenomenal, to women's inclusion. Backlash, particularly when it is violent (both physically and structurally), bounds women's agency yet again. Women may not run for office, speak their minds, assert their economic rights, or leave abusive situations for fear of reprisal. This fear is warranted by the very real experiences women have with violence in response to exerting their authority and inclusion.

While this book has focused on the limits of women's inclusion, that violence accompanies the promotion of all of these policies in indicating that women's inclusion *is* challenging existing male-dominated power structures. Everywhere one looks, men are using violence and exclusion to re(assert) male dominance and a patriarchal system privileging masculine authorities.[16] If there weren't challenges, there would be no need to (re)assert male authority and privilege. Backlash can include actions of individual men against women but can also be backlash of states against women's inclusion more generally, both often using violence as a means of enforcement of male domination but more so masculinities. In a recent interview, Amanullah de Sondy, author of *The Crisis of Islamic Masculinities*, argued that: "The issue is the global crisis of Islamic masculinity. Women are finding their voice and position in society through God and *this unsettles patriarchy*."[17] And this is not just happening in the context of religiously informed masculinities, but it is happening under different rubrics everywhere where women challenge exclusion and violence—which is interpreted as challenging men—and this is sometimes accompanied by a backlash against women promoting their inclusion.

The first issue is backlash directed against women. As Jacqui True has noted, violence against women is "becoming more both more common and more egregious" in many parts of the world.[18] As scholars have long noted, global arenas of markets, states, and trade are "arenas" for gender formation.[19] The "globalizing masculinities" generated via global political processes are informed and shaped by shifts to the system.[20] As neoliberal order continues to promote decentralization of production and state organization, masculinities get destabilized, and men find ways to re-assert and re-stabilize masculinities. As production and company headquarters keep moving to the Global South, men in the Global North find their work sectors shrinking and the increased push for consumer-driven service economies shift preferences to women's and other marginalized group's labor. And with increased pressures from climate change and decreased state support, women and men in the Global South deal with daily vulnerabilities and insecurities but still in a patriarchal system privileging masculinities; thus violence is also used in these contexts.

There is a growing body of work on violence against women in politics.[21] Gabrielle Bardall's work on electoral violence has identified an important phenomena of violence directed at elected women and the numbers are staggering. Electoral violence is defined as "any random or organized act or threat to intimidate, physically harm, blackmail, or abuse a political stakeholder in seeking to determine, delay, or to otherwise influence an electoral process."[22] But such violence can be "gendered" when violence targets women, which is predominantly via intimidation, verbal harassment, and group clashes. Women who are political candidates or party supporters made up the majority of the victims (nearly half).[23] This violence is contextualized as backlash to women's increased representation and participation.[24] In the context of post-conflict transitions, where women have had more autonomy when men are absent, there may be violence targeted at women's political participation more generally; they do not even have to run for office, just have an interest in politics. While men still face more incidents of physical harm than women, their data shows women are more likely to be arbitrarily detained, intimidated, or psychologically abused. In Afghanistan nine out of ten threats against candidates were against female candidates. The report describes one incident where ten women volunteers of a woman candidate (Fauzia Gilani) were kidnapped to try to get her to quit, and five women were killed when she refused.[25] The report includes several stories such as this one, and it is hard to read about the power of misogyny working against women exerting their agency, and how this backlash can even include death.

Backlash can take the form of verbal harassment as well. U.S. Senator Kirsten Gillibrand, in her book *Off the Sidelines*, chronicles the sexual harassment she experienced in the United States Congress, including one male congressman who told her, "Don't lose too much weight now . . . I like my girls chubby." Perhaps even more distressing has been the media backlash in which one reporter accused her of lying and several others complained she did not "name names."[26] But the point is, it does not matter what she did, men saw it as an attack on men and internalized it as an attack on male privilege and would have criticized any response. Men want her to name names in order to be off the hook for being part of a sexist culture by specifying it is only a few men who did this, but Gillibrand, in not naming, is emphasizing this is a masculinist culture that makes such comments okay in the first place, and men who are bystanders are implicated as well. When women in office have to deal with persistent sexual harassment and backlash to their mere presence, they are hindered in fully effectuating their jobs.

There has also been backlash at other levels, which matters in understanding resistance to implementing laws or even passing them to promote women's inclusion. Chapter 6 noted how this push for violence against women legislation has actually created a backlash against women's rights in some cases. In Tajikistan, a resurgence of "traditional" values, particularly kinship networks focusing on "protecting" women, has shaped the discourse on violence against women by reinforcing patriarchal ideas about violence in the family, so forced pregnancy and beatings are not considered violence by family members.[27]

It is imperative to contextualize backlash and its gendered dynamics. Centrally, *backlash against women and women's inclusion is not epiphenomenal but endemic to promoting women's inclusion.* Kyriarchy produces male dominance, and masculinities promote violence as a central strategy in protecting this dominance. When add-women strategies do not situate women's inclusion in this larger context of kyriarchy, we continue to treat backlash as isolated events when it is actually a central part of the global system.

There Is No Such Thing as "Informal"

One striking feature of women's inclusion is how informal dynamics—such as a police officer's beliefs, the sex of a political gatekeeper, or the misogyny of the voting public—are important in shaping the implementation of policies and women's general experiences with representation, recognition, and protection.[28] And based on this, I question the usefulness of the typical formal/informal dichotomy in understanding the importance of gender in shaping women and men's experiences with institutions. If informal dynamics shape all institutions, like government, family, and states, and profoundly affect women's and other marginalized groups' access to these institutions, then to what degree are informal dynamics actually always a formal part of institutions? In other words, if one rejects the formal/informal dichotomy, is it possible to more systematically engage how unwritten rules and behaviors in institutional design act as a formal component of institutions? And if these "formalized informal" dynamics were engaged the same way traditionally formal aspects were engaged, would one develop a different assessment of how to implement women's inclusion? For example, if less competitive and prestigious offices have more women, then measuring competiveness of institutions based on size and power could become a key point of analysis or a new measure of democratic institutions (besides only measuring change in leadership as a measure of competitiveness, as "Polity" democracy scores measure). It would also help illustrate why changing the sex composition of an institution may not sufficiently change how it is gendered. Moreover, if women's activism is consistently a central explanation for women's inclusion (as demonstrated throughout this book) then it ceases to be an informal force. Rather, women's activism acts as a formal dynamic to women's inclusion and should be theorized and given the same weight that electoral systems and level of democracy are. Informal dynamics behave like rules and regulations in producing patterned behaviors and research should scrutinize and hypothesize these in the same manner as formal explanations.

Men and Masculinities

One way to move beyond women's inclusion and add-women politics is to bring men and masculinities into the conversation. Bina Shah, a Pakistani writer-activist recently wrote, "Want to end sexual violence against women? Fix the men."[29] She wrote this in response to the Global Summit to End Violence against Women in Conflict in 2014 where she found out of 175 events, only two "fringe" events focused on the role men play in ending conflict-related violence against women. This can happen in two ways: in generating programs and policies aimed at men and masculinities but also in promoting this focus on masculinities in academic research on women's inclusion and movements for gender equality.

I first will begin by focusing on what is happening to target men and masculinities. In Niger there is a "school for husbands," a UN-sponsored program that works with the government to encourage contraceptive use to bring down the birth rate. Though it does not appear to directly challenge male dominance, it does seek to challenge men's virility as a standard of masculinity and success.

Such programs focus on changing how men think about women. One example is the White Ribbon Campaign based out of Canada, which seeks to inform men about the link between masculinity and violence. In Bosnia and Serbia, there is a program, Young Men's Initiative, which builds a curriculum for adolescents to "deconstruct masculinity and reflect on how unhealthy gender norms lead to the inequitable treatment of women and girls."[30] Another program, supported by CARE International, is the Rwanda Men's Resource Center, organized by men in response to gender-based violence and, according to their website, aims to "serve as role models for the promotion of positive masculine behaviors."[31]

While it is important to "fix men," that will not really happen without fixing the broken kyriarchical system that produces "broken" men and women. In this sense, fixing men means: 1) fixing masculinities so that violence, heterosexuality, and domination are no longer valued as central to its definition 2); understanding how masculinities and femininities are informed by and inform domination in the context of race, class, sexuality, and imperialism; and 3) either challenging or deconstructing the different valorization between and around masculinities and femininities so we may value femininities as worthwhile for all humans, men and women alike. As I have indicated, since women's increased economic and political agency is sometimes correlated with increased violence, figuring out how to eradicate violence becomes an issue of how to expose and challenge masculinity's instability and how instability is further complicated by other social identities. Policies and practices that identify how masculinity is made fragile would change the dialogue about why men are violent (and not just towards women but one another as well).

I do not know if this means eventually doing away with these categories. This would seem useful if there were alternative frames for thinking about human organization that brought together both masculine and feminine ideas, and others outside either category, but is it possible to do so without simply (re)creating new binaries and categories? Difference itself is not the problem; it is how we value certain differences over others and give these differences power. Perhaps we are limited in our language in what we call identities, but there is much that can be done so that we value femininities and change masculinities so they do not depend on violence and exclusion in order to function. One can change the power dynamics among these categories, illustrating their fragile nature and need for continued (re)enforcement through our behaviors, rejecting them as distinct and acknowledging them as relational. One idea is to talk and think about identities as three-dimensional. This means acknowledging that we all occupy many identities, many of which exist along continuums that intersect in space and produce infinite possibilities for "who we are." In this sense, we would have to think more abstractly and bigger about the identities informing our existence.

I mentioned the other way to challenge the "women = gender" paradigm is for academic work in politics and international relations to focus on men and masculinities. However, as the field of international relations has long focused primarily on men and what they do, what I mean is to use analytical gender and critical feminism in examining men and masculinities, and how they shape political processes. Feminist international relations has a long history of this, but outside of explicitly critical feminist work, men and masculinities have lagged, though importantly this appears to be changing. In electoral politics, scholars are starting to focus on male dominance.[32] Elin Bjarnegård has a recent book out focusing on male dominance in parliaments, starting with the observation "men are politically overrepresented everywhere in the world."[33] Drude Dahlerup and Monique Leyenaar have also recently edited a book, *Breaking Male Dominance in Old Democracies*, which seeks to challenge the idea "gender equality is almost here."[34] Political scientist Rainbow Murray suggested that states use "ceiling quotas" for men, rather than use quotas for women in parliament, to increase merit-based promotion and equal scrutiny of anyone running for office, not just women.[35] Then men's leadership would also be judged in terms of competency. In this sense, there has been a shift in the study of adding women and women's underrepresentation to the discourse on why men still continue to dominate, an imperative discussion to make sense of the limits of women's inclusion.

Critical global political economy (GPE) has long focused on men and masculinities as central to (re)producing unequal global economic processes.[36] But GPE, as a transdisciplinary field, gets treated as a separate entity from more mainstream international political economy (IPE), which continues to confuse women and gender in its assessments of globalization. Much of this research I cited in chapter 2 on "gender equality" and informs the World Bank and assessments of women as smart economics in chapter 5. This appears an important point for inter-vention—to assert gender and women are not synonymous and gender equality is not what is being promoted by pursuing higher productivity among the world's women.

Feminist security studies has also long focused on critical assess-ment of men and masculinities in women's (in)securities.[37] While there is other security work focusing primarily on women, these stud-ies often (re)produce the "gender = women" narrative and rely on es-sentializing logics to make the case for women's inclusion.[38] But more generally, work on violence against women could include more critical assessments of violent men and movements to addressed masculinized violence.

Transnational feminist scholarship has also long engaged gender as an intersectional identity. Scholarship in this field has long fo-cused on the centrality of marginalized identities in the reproduction of neoliberal world order.[39] This transdisciplinary work is important for including ideas about and scholarship produced from the global periphery.

Another burgeoning field in international relations (IR) that is challenging gender and sexual categories is queer IR. Scholarship in this field links sex, gender, and sexuality in ways that overtly expose and challenge binary thinking. Political scientist Cynthia Weber has recently written about how in IR discourses about statecraft, the pro-duction of the "homosexual" is central to understanding IR theories and practices.[40] Heteronormativity plays a key role in explaining why women are promoted as part of good governance and smart econom-ics. Women's domestic roles as child bearers and community organizers are rooted in assumptions about heterosexual kinship networks. Quali-ties such as honesty and selflessness are cited as reasons why women make good politicians or employees. But these are also the qualities of a "good wife and mother." Further interrogation of heterosexual norms and their impact on masculine and feminine practices in public office, economies, and domestic life will expose the complexities of women and men's lived experiences and the fragility of binary thinking.

If gender is relational, then our analyses should focus on the pro-duction of the relationalities of masculinities and femininities that then inform men and women's lived experiences. And there is a lot of this work happening, as evidenced by all the studies above, but these have yet to really inform the governments and public who continue to uncritically promote women without the discussion of why they are excluded in the first place.

New Ideas for Gender Equality

It is time for renaming and reframing gender equality. Let's by no means abandon women's inclusion and the policies being pursued to promote women. But if these are women's inclusion policies, then what policies and practices would constitute gender equality? This is not an easy question, but hopefully one scholars and practitioners can begin to have as we arrive at an opportune moment to define how gender equality will be pursued in this century. Marriage equality is gaining momentum and this movement may promote equality of genders by allowing space for feminine-identified relationships.[41] Other potential issues that may become central to the promotion of gender equality in the twenty-first century are: reproductive justice, transgender rights, and disarmament and demilitarization.

Marriage equality has been adopted among most Western democracies, and some Latin American states (Argentina, Brazil, and Uruguay).[42] I am skeptical that the promotion of such a heteronormative institution should be categorized as an act to advance gender equality and this deserves critical discussion. At the same time, LGBTQ movements have also experienced a backlash in other parts of the world, such as Russia and increasingly the United States.[43] The larger movements for LGBTQ rights appear to be gaining momentum in many parts of the world, from decriminalizing homosexuality to the promotion of anti-discrimination policies in housing and work. While gaining momentum, there is still a long way to go for states to let go of their commitments to gender order and how issues of marriage and family challenge this. Because sexuality and gender are interdependent, often LGBTQ rights are denied based on ideas about masculinities and femininities and how these are translated to men, women, sexual desire, and heteronormative reproduction. When binary sexuality and even discretely categorized sexuality is challenged, gender cannot help but also be challenged in the process.

One central issue for women in some capacity nearly everywhere is reproductive justice. "Reproductive justice" is a term introduced and used by women of color in the United States to link reproductive rights and social justice and shift the discourse beyond individual-level "privacy-based" advocated for by mainstream pro-choice movements. One key organization of reproductive justice is Sistersong in the United States, and they write that reproductive justice "represents a shift for women advocating for control of their bodies, from a narrower focus on legal access and individual choice (the focus of mainstream organizations) to a broader analysis of racial, economic, cultural, and structural constraints on our power."[44] I find this framework immensely helpful for broadening the discourses on reproduction past birth control and abortion, which seems to dominate the discussion in the U.S. and some international communities. The goal is to situate women's reproductive realities in larger structural forces. Women's reproductive decisions continue to be controlled by kyriarchical social structures all over the world and it remains a central and powerful way to control women. I cannot help but think this is one of the central issues facing women as a group today, though which issues are most salient to women varies as much as women themselves vary.

Women's reproductive choices are shaped by families, communities, social conventions, and state apparatuses. Until women have primary control over their bodies everywhere in the world, including access to contraception, abortion, sexual knowledge, sexual decision-making, and freedom from practices that impact reproduction such as forced sterilization, cutting, and social pressure to have or not have children, women will continue to be subordinate to the sociopolitical control of others. So while increasing access to birth control and "family planning" continues to be a problem in many places, efforts to do so still need to be accompanied by discussions about valuing women and motherhood and the tensions in states that still want to "control" women's fertility. When the World Bank cites instrumental reasons for lowering women's fertility—it improves human capital, and increases growth and women's productivity in the economy—we should hesitate in supporting such efforts in which women's bodies remain central to economic growth and development.

While I focused on LGBTQ rights a little above, I think it is worth emphasizing transgender rights as central to gender equality, in part because of the resistance to include transgender rights within some feminist movements. The movement for gender equality in the twenty-first century cannot be just about "women." In the same ways early suffragettes failed feminism and many women by excluding women of color and compartmentalizing emancipation, I would contend the exclusion of transgender issues by second-wave feminists also fails to realize the importance of a feminist movement against all oppression, not just the oppression of (some) women. The promotion of transgender rights, which has started to gain ground, are not a distinct movement from feminism, though it appears some feminists want to treat it as such. Rather, at stake is the issue of controlling one's own definition of gender, one's own identity and body more generally, which are at the core of much feminist work throughout history.

In Argentina, people may change their genders on their birth certificates after a 2012 law. And in Nepal, India, Australia, New Zealand, and Pakistan the government recognizes a category of "third gender" if one does not identify as male or female.[45] Adding a gender is a first step in challenging a gender binary for sure, even though it also perpetuates it by producing a male/female/other dichotomy. In practice it is a pragmatic and substantive tool for those who do not identify with historical male/female categories.

But in many European countries, in order to "switch" one's gender, it requires a medical expert statement or psychiatric diagnosis—meaning in most states one cannot "self-determine" one's own gender and it is considered a medical disease or issue in legal terms. Even more troubling is how, in many countries in Europe, to change one's gender means undergoing forced sterilization (through insistence on surgery).[46] These policies are slowly changing but are not widely known. In the United States, while some states and cities have outlawed discrimination against transgendered people, other states are actively adopting anti-transgender policies.

Along these same lines, there needs to be a prioritization of marginalized groups within the feminist movement and rights centered on intersectional forms of oppression. The women's movement in the U.S., long dominated by white middle-class women, is facing a reckoning in its relationship with the Black Lives Matter movement. Gender equality is about emancipation from domination. As Audre Lorde stated:

> From my membership in all of these groups I have learned that oppression and the intolerance of difference come in all shapes and sexes and colors and sexualities; and that among those of us who share the goals of liberation and a workable future for our children, there can be no hierarchies of oppression. I have learned that sexism and heterosexism both arise from the same source as racism.[47]

Domination is generated through unequal valorizations of difference, and when one valorizes masculine over feminine it stems from the same logic of valorizing white over black, or wealthy over poor. That is not to say these social categories are equal or comparable—our identities are fluid, contingent, and contextual—but it does mean to advocate for challenging how we value difference in one category should never come at the cost of perpetuating the different valorizations in any other category. Gender equality is about showing up, not just for a women's rights parade and protest but also for the anti-capitalist, civil rights, and LGBTQ parades and protests also.

Another important issue for gender equality is disarmament and challenging increased militarism and militarization of states, including continued pursuit of weapons of mass destruction (WMD) programs and small arms trade. Some feminists have long argued weapons and weapons programs impact women through reallocation of resources and threat of personal violence. The 1970s women's conferences exposed how nuclear arms were a threat to women in promoting the militarization of states and shifting potential funding from state welfare programs to defense. So on a resource level, many feminists have long assessed WMD programs as gendered and important in women's security because they emphasize militarization of states and justify resource allocation in a way that directly impacts women.[48] This has been extended to a focus on small arms trade and the influx of weapons shape women's experiences of violence before, during, and after conflict. These arms in the world system making conflict easier and deadlier.[49] I find this to be a central issue for gender equality because to address nuclear proliferation and small arms trades will require a discussion about states, masculinities, and neoliberal militarization and how such systems produce immense (in)security for women and others.

More generally, this speaks to a need for resistance to neoliberalism as the model of political economic order. In the 1970s global economic order and its inequalities were front and center in discussions of women and development, but these have become increasingly marginalized among powerful global actors. To challenge a kyriarchical system means to challenge a neoliberal capitalist system built on marginalization and domination. This system uses differences like gender, class, race, sexuality, and geography to perpetuate a status quo of inequality. Neoliberal order is steeped in a logic of perpetual growth, which can only be sustained through the maintenance of differences in order to justify an unequal status quo. In challenging what counts as gender equality, and equality more generally, we can begin to expose the degree to which this current economic order is entirely incapable of rectifying the marginalization of so many people. Alternative economic orders are needed, ones not centered on infinite growth lobbied for and constructed by the most powerful states, corporations, and international organizations. We need alternative logics of political and economic order centered on principles of basic needs and low/no growth, and respect for human and natural resources. Resisting gender equality as a universally progressive and positive development is an important part of this.

Ultimately, we have let states and international organizations off the hook for their role in perpetuating women's and other marginalized groups' subordination by letting them co-opt political feminist ideas, but I am not sure there is any way to prevent this from happening. Anytime activists promote radical ideas to promote social change through the state, there will be trade-offs. States may be a major catalyst for changing rules and regulations but they may also take these ideas and use them in ways activists do not intend, or for reasons other than justice. And liberal feminist logic helped them do it. It is time to re-claim these radically feminist ideas and to put states and international organizations back on the hook for all the ways they are failing, not just women and men, but racial, ethnic, and sexual minorities as well. In 2004, Cynthia Enloe wrote we need a feminist consciousness to accompany our study of and engagement with gender because this feminist consciousness "keeps one taking seriously—staying intellectually curious about—the experiences, actions, and ideas of women and girls."[50] Take away an explicit interest in femininities, and it will be impossible to develop a reliable analysis of masculinity. Engaging women's inclusion as a liberal feminist approach that works to add-women without challenging gender is an important step in illustrating its limits and the need to engage feminist approaches to gender. Perhaps the cases in this book will illustrate how challenging male domination is important, but insufficient, in ending women's subjugation, poverty, and insecurity.

NOTES

CHAPTER 1. ADD GENDER AND STIR

1 Michelle Bachelet is the former head of UN Women and President of Chile. This quote is from a speech titled "The Century of Inclusion and Women's Full Participation," February 21, 2013, Dublin, Ireland.

2 World Health Organization 2013; True 2012, 3.

3 Some scholars are right in challenging how certain states have effectively implemented many of these policies, particularly in Scandinavia. This book walks a fine line of illustrating the importance of such policies, while maintaining they are not a panacea to women's inequality or gender equality. The latter requires a shift in understandings of gender and other social identities and stronger efforts to disrupt gendered binaries, particularly in the context of neoliberal world order. Additionally, even in Scandinavian states, gender as masculinities/femininities still remains, and thus still affects policies.

4 Enloe 2014, 3.

5 As further discussed in chapter 1, many of these policies do not emerge only from liberal feminism; some emerge from socialist and radical feminism as well. But because these policies are not meant to deconstruct gender binaries, they still work in a liberal feminist model of emancipation and have been integrated through less radical interpretation and discourses.

6 Tickner 2001, 13.

7 Fiorenza 2001; Fiorenza 1992, 8 cited from Pui-Lan 2009.

8 Carver 1996; Harding 1987; Peterson 2005; Sjoberg 2013; Tickner 2001; Wibben 2011.

9 There are many great definitions of gender; what is important is they all share a commitment to masculinities and femininities and their social construction.

10 Peterson 1992; Scott 1986; Tickner 2001.

11 Tickner and Sjoberg 2011, 3.

12 Scott 1986.

13 Ibid.

14 Peterson 2005.

15 See Enloe 2007; 2014.

16 Peterson 1992; 2003.

17 Fausto-Sterling 2005, 2.

18 Runyan and Peterson 2014.

19 Peterson 2005.

20 See Htun and Weldon 2012; Hughes, Krook, and Paxton 2015; True and Mintrom 2001; Krook 2009.

21 Peterson and Runyan 2010.

22 Barker 2005; Eisenstein 2005; 2009; Fraser 2009; 2013; Hartsock 2006; Peterson 2003; 2005.

23 Fraser 2013.

24 Peterson 2005.

25 For discussions of different types of feminism, see Lorber 2010; Tong 2009; Tickner 2001.

26 Harding 1987; Whitworth 2004, 401.

27 Runyan and Peterson 2014, 13.

28 Basu 2011, 111; Giddens 1984.

29 Peterson 2003; Peterson and Runyan 2010; Tickner and Sjoberg 2011.

30 Sjoberg 2013; Sjoberg and Tickner 2011, 4.

31 I use the term "geography" to note how one's identity is shaped by "place." As such, imperialist, colonial, and neocolonial politics are also central to one's identity. For example, the Global South is often treated as less progressive and thus women in the Global South are seen as having less agency.

32 Adewunmi 2014.

33 Crenshaw 1991.

34 Grillo 1995.

35 Collins 1998; Lorde 1970.

36 Ackerly, Stern, and True 2006, 6.

37 Tickner 2006, 24.

38 Ackerly, Stern, and True 2006, 6.

39 McKee 2003, 1.

40 Weldon and Htun 2013.

CHAPTER 2. GENDER EQUALITY AND THE ILLUSION OF PROGRESS

1 Inglehart and Norris 2003; Squires 2007; Zentai 2006.

2 There are notable exceptions; often explicitly critical feminist work acknowledges gender as more complex than man/women or male/female. See Runyan and Peterson 2014.

3 Paxton, Hughes, and Green 2006; UN Women 2016a.

4 Missing data make it difficult to assess the actual number.

5 Jacob, Scherpereel, and Adams 2013. This is based on the data of the UN Women's "Women in Politics 2015" publication. Out of 101 countries listed, only eight had zero women in cabinets.

6 Caul 2001; McBride and Mazur 2010; Hughes, Krook, and Paxton 2015; Franceschet and Piscopo 2008.

7 Ellerby 2011. A transition was defined as a positive change of at least two according to Polity Scores two years prior to adoption year (Russett 1998).

8　Paxton and Hughes 2015.

9　Based on data from the Quota Project, August 2016 (International IDEA, Inter-Parliamentary Union, and Stockholm University 2016).

10　Williams and Thames 2008.

11　Ibid.

12　Thames and Williams 2013, 67. The authors note a lot of missing data on lower courts, where women are more likely to be, so it is very likely this percent is lower than it should be.

13　Jalalzai 2013, 36.

14　Ibid., 32.

15　Inter-Parliamentary Union 2014.

16　ILO 2015.

17　World Bank 2012, 9.

18　UN Women 2011, 104.

19　Elborgh-Woytek et al. 2013, 6.

20　World Bank 2012, 8, 55.

21　Hallward-Driemeier, Hasan, and Rusu 2013a, 2.

22　These data were compiled by changes in laws rather than changes per country. This means some countries updated laws more than once. For example, about half of the laws changed regarding unmarried women were from countries that changed them more than once and the same is true for married women's property rights. In this sense, the data double and triple count. However, the data reported focuses of the number of countries with any changes to laws.

23　UN Women 2015c, 31.

24　Hallward-Driemeier, Hasan, and Rusu 2013a, 12.

25　McGee and Moore 2014.

26　Ibid., 33.

27　Hallward-Driemeier, Hasan, and Iqbal 2013.

28　World Economic Forum 2013.

29　Weldon 2006.

30　UN Women 2015c, 29.

31　Htun and Weldon 2012.

32　According to the United Nations Office on Drugs and Crime (2016b), trafficking is defined in article 3 of the *Protocol to Prevent, Suppress and Punish Trafficking in Persons* as "the recruitment, transportation, transfer, harboring or receipt of persons, by means of the threat or use of force or other forms of coercion, of abduction, of fraud, of deception, of the abuse of power, or of a position of vulnerability or of the giving or receiving of payments or benefits to achieve the consent of a person having control over another person, for the purpose of exploitation. Exploitation shall include, at a minimum, the exploitation of the prostitution of others or other forms of sexual exploitation, forced labor or services, slavery or practices similar to slavery, servitude or the removal of organs."

33　United Nations Office on Drugs and Crime 2014.

34 United Nations Office on Drugs and Crime 2009, 8.

35 Department of State 2016.

36 This is based on data from the United Nations Office on Drugs and Crime's (2016a) Database on Legislation.

37 United Nations 2014.

38 See Sjoberg 2013; True 2012.

39 For a discussion of how these data were categorized, see Ellerby 2015; 2016a.

40 Kent 2015; UN Women 2015a.

41 Inter-Parliamentary Union 2015.

42 Inter-Parliamentary Union 2014.

43 Ibid.

44 UN Women 2015b.

45 Ibid.

46 UN Women 2011, 105.

47 World Bank 2012, 198.

48 UN Women 2011, 104.

49 Ibid.

50 Darnaud 2016; Food and Agricultural Organization 2011.

51 World Economic Forum 2014, 7, 14. This number is the same as 2013's report.

52 World Economic Forum 2014.

53 UN Women 2015c.

54 ILO 2015.

55 The ILO defines gender gap as "those that disadvantage women compared to men" (2012a, 1).

56 Ibid., v–vi.

57 Anyanwu and Augustine 2013.

58 ILO 2015.

59 UN Women 2015c, 80.

60 United Nations 2014, 40.

61 Ford 2015.

62 European Union Agency for Fundamental Rights 2014; UN Women 2015c; World Health Organization 2013.

63 True 2012, 3.

64 United Nations 2006, 42.

65 Jagori and UN Women 2011, xi.

66 World Health Organization 2013, 17.

67 Montoya 2013, 4.

68 World Health Organization 2013, 17.

69 World Health Organization 2013.

70 Ibid., 19.

71 United Nations Refugee Agency 2013.

72 United Nations 2013.

73 Krook and True 2010; Squires 2007.

74 Caprioli 2005.

75 For fertility rates, see Regan and Paskeviciute 2003. For labor force participation, see Gray, Kittilson, and Sandholtz 2006; Drury and Peksen 2012; Demeritt, Nichols, and Kelly 2014. See Hill and Karim 2016 for an overview of scholarship using gender equality measures.

76 Caprioli 2005.

77 Peterson 2003; True 2012.

78 As the study starts in 1960s when the Pill first emerged, fertility was physiologically harder for women to manage prior to contraception, so this is probably not a useful predictor of lower fertility rates in the 1960s to early 1970s since it was not widely available.

79 Caprioli 2005.

80 Vasquez del Aguila 2006.

81 Hartmann 2011; Ko 2016; Tillet 2013.

82 Inglehart and Norris 2003.

83 Dorius and Firebaugh 2010.

84 Rees and Riezman 2012.

85 Cooray, Mallick, and Dutta 2014.

86 Anyanwu and Augustine 2013.

87 Cuberes and Teignier 2014; emphasis added.

88 Runyan and Peterson 2014, 5. Reproductive work is contrasted with productive labor, or that which is paid in the formal workforce. Reproductive labor refers to the unpaid (though vital) "work" that happens in the domestic sphere, including child-rearing, socialization, and emotional and caring labor.

89 Viterna and Fallon 2008.

90 UN Women, n.d.

91 United Nations Development Programme 2014b, 4.

92 Lombardo and Meier 2008; Lombardo, Meier, and Verloo 2010.

93 Lombardo, Meier, and Verloo 2010.

94 Montoya 2013; Towns 2010.

95 Lorber 2010, 10.

96 Zalewski 2000, 6.

97 Arat 2015.

98 Lorber 2010, 25–27.

99 Tickner 2001, 12.

100 Lorber 2010; Zalewski 2000.

101 Zalewski 2000, 7–9.

102 The term "institutions" here is used to mean both actual physical institutions (such as governments) as well as "sets of rules" (such as laws). This is based upon the overview on international institutions provided by Simmons and Martin 2002.

103 This term is in quotes to indicate many feminists (including myself) understand female itself to be socially constructed and thus (re)produces an artificial dichotomy between sex and gender and male/female.

104 Plattner 1998; Towns 2010.

105 Young 2000, 5.

106 Taylor 1998.

107 Bunch and Frost 2000; Dovi 2002; Taylor 1998; Young 2000.

108 Bunch and Frost 2000.

109 Phillips 1998, 228.

110 Ibid.

111 Ibid., 229.

112 Ibid., 233.

113 Ibid., 229.

114 This is based upon data from the Inter-Parliamentary Union (2016).

115 Young 2000, 5.

116 Taylor 1998, 37–38.

117 Fraser 2000.

118 Plattner 1998.

119 Towns 2010, 57.

120 Ibid., 65–66.

121 Ibid., 75–77.

122 Harvey 2005, 2.

123 Richardson 2001.

124 Eisenstein 2009; Klein 2007.

125 Fraser 2009.

126 Ibid.

127 Eisenstein 2009.

128 Arat 2015; Eisenstein 2009.

129 Htun and Weldon 2012.

130 Pierotti 2012.

131 Arat 2015.

132 Haritaworn, Kuntsman, and Posocco 2013.

133 Butler 2004; Spade 2011; Puar 2007; Mbembe 2003.

134 Dutta 2013; Gosine 2013; Scott 2013.

135 Lind and Keating 2013.

136 Scott 2013.

CHAPTER 3. DUAL AND DUELING GENDER IN GLOBAL NARRATIVES

1 I call this narrative somewhat feminist because, while the discussions allude to patriarchal structures and the power of gender, these declarations never actually use the term "patriarchy" or any reference to structural forms of oppression.

2 Fraser 2009.

3 Article 12, Paragraph 4 in the Geneva Convention IV, "Relative to the Protection of Civilian Persons in Time of War, 1949."

4 Article 76 of the 1977 Additional Protocol to the Geneva Conventions; emphasis added.

5 United Nations 1995a, 11.

6 Some other issues include (though this is not an exhaustive list) health, foreign occupation, migration and displacement, specific conflicts, drug trafficking, and disappeared persons.

7 United Nations 1975, 109.

8 United Nations 1975, 19.

9 United Nations 1980, 21.

10 United Nations 1985, 24.

11 Krook and True 2010.

12 United Nations 1975, 22.

13 Ibid., 104.

14 Ibid., 58.

15 Ibid., 29.

16 United Nations 1980, 8, 87.

17 Ibid., 98.

18 United Nations 1985, 26, 39.

19 Fraser 2009.

20 United Nations 1975, 23.

21 There remains quite a lot of debate about trafficking and how to eradicate it, particularly sex trafficking. See Lobasz 2009 for an overview of these approaches.

22 United Nations 1980, 104.

23 Ibid., 67.

24 United Nations 1985, 70.

25 United Nations 1975, 106, 107.

26 United Nations 1980, 133.

27 United Nations 1985, 63.

28 Zwingel 2011.

29 United Nations 1979.

30 Parts V and VI are technical sections on monitoring and maintaining CEDAW. It outlines a committee for monitoring implementation, which will be supported by the Secretary-General of the UN. It also clarifies that states will need to report to the committee on progress at least every four years.

31 United Nations 1985, 6.

32 Sex roles, in this context, are what most would now call "gender roles," to acknowledge how "roles" are socially produced and not biologically determined. But because there is little specificity in what such roles mean or how they are produced, the term "sex roles" adequately describes how behaviors for male and female bodies are socially produced.

33 United Nations 1980, 17, 94.

34 United Nations 1975, 60.

35 Ibid., 161.

36 United Nations 1980, 5; emphasis added.

37 Ibid., 11.

38 United Nations 1985, 29.
39 Ibid., 7.
40 United Nations 1980, 129.
41 United Nations 1985, 7.
42 United Nations 1975, 21, 90.
43 United Nations 1980, 27.
44 Ibid., 60.
45 United Nations 1985, 10; emphasis added.
46 United Nations 1980, 26.
47 Ibid., 128.
48 Joachim 2007, 105.
49 Quoted in Joachim 2007, 113.
50 Ibid., 122.
51 United Nations 1985, 12.
52 While I do not exhaustively cover all of them here, I focus on the ones cited within the literature and other reports as precedent-setting (Bunch and Reilly 1994; Joachim 2007).
53 Bunch 1990.
54 Joachim 2007, 124.
55 United Nations 1993, 5.
56 Joachim 2007, 130.
57 United Nations 1993.
58 United Nations 1995b, 44.
59 United Nations 1995b; emphasis added.
60 Anderlini 2010; Krook 2009.
61 United Nations 1995a, 7.
62 True and Mintrom 2001.
63 NGOs were not official participants of the conferences in which states and governmental organizations participated, but there was a simultaneous conference exclusively for NGOs. These NGOs, however, were heavily consulted prior to Beijing with a series of smaller regional conferences.
64 United Nations 1995a, 16.
65 Dahlerup 2006.
66 Krook and True 2010.
67 United Nations 1995a, 86; hereafter cited parenthetically in the text.
68 See Peterson 1992, 2014; Enloe 2014; Sjoberg 2013; Tickner 2001 as examples.
69 Anderlini 2007, 6.
70 United Nations 1995a, 57; hereafter cited parenthetically in the text.
71 Cockburn 2007, 140.
72 Cohn, Kinsella, and Gibbings 2004; Cockburn 2007, 140.
73 For a more extensive discussion of the process, see Anderlini 2007; Willett 2010; Tryggestad 2009; Cockburn 2007; Hill, Aboitiz, and Poehlman-Doumbouya 2003.
74 Cockburn 2007, 143.

75 Ibid., 152.

76 Ellerby 2015.

77 Cockburn 2007, 147.

78 Cohn 2008.

79 Cockburn 2007, 148.

80 Whitworth 2004, 137.

81 I believe the new UN gender entity being described in Resolution 1888 is UN Women, which unified several previous departments working on women's issues, including UNIFEM, Division for the Advancement of Women, Office of Special Adviser on Gender Issues and Advancement of Women, and International Research and Training Institute for the Advancement of Women.

CHAPTER 4. THE "PROBLEM" WITH WOMEN'S REPRESENTATION IN GOVERNMENT

1 Johnson 2016.

2 Squires 2007, 34.

3 Stetson and Mazur 1995; True and Mintrom 2001.

4 Squires 2007, 38.

5 McBride and Mazur 2010, 7.

6 Squires 2007, 62.

7 Lovenduski 2005; Mazur and McBride 2007.

8 See Krook 2009 for a thorough review of the literature.

9 Araújo 2003; Hassim 2002; Meier 2004; Opello 2006.

10 Baldez 2006; Caul 2001; Goetz and Hassim 2003; Matland and Studlar 1996; Schmidt 2003.

11 Bruhn 2003; Kittilson 2006; cf. Krook 2009.

12 Connell 1998.

13 Bauer and Britton 2006; Reyes 2002; Towns 2010.

14 Bauer 2002; Ballington and Dahlerup 2006; Bush 2011; Towns 2012.

15 Ellerby 2013.

16 Krook 2006; Norris and Dahlerup 2015; Towns 2010.

17 Krook 2009, 24.

18 Ibid., 19.

19 Dahlerup 2006; Htun and Jones 2002; Krook 2009.

20 Krook 2009.

21 Ibid., 12–13.

22 Ibid.

23 Bauer and Okpotor 2013; Davis 1997; Escobar-Lemmon and Taylor-Robinson 2005; Jalalzai 2013; Thames and Williams 2013; Tremblay and Stockemer 2013.

24 Nwankwor 2014.

25 Bauer and Tremblay 2011.

26 Bauer and Okpotor 2013.

27 Tripp et al. 2009; Bauer and Okpotor 2013.

28 Whitford, Wilkins, and Ball 2007.
29 Bauer and Tremblay 2011, 182.
30 Jacob, Scherpereel, and Adams 2013.
31 Russell and DeLancey 2002, 148.
32 Bauer and Tremblay 2011.
33 Ibid.
34 Bauer and Okpotor 2013.
35 Ibid.
36 Escobar-Lemmon and Taylor-Robinson 2009.
37 Studlar and Moncrief 1999.
38 Jalalzai and Krook 2010; Bauer and Tremblay 2011, 179; Whicker and Isaacs 1999.
39 Jalalzai 2013, 14, 37.
40 Ibid., 37.
41 Bauer and Tremblay 2011, 182.
42 Williams and Thames 2008.
43 Kalantry 2012.
44 Ibid.
45 Bauer and Tremblay 2011; Jalalzai and Krook 2010; Nwankor 2014.
46 This is based on research from Bauer and Okpotor 2013; Davis 1997; Escobar-Lemmon and Taylor-Robinson 2005; Krook and O'Brien 2012; Thames and Williams 2013; Tremblay and Stockemer 2013.
47 Krook and O'Brien 2012.
48 Kittilson and Schwindt-Bayer 2010; Krook and O'Brien 2012.
49 Bauer and Tremblay 2011.
50 Bauer and Okpotor 2013.
51 Bauer and Tremblay 2011, 179.
52 Krook and O'Brien 2012.
53 Arriola and Johnson 2014.
54 Matland and Studlar 1996; Whitford, Wilkins, and Ball 2007.
55 Bauer and Tremblay 2011, 182.
56 Jalalzai and Krook 2010.
57 Studlar and Moncrief 1999.
58 Bauer and Tremblay 2011, 182.
59 Caul 1999; Kobayashi 2004.
60 Jacob, Scherpereel, and Adams 2013; Hughes, Krook, and Paxton 2015; Paxton, Hughes, and Green 2006.
61 Jacob, Scherpereel, and Adams 2013.
62 Russell and DeLancey 2002, 148.
63 Paxton, Hughes, and Green 2006, 89.
64 Hughes and Tripp 2015.
65 Paxton, Painter, and Hughes 2010.
66 Viterna and Fallon 2008.

67 Escobar-Lemmon and Taylor-Robinson 2009; Krook 2009; Squires 2007; Towns 2010.
68 Bush 2011; Towns 2012.
69 Dahlerup 2006; Paxton, Painter, and Hughes 2010.
70 Krook 2016.
71 Williams and Thames 2008.
72 Ibid.
73 Jacob, Scherpereel, and Adams 2013.
74 Krook and O'Brien 2012.
75 Hughes, Krook, and Paxton 2015; Krook 2016.
76 Krook 2016.
77 Hughes, Krook, and Paxton 2015.
78 Franceschet and Thomas 2015.
79 Benstead 2015; Bjarnegård 2013, 185.
80 Cheng and Tavits 2011; Johnson 2016.
81 Inter-Parliamentary Union 2000, 97; Paxton and Hughes 2007, 142.
82 Beckwith 2015; O'Brien et al. 2015.
83 Johnson 2016; Krook 2016; Sineau 2005.
84 Whicker and Isaacs 1999.
85 Franceschet and Thomas 2015; Jacob, Scherpereel, and Adams 2013.
86 Kobayashi 2004.
87 Kittilson and Schwindt-Bayer 2010.
88 Hodson 1997; Richter 1990.
89 Johnson 2016.
90 Jalalzai and Krook 2010.
91 Jalalzai 2004.
92 Franceschet and Piscopo 2008, 418; Krook 2009; 2016.
93 Krook and O'Brien 2012.
94 O'Brien et al. 2015.
95 Escobar-Lemmon and Taylor-Robinson 2009; Krook 2009.
96 Mansbridge 2003; Bird 2015.
97 Fleschenberg 2011, 26; Forest 2011, 66; Krook and O'Brien 2012; O'Brien et al. 2015.
98 Pinto 2011; Tremblay and Stockemer 2013.
99 Jalalzai 2004.
100 Pinto 2011, 20.
101 Jalalzai 2004.
102 Bjarnegård 2013, 186.
103 Johnson 2016.
104 Benstead 2015.
105 Ibid.
106 Bjarnegård 2013.

107 Benstead 2015; Dolan 2005; Rosenwasser and Dean 1989, 3; Huddy and Terkildsen 1993.

108 Falk and Kenski 2006.

109 Ibid.

110 Paxton and Kunovich 2003.

111 Abou-Zeid 2006; Pinto 2011.

112 Kobayashi 2004.

113 Pinto 2011; Bauer and Tremblay 2011.

114 Escobar-Lemmon and Taylor-Robinson 2009.

115 Krook and O'Brien 2012.

116 Bligh et al. 2012.

117 Mansbridge 2003; Dovi 2002.

118 Benstead 2015; Lu and Breuning 2014.

119 Dolan 1997.

120 Bauer and Tremblay 2011, 179.

121 Htun and Ossa 2013.

122 Dovi 2002; Mansbridge 2003.

123 Dovi 2002.

124 Young 1997, 350.

125 Dovi 2002.

126 Krook and O'Brien 2012; Bauer and Tremblay 2011, 180.

127 Escobar-Lemmon and Taylor-Robinson 2009.

128 Tremblay and Stockemer 2013.

129 Krook and O'Brien 2012.

130 O'Brien et al. 2015.

131 Nwankwor 2014.

132 Hughes 2011.

133 Hughes 2013.

134 Ibid.

135 Bird 2015.

136 Htun and Ossa 2013.

137 Jensenius 2016.

138 Baldez 2006.

139 Tickner 2001, 12.

140 Krook 2006.

141 Towns 2010, 158.

142 World Bank 2001, 95.

143 World Bank 2014, 16, 17.

144 Krook 2009; Squires 2007; Baldez 2006.

145 Squires 2007, 33.

146 Franzway, Connell, and Court 1989, 135; Squires 2007, 36.

147 Hughes, Krook, and Paxton 2015.

148 Bjarnegård 2013, 7.

149 Sapiro 1991, 177.
150 Lovenduski 2005, 348.
151 Baldez 2006.
152 McBride and Mazur 2010.
153 Such as Bjarnegård 2013 and Krook 2009.

CHAPTER 5. THE "PROBLEM" WITH RECOGNIZING WOMEN'S ECONOMIC RIGHTS

1 World Bank 2012, xiii; emphasis added.
2 A Google search of the term "women as smart economics" will bring up multiple World Bank documents and web links.
3 World Bank 2012, xx.
4 Ibid., 13.
5 ILO 2012b, v.
6 Sweeney 2007, 234.
7 Giri 2012.
8 Hallward-Driemeier, Hasan, and Rusu 2013a.
9 Sweeney 2007, 235.
10 Hallward-Driemeier, Hasan, and Rusu 2013a, 10.
11 Giri 2012.
12 Giri 2012; Hallward-Driemeier, Hasan, and Rusu 2013a, 26.
13 Hallward-Driemeier, Hasan, and Rusu 2013a, 27.
14 UN Women 2011, 105.
15 World Bank 2012, 198.
16 ILO 2015.
17 UN Women 2015c, 80.
18 Ford 2015.
19 Ibid.
20 Hallward-Driemeier, Hasan, and Rusu 2013b, 10.
21 Budlender and Alma 2011, 3.
22 Buchy 2012.
23 Giri 2012.
24 Buchy 2012, 4; Eaton 2016.
25 Hallward-Driemeier, Hasan, and Rusu 2013a, 15.
26 Doss et al. 2013.
27 Ibid. Doss et al. 2013 make an important point that how land ownership is defined and documented affects the data and findings quite significantly.
28 World Bank 2012, 230.
29 OECD 2012; World Bank 2012, 206, 225.
30 Cited in World Bank 2012, 232.
31 Ford 2015.
32 World Bank 2014, 19.
33 UN Women 2015, 18, 20.

34 Anyanwu and Augustine 2013; UN Women 2011.

35 UN Women 2011, 207.

36 ILO 2012b.

37 UN Women 2015c.

38 ILO 2012b, viii.

39 Anyanwu and Augustine 2013.

40 UN Women 2015c.

41 Runyan and Peterson 2014; World Bank 2012, 206–7.

42 Giri 2012; Udry et al. 1995; World Bank 2012.

43 World Bank 2012, 227.

44 Thomas and Skeat 1990.

45 Budlender and Alma 2011.

46 However, it is worth noting that customary law was often shaped by colonial practices, so in some cases there is little distinction between customary and civil legal codes because both were shaped by colonialism (Thipe 2013).

47 Hallward-Driemeier and Gajigo 2013, 15.

48 Ibid.

49 Budlender and Alma 2011, 41.

50 Thipe 2013.

51 Dlamini, quoted in Thipe 2013.

52 World Bank 2014, 18–19.

53 UN Women 2015c, 146.

54 Correll et al. 2007; Steinpreis et al. 1999.

55 Moss-Racusin et al. 2012.

56 Levinson and Young 2010.

57 Raymond 2013.

58 Derous, Ryan, and Serlie 2014.

59 UN Women 2015c, 33.

60 World Bank 2014.

61 Ford 2015.

62 Deere and León 2001, 3.

63 Giri 2012.

64 Agarwal 2003; Giri 2012.

65 For example, most children carry their father's surnames, myself included.

66 Deere and León 2001, 3; Thipe 2013.

67 Himmelweit et al. 2013.

68 Agarwal 2003; Deere and León 2001; Jackson 2003.

69 Deninger 2005; Doss 2006; Quisumbing and Maluccio 2003; Rees and Riezman 2012.

70 Rashad 1999.

71 UN Women 2015c, 27.

72 Giri 2012.

73 Hallward-Driemeier, Hasan, and Rusu 2013a, 10.

74 Budlender and Alma 2011, 42.

75 Ibid.

76 Ibid., 53.

77 Ibid., 55.

78 UN Women 2015c, 216.

79 Ibid.

80 Ford 2015.

81 UN Women 2015c, 220; hereafter cited parenthetically in the text.

82 Runyan and Peterson 2014.

83 Thomas and Skeat 1990.

84 Thipe 2013.

85 The "poorest" population is defined as the bottom twenty percent of a population (UN Women 2015c, 45).

86 UN Women 2015c, 73.

87 Duncan 2014.

88 Ibid., 146.

89 Ford 2015; UN Women 2015c, 44.

90 BBC News 2016.

91 UN Women 2015c, 27.

92 Food and Agricultural Organization 2011, 2.

93 Agarwal 2003; Buchy 2012; Budlender and Alma 2011; Food and Agricultural Organization 2011; Hallward-Driemeier, Hasan, and Rusu 2013b; Thomas and Skeat 1990; UN Women 2011.

94 UN Women 2015c, 14.

95 Eastin and Prakash 2013; Gray, Kittilson, and Sandholtz 2006; Richards and Gelleny 2007, United Nations 2015.

96 Abu-Ghaida and Klasen 2004; World Bank 2006; Yukhananov 2013.

97 Goldin 1995; Anyanwu and Augustine 2013.

98 Rees and Riezman 2012.

99 Agarwal 2003; Deininger 2003; OECD 2012.

100 Agarwal 1994; 2003; Deere and León 2001; Deininger 2003; Hallward-Driemeier, Hasan, and Rusu 2013a; Udry et al. 1995; World Bank 2012.

101 Anyanwu and Augustine 2013.

102 World Bank 2012.

103 Hallward-Driemeier, Hasan, and Rusu 2013a.

104 Agarwal 2003.

105 Hallward-Driemeier and Hasan 2013.

106 Udry et al. 1995.

107 Field 2007.

108 Kalpana 2011, 55.

109 Maclean 2010.

110 World Bank 2012, 226.

111 Keating, Rasmussen, and Rishi 2010.

112 Drolet 2010.

113 Keating, Rasmussen, and Rishi 2010.

114 Ibid.

115 Maclean 2010.

116 For a discussion of these different models of microfinance and types of organizations, see Drolet 2010; Mayoux 2002; Visvanathan and Yoder 2011.

117 Rhyne 1998, 6.

118 Yunus 2005; my emphasis.

119 Keating, Rasmussen, and Rishi 2010.

120 United Nations, quoted in Keating, Rasmussen, and Rishi 2010.

121 Bajaj 2011; Banerjee et al. 2013; Drolet 2010.

122 Keating, Rasmussen, and Rishi 2010.

123 Polgreen and Bajaj 2010.

124 Bajaj 2011; Banerjee et al. 2013.

125 World Bank 2012, 226.

126 Maclean 2010.

127 Cheston and Kuhn 2002.

128 Polgreen and Bajaj 2010.

129 Kalpan 2011, 58.

130 Keating, Rasmussen, and Rishi 2010.

131 Kalpana 2011, 57.

132 Keating, Rasmussen, and Rishi 2010.

133 World Bank 2006, 238.

134 Azmat and Petrongolo 2014.

135 World Bank 2012, 238.

136 Ibid., 236.

137 UN Women 2015c; World Bank 2012, 170–71.

138 World Bank 2012, 170–71.

139 In its recent report on the status of the world's women, UN Women does note the need to better value reproductive labor, but still emphasizes the need for women to participate in formal economies.

140 Blackmon 2009.

141 Peterson 2003; Agarwal 2003.

142 UN Women 2011, 111.

143 Runyan and Peterson 2013; True 2012.

144 ILO 2012a, vi.

145 Baird, Friedman, and Schady 2007; United Nations Development Programme 2014c, 19, 74. Importantly the World Bank's 2014 development report was virtually silent on the economic crisis. Wendy Harcourt's assessment of the 2012 World Bank report points to this: "The report is silent on the impact on women's lives of the multiple crises of finance, food, energy, climate, land grabbing, and resource extraction."

146 Peterson 2003; 2010; Rupert and Solomon 2006; True 2012.

147 Wallerstein 1983.

148 Mittelman, quoted in Gills 2010.

149 Beneria 2003; Peterson 2003; 2010.

150 Jayarajah, Branson, and Sen 1996.

151 Mosley 1991.

152 Peterson 2003, 70.

153 Ibid., 73.

154 Beneria 2003; Hughes 2000.

155 Tzannatos 2006, 18.

156 Beneria 2003.

157 Wood 2006, 144.

158 World Bank 2001, 213.

159 ILO 2012a, 22.

160 Anyanwu and Augustine 2013.

161 Beneria 2003.

162 United Nations 2014, 3.

163 Ferris, Petz, and Stark 2013, 71, 72.

164 United Nations 2014, 48.

165 Razavi 2012.

166 Chant and Sweetman 2012.

167 Elson 2009.

168 Goodhart 2008, 139.

169 Peterson 2010.

CHAPTER 6. THE "PROBLEM" WITH PROTECTING WOMEN
FROM VIOLENCE

1 Brunell and Johnson 2010.

2 Sen 2003, 119.

3 European Union Agency for Fundamental Rights 2014; UN Women 2015c.

4 Tran 2013.

5 Peterson and Runyan 2010, 166.

6 Ibid., 149.

7 Shelley 2011, 39.

8 Ibid.

9 Waters et al. 2004.

10 Shelley 2011, 40.

11 McCann 2005, 13.

12 Htun and Weldon 2012; Johnson 2007; Montoya 2013; Weldon 2002; Weldon and Htun 2013.

13 Htun and Weldon 2012.

14 Weldon 2002, 195.

15 Montoya 2013.

16 Ellerby 2016a.

17 Carrillo and Chinchilla 2010, 146.
18 Tripp et al. 2009, 211.
19 Ibid.
20 McBride and Mazur 2010; Weldon 2002, 5.
21 Franceschet 2010; Johnson 2007; Weldon 2002.
22 Ellerby 2013.
23 Luciak 2001.
24 Zippel 2004.
25 Montoya 2013, 166.
26 Krizsan and Popa 2010.
27 Johnson 2007.
28 Avdeyeva 2007.
29 Whitman 2007.
30 Nabukeera-Musoke 2009.
31 Tripp et al. 2009; Agbalajobi 2009.
32 United Nations 2007.
33 UN Women 2011, 34.
34 Pierotti 2012.
35 Avdeyeva 2007.
36 Brunell and Johnson 2010; Htun and Weldon 2012; Johnson and Zaynullina 2010;
    Zippel 2004.
37 Htun and Weldon 2012.
38 Weldon and Htun 2013.
39 McCann 2005, 23.
40 Montoya 2013, 160.
41 European Union Agency for Fundamental Rights 2014.
42 UN Women 2015c, 50, 94.
43 Chivens 2010.
44 Avdeyeva and Fábián 2010; Arce and Essau 2012.
45 Johnson 2007.
46 United Nations Office on Drugs and Crime 2009, 6.
47 Ibid., 40.
48 Ellerby 2013.
49 UN Women 2014a.
50 UN Women 2011, 11.
51 Ibid., 51.
52 Johnson 2007; Weldon 2002.
53 Hrycak 2010, 55.
54 Johnson 2007.
55 Ellerby 2016b.
56 Luciak 2001, 39.
57 Weldon 2002.
58 Johnson 2007.

59 Franceschet 2010.

60 Quoted in Luciak 2001, 7.

61 Luciak 1998.

62 An important caveat is that the United States has also not ratified.

63 Johnson 2007.

64 This assessment is based on findings from Weldon and Htun 2013.

65 Weldon and Htun 2013.

66 While criminalization of violence against women is meant to *prevent* violence through fear of punishment and signaling culturally that it is wrong, this only works to the extent the violence is known and prosecuted, both of which are issues with violence against women policies. So violence against women polices may punish perpetrators, but this does not necessarily translate into prevention of violence.

67 Sjoberg and Gentry 2008.

68 Arce and Essau 2012, 378.

69 Victorian Health Foundation 2009, 7–8.

70 UN Women 2011, 32, 33.

71 Victorian Health Foundation 2009.

72 UN Women 2011.

73 Ibid., 25.

74 Victorian Health Foundation 2009; White Ribbon Scotland 2013.

75 Beske 2012.

76 Sharipova and Fábián 2010.

77 Robnik 2010, 196.

78 McGee and Moore 2014.

79 Baaz and Stern 2013.

80 Weldon and Htun 2013.

81 Crenshaw 1991.

82 Agnes 1992.

83 Sokoloff and Dupont 2005.

84 Busza, cited in Miller 2004.

85 Montoya and Agustin 2013.

86 World Bank 2013; my emphasis.

87 UN Women 2011, 53.

88 Beske 2012, 391.

89 True 2012, 39.

90 Runyan and Peterson 2014, 183.

91 True 2012, 39.

92 Ibid.

93 Ellerby 2015.

94 Baaz and Stern 2013, 112.

95 True 2012, 126.

96 Cohn, Kinsella, and Gibbings 2004.

97 UN Women 2011.

98 Victorian Health Foundation 2009.

CHAPTER 7. BEYOND ADD-WOMEN POLITICS

1   Brokaw 2013; Kristof and WuDunn 2009, 1; UN Women 2011.

2   Lovenduski 2005.

3   Fleschenburg 2011, 24.

4   Franceschet 2010.

5   Escobar-Lemmon and Taylor-Robinson 2005.

6   Bauer and Tremblay 2011, 180; Williams and Thames 2013, 68.

7   As GDP per capita is tested in most quantitative models on these policies, clearly someone thinks it matters.

8   Towns 2010; 2012.

9   Towns 2010, 134.

10 Based on data drawn from Jalalzai and Krook 2010.

11 Nwankwor 2014.

12 Jalalzai and Krook 2010.

13 Hallward-Driemeier and Gajigo 2013.

14 World Bank 2012, 9, 56.

15 Weldon and Htun 2013.

16 Beske 2012, 391.

17 Quoted in Shah 2014.

18 True 2012, 3.

19 Connell 1998.

20 True 2012.

21 National Democratic Institute 2016.

22 Fischer 2002.

23 Bardall 2011, 11.

24 Gottardo and Rojas, cited in Bardall 2011.

25 Bardall 2011, 13.

26 Carmon 2014.

27 Sharipova and Fábián 2010.

28 Krook and Mackay 2011.

29 Shah 2014.

30 International Center for Research on Women 2014.

31 Rwanda Men's Resource Center 2016.

32 For examples of research that focuses on men and masculinities, see Cohn 1987; Enloe 2000; 2014; Peterson 1992; Shepherd 2008; True 2012.

33 Bjarnegård 2013, 1.

34 Dahlerup and Leyenaar 2013.

35 Murray 2014.

36 Barker 2005; Kuiper and Barker 2006; Chowdhry and Nair 2002; Dickinson and Schaeffer 2001; Hewitson 1999; Hoskyns and Rai 2007; Marchand and

Runyan 2011; Nagar et al. 2002; Peterson 2003; Safri and Graham 2010; True 2012.

37 Baaz and Stern 2013; Enloe 2000; Shepherd 2008; Wibben 2011; Sjoberg 2013.

38 Caprioli 2003; 2005; Hudson et al. 2008; Carpenter 2003.

39 See Grewal and Kaplan 1994; 2001; Mohanty 1988; 2003; Swarr and Nagar 2010.

40 Weber 2016, 49. See also Peterson 2014; Agathangelou 2013.

41 There are limits to these policies. Marriage equality does not deconstruct the value of marriage in the first place, which has long been a repressive institution for women who were treated as property. Additionally, as marriage is often steeped in patriarchal religious structures, one could also argue this is not gender equality because it remains heteronormative and involves state control of people's sexuality. And efforts to "add genders" still means states want to classify its citizens based on narrow categories.

42 Kollman 2013.

43 Saner 2013; 2014.

44 Sistersong 2014.

45 Knight 2012.

46 Saner 2014.

47 Lorde 1983.

48 Cohn and Ruddick 2003.

49 Cockburn 2007, 151.

50 Enloe 2004.

REFERENCES

Abou-Zeid, Gihan. 2006. "The Arab Region: Women's Access to the Decision-Making Process Across the Arab Nation." In *Women, Quotas, and Politics*, edited by Drude Dahlerup. New York: Routledge, 168–93.

Abu-Ghaida, Dina, and Stephan Klasen. 2004. "The Costs of Missing the Millennium Development Goal on Gender Equity." *World Development* 32 (7): 1075–1107.

Ackerly, Brooke, Maria Stern, and Jacqui True, eds. 2006. *Feminist Methodologies for International Relations*. New York: Cambridge University Press.

Adewunmi, Bim. 2014. "Kimberlé Crenshaw on Intersectionality." *New Statesman*, April 2. www.newstatesman.com.

Agarwal, Bina. 1994. *A Field of One's Own: Gender and Land Rights in South Asia*. Cambridge: Cambridge University Press.

———. 2003. "Gender and Land Rights Revisited: Exploring New Prospects via the State, Family, and Market." *Journal of Agrarian Change* 3 (1/2): 184–224.

Agathangelou, Anna M. 2013. "Neoliberal Geopolitical Order and Value." *International Feminist Journal of Politics* 15 (4): 453–76.

Agbalajobi, Damolola Taiye. 2009. "The Role of African Women in Peace Building and Conflict Resolution: The Case of Burundi." *Global Media Journal* 8 (15).

Agnes, Flavia. 1992. "Protecting Women against Violence? Review of a Decade of Legislation, 1980–89." *Economic and Political Weekly* 27 (17): 19–33.

Anderlini, Sanam. 2007. *Women Building Peace: What They Do, Why It Matters*. Boulder, CO: Lynne Rienner.

———. 2010. *What the Women Say: Participation and UNSCR 1325*. Cambridge, MA: International Civil Society Action Network and MIT Center for International Studies. http://web.mit.edu.

Anyanwu, John C., and Darline Augustine. 2013. "Gender Equality in Employment in Africa: Empirical Analysis and Policy Implications." *African Development Review* 25 (4): 400–420.

Arat, Zehra F. Kabasakal. 2015. "Feminisms, Women's Rights, and the UN: Would Achieving Gender Equality Empower Women?" *American Political Science Review* 109 (4): 674–89.

Araújo, Clara. 2003. "Quotas for Women in the Brazilian Legislative System." *Implementation of Quotas: Latin American Experiences*. Lima: International IDEA. http://www.quotaproject.org.

Arce, Carmen Camacho, and Cecelia A. Essau. 2012. "Domestic Violence in Bolivia." In *Violence and Abuse in Society: Understanding a Global Crisis*, edited by Angela Browne-Miller. Santa Barbara, CA: Praeger, 373–86.

Arriola, Leonardo, and Martha Johnson. 2014. "Ethnic Politics and Women's Empowerment in Africa: Ministerial Appointments to Executive Cabinets." *American Journal of Political Science* 58 (2): 495–510.

Avdeyeva, Olga. 2007. "When Do States Comply with International Treaties? Policies on Violence against Women in Post-Communist Countries." *International Studies Quarterly* 51 (4): 877–900.

Avdeyeva, Olga, and Katalin Fábián. 2010. "The Promise and Perils of International Treaties." In *Domestic Violence in Post-Communist States*, edited by Katalin Fábián. Bloomington: Indiana University Press, 308–36.

Azmat, Ghazala, and Barbara Petrongolo. 2014. *Gender and the Labor Market: What Have We Learned from Field and Lab Experiments?* Bonn, Germany: Institute for the Study of Labor. www.econstor.eu.

Baaz, Maria Eriksson, and Maria Stern. 2013. *Sexual Violence as a Weapon of War? Perceptions, Prescriptions, Problems in the Congo and Beyond.* London: Zed Books.

Bajaj, Vikas. 2011. "In India, Microcredit Has Suffered a Black Eye." *New York Times*, January 6. www.nytimes.com.

Baldez, Lisa. 2006. "The Pros and Cons of Gender Quota Laws: What Happens When You Kick Men Out and Let Women In?" *Politics and Gender* 2 (1): 102–9.

Ballington, Julie, and Drude Dahlerup. 2006. "Gender Quotas in Post-Conflict States: East Timor, Afghanistan, and Iraq." In *Women, Quotas and Politics*, edited by Drude Dahlerup, 249–58. New York: Routledge.

Banerjee, Abhijit, Esther Duflo, Rachel Glennester, and Cynthia Kinnan. 2013. "The Miracle of Microfinance? Evidence from a Randomized Evaluation." *American Economic Journal: Applied Economics* 7 (1): 22–53.

Bardall, Gabrielle. 2011. *Breaking the Mold: Understanding Gender and Electoral Violence.* Washington, DC: International Foundation for Electoral Systems.

Barker, Drucilla K. 2005. "Beyond Women and Economics: Rereading 'Women's Work.'" *Signs* 30 (4): 2189–2209.

Basu, Soumita. 2011. "Security as Emancipation." In *Feminism and International Relations: Conversations about the Past, Present, and Future*, edited by J. Ann Tickner and Laura Sjoberg. London and New York: Routledge, 98–114.

Bauer, Antje. 2002. *Afghan Women and the Democratic Reconstruction of Afghanistan: Findings and Interviews from a Journalist's Field Trip.* Berlin: Berghof Research Center for Constructive Conflict Management.

Bauer, Gretchen, and Hannah Britton. 2006. *Women in African Parliaments.* Boulder, CO: Lynne Rienner.

Bauer, Gretchen, and Jennie E. Burnet. 2013. "Gender Quotas, Democracy, and Women's Representation in Africa: Some Insights from Democratic Botswana and Autocratic Rwanda." *Women's Studies International Forum* 41 (2): 103–12.

Bauer, Gretchen, and Faith Okpotor. 2013. "'Her Excellency': An Exploratory Overview of Women Cabinet Ministers in Africa." *Africa Today* 60 (1): 76–97.

Bauer, Gretchen, and Manon Tremblay. 2011. *Women in Executive Power: A Global Overview*. New York: Taylor and Francis.

BBC News. 2016. "Gender Equality in Workplace Could Add Trillions to US Economy." *BBC News*, April 7. www.bbc.com.

Beckwith, Karen. 2015. "Before Prime Minister: Margaret Thatcher, Angela Merkel, and Gendered Party Leadership Contests." *Politics and Gender* 11: 718–45.

Bell, Christine, and Catherine O'Rourke. 2010. "Peace Agreement Database." Transitional Justice Institute. http://www.transitionaljustice.ulster.ac.uk.

Beneria, Lourdes. 2003. *Gender, Development, and Globalization: Economics as if All People Mattered*. New York: Routledge.

Benstead, Lindsay J. 2015. "Why Quotas Are Needed to Improve Women's Access to Services in Clientelistic Regimes." *Governance* 29 (2): 185–205.

Beske, Melissa A. 2012. "Assimilating Adversity: Gender, Family, and the Cultural Normalization of Intimate Partner Violence in Western Belize." In *Violence and Abuse in Society: Understanding a Global Crisis*, edited by Angela Browne-Miller. Santa Barbara, CA: Praeger, 387–402.

Bird, Karen. 2015. "Intersections of Exclusion: The Institutional Dynamics of Combined Gender and Ethnic Quota Systems." *Politics, Groups, and Identities* (June): 1–23.

Bligh, Michelle C., Michele M. Schlehofer, Bettina J. Casad, and Amber M. Gaffney. 2012. "Competent Enough, but Would You Vote for Her? Gender Stereotypes and Media Influences on Perceptions of Women Politicians." *Journal of Applied Social Psychology* 42 (3): 560–597.

Bjarnegård, Elin. 2013. *Gender, Informal Institutions and Political Recruitment: Explaining Male Dominance in Parliamentary Representation*. New York: Palgrave Macmillan.

Blackmon, Pamela. 2009. "Factoring Gender into Economic Development: Changing the Policies of the International Monetary Fund and the World Bank." *Women's Studies* 38 (2): 213–37.

Brokaw, Tom. 2013. "Welcome to the Century of Women." *Lean In*, April 29. Accessed August 31, 2014. www.leanin.org.

Bruhn, Kathleen. 2003. "Whores and Lesbians: Political Activism, Party Strategies, and Gender Quotas in Mexico." *Electoral Studies* 22 (1): 101–19.

Brunell, Laura, and Janet Else Johnson. 2010. "The New WAVE: How Transnational Feminist Networks Promote Domestic Violence Reform in Post-Communist Europe." In *Domestic Violence in Post-Communist States*, edited by Katalin Fábián. Bloomington: Indiana University Press, 261–92.

Buchy, Marlene. 2012. *Securing Women's Tenure And Leadership for Forest Management: A Summary of the Asian Experience*. Washington, DC: Rights and Resources Institute. www.rightsandresources.org.

Budlender, Debbie, and Eileen Alma. 2011. *Women and Land: Securing Rights for Better Lives*. Ottawa: International Development Research Centre.

Bunch, Charlotte. 1990. "Women's Rights as Human Rights: Toward a Re-Vision of Human Rights." *Human Rights Quarterly* 12 (4): 486–98.

Bunch, Charlotte, and Samantha Frost. 2000. "Women's Human Rights: An Introduction." In *Routledge International Encyclopedia of Women: Global Women's Issues and Knowledge*, edited by Cheris Kramarae and Dale Spender. New York: Routledge.

Bunch, Charlotte, and Niamh Reilly. 1994. *Demanding Accountability: The Global Campaign and Vienna Tribunal for Women's Human Rights*. New York: United Nations Development Fund for Women.

Bush, Sarah Sunn. 2011. "International Politics and the Spread of Quotas for Women in Legislatures." *International Organization* 65 (1): 103–37.

Butler, Judith. 2004. *Precarious Life: The Power of Mourning and Violence*. New York: Verso Books.

Caprioli, Mary. 2003. "Gender Equality and State Aggression." *International Interactions* 29: 195–214.

———. 2005. "Primed for Violence: The Role of Gender Inequality in Predicting Internal Conflict." *International Studies Quarterly* 49(2): 161–78.

Carmon, Irin. 2014. "Why Senator Kirsten Gillibrand Should Not Have to Name Names." *MSNBC.com*, August 31. http://www.msnbc.com.

Carpenter, Charli. 2003. "Women and Children First: Gender, Norms, and Humanitarian Evacuation in the Balkans 1991–1995." *International Organization* 57 (4): 661–694.

Carrillo, Anna Lorena, and Norma Stoltz Chinchilla. 2010. "From Urban Elite to Peasant Organizing: Agendas, Accomplishments, and Challenges of Thirty-Plus Years of Guatemalan Feminism, 1975–2007." In *Women's Activism in Latin America and the Caribbean*, edited by Elizabeth Maier and Nathalie Lebon. New Brunswick, NJ: Rutgers University Press, 140–58.

Carver, Terrell. 1996. *Gender Is Not a Synonym for Women*. Boulder, CO: Lynne Rienner.

Catalano, Shannan. 2012. *Intimate Partner Violence, 1993–2010*. Washington, DC: Bureau of Justice Statistics. www.bjs.gov.

Caul, Miki. 1999. "Women's Representation in Parliament: The Role of Political Parties." *Party Politics* 5 (1): 79–98.

———. 2001. "Political Parties and the Adoption of Candidate Gender Quotas: A Cross-National Analysis." *Journal of Politics* 63 (4): 1214–29.

Chant, Sylvia, and Caroline Sweetman. 2012. "Fixing Women or Fixing the World? 'Smart Economics,' Efficiency Approaches, and Gender Equality in Development." *Gender and Development* 20 (3): 517–29.

Cheng, Christine, and Margit Tavits. 2011. "Informal Influences in Selecting Female Political Candidates." *Political Research Quarterly* 64 (2): 460–71.

Cheston, Susy, and Lisa Kuhn. 2002. *Empowering Women Through Microfinance*. New York: UNIFEM.

Chivens, Thomas. 2010. "The Politics of Awareness: Making Domestic Violence Visible in Poland." In *Domestic Violence in Post-Communist States*, edited by Katalin Fábián. Bloomington: Indiana University Press, 171–94.

Chowdhry, Geeta, and Sheila Nair, eds. 2002. *Power, Postcolonialism, and International Relations: Reading Race, Gender, and Class.* London: Routledge.

Christensen, Iverson. 2016. "Worldwide Guide to Women in Leadership." *Guide 2 Women Leaders.* Accessed July 6, 2016. www.guide2womenleaders.com.

Cockburn, Cynthia. 2007. *From Where We Stand: War, Women's Activism, and Feminist Analysis.* London: Zed Books.

Cohn, Carol. 1987. "Sex and Death in the Rational World of Defense Intellectuals." *Signs: Journal of Women in Culture and Society* 12 (4): 687.

———. 2008. "The Relevance of Gender for Eliminating Weapons of Mass Destruction." In *Global Governance: Feminist Perspectives*, edited by Shirin Rai and Georgina Waylen. London: Palgrave Macmillan, 185–206.

Cohn, Carol, Helen Kinsella, and Sheri Gibbings. 2004. "Women, Peace and Security Resolution 1325." *International Feminist Journal of Politics* 6 (1): 130–140.

Cohn, Carol, and Sara Ruddick. 2003. *A Feminist Ethical Perspective on Weapons of Mass Destruction.* Boston, MA: Consortium on Gender, Security, and Human Rights. www.genderandsecurity.org.

Collins, Patricia Hill. 1998. "Intersections of Race, Class, Gender, and Nation: Some Implications for Black Family Studies." *Journal of Comparative Family Studies* 29 (1): 27–36.

Connell, Dan. 1998. "Strategies for Change: Women and Politics in Eritrea and South Africa." *Review of African Political Economy* 25 (76): 189–206.

Cooray, Arusha, Sushanta Mallick, and Nabamita Dutta. 2014. "Gender-Specific Human Capital, Openness, and Growth: Exploring the Linkages for South Asia." *Review of Development Economics* 18 (1): 107–22.

Crenshaw, Kimberlé. 1991. "Mapping the Margins: Intersectionality, Identity Politics, and Violence against Women of Color." *Stanford Law Review* 43 (6): 1241–99.

Cuberes, David, and Marc Teignier. 2014. "Gender Inequality and Economic Growth: A Critical Review." *Journal of International Development* 26 (2): 260–76.

Dahlerup, Drude. 2006. "Introduction." In *Women, Quotas and Politics*, edited by Drude Dahlerup. London: Routledge, 3–32.

Dahlerup, Drude, and Monique Leyenaar, eds. 2013. *Breaking Male Dominance in Old Democracies.* New York: Oxford.

Darnaud, Gina. 2016. "If You Give a Piece of Land to a Female, It Will Change the World . . . Literally." *Global Citizen*, March 31. Accessed March 31, 2016. www.globalcitizen.org.

Davis, Rebecca Howard. 1997. *Women and Power in Parliamentary Democracies: Cabinet Appointments in Western Europe, 1968–1992.* Lincoln: University of Nebraska Press.

Deere, Carmen Diana, and Magdalena León. 2001. *Empowering Women: Land and Property Rights in Latin America.* Pittsburgh: Pittsburgh University Press.

Deininger, Klaus. 2003. *Land Policies for Growth and Poverty Reduction*. Washington, DC: World Bank. www.worldbank.org.

Demeritt, Jacqueline H.R., Angela D. Nichols, and Eliza G Kelly. 2014. "Female Participation and Civil War Relapse." *Civil Wars* 16 (3): 346–68.

Department of State. 2016. "International Conventions Relevant to Combating Trafficking in Persons." Washington, DC: Office of Website Management, Bureau of Public Affairs. Accessed August 6, 2016. www.state.gov.

Derous, Eva, Ann Marie Ryan, and Alec W. Serlie. 2014. "Double Jeopardy Upon Resumé Screening: When Achmed Is Less Employable than Aïsha." *Personnel Psychology* 68 (3): 659–96.

Dickinson, Torry D., and Robert K. Schaeffer. 2001. *Fast Forward: Work, Gender, and Protest in a Changing World*. Boulder, CO: Rowman and Littlefield.

Dolan, Kathleen. 1997. "Gender Differences in Support for Women Candidates." *Women and Politics* 17 (2): 27–41.

———. 2005. "Do Women Candidates Play to Gender Stereotypes? Do Men Candidates Play to Women? Candidate Sex and Issues Priorities on Campaign Websites." *Political Research Quarterly* 58 (1): 31–44.

Dorius, Shawn F., and Glenn Firebaugh. 2010. "Trends in Global Gender Inequality." *Social Forces* 88 (5): 1941–68.

Doss, Cheryl. 2006. "The Effects of Intrahousehold Property Ownership on Expenditure Patterns in Ghana." *Journal of African Economies* 15(1): 149–80.

Doss, Cheryl, Chiara Kovarik, Amber Peterman, Agnes R. Quisumbing, and Mara van den Bold. 2013. *Gender Inequalities in Ownership and Control of Land in Africa: Myth versus Reality*. Washington, DC: International Food Policy Research Institute.

Dovi, Suzanne. 2002. "Preferable Descriptive Representatives: Will Just Any Woman, Black, or Latino Do?" *American Political Science Review* 96 (4): 729–44.

Drolet, Julie. 2010. "Feminist Perspectives in Development: Implications for Women and Microcredit." *Affilia* 25 (3): 212–23.

Drury, Cooper A., and Dursun Peksen. 2012. "Women and Economic Statecraft: The Negative Impact International Sanctions Visit on Women." *European Journal of International Relations*: 463–90.

Duncan, Natricia. 2014. "Land Rights in Latin America: Where Are the Voices of Indigenous Women?" *Guardian*, July 23. www.theguardian.com.

Dutta, Aniruddha. 2013. "Legible Identities and Legitimate Citizens." *International Feminist Journal of Politics* 15 (4): 494–514.

Eastin, Joshua, and Aseem Prakash. 2013. "Economic Development and Gender Equality: Is There a Gender Kuznets Curve?" *World Politics* 65 (1): 156–86.

Eaton, Sam. 2016. "These Indian Women Said They Could Protect Their Local Forests Better than the Men in Their Village. The Men Agreed." *Public Radio International*, March 29. www.pri.org.

Eisenstein, Hester. 2005. "A Dangerous Liaison? Feminism and Corporate Globalization." *Science and Society* 69 (3): 487–518.

————. 2009. *Feminism Seduced: How Global Elites Use Women's Labor and Ideas to Exploit the World*. Boulder, CO: Paradigm.

Elborgh-Woytek, Karin, Monique Newiak, Kalpana Kochhar, Stefania Fabrizio, Kangni Kpodar, Philippe Wingender, Benedict J. Clements, and Gerd Schwartz. 2013. *Women, Work, and the Economy: Macroeconomic Gains from Gender Equity*. Washington, DC: International Monetary Fund. www.imf.org.

Ellerby, Kara. 2013. "(En)gendered Security? The Complexities of Women's Inclusion in Peace Processes." *International Interactions* 39 (4): 435–60.

————. 2015. "(En)gendered Security? Gender Mainstreaming and Women's Inclusion in Peace Processes." In *A Systematic Understanding of Gender, Peace and Security: Implementing UNSCR 1325*, edited by Ismene Gizelis and Louise Olsson. New York: Routledge, 185–209.

————. 2016a. "A Seat at the Table Is Not Enough: Understanding Women's Substantive Representation in Peace Processes." *Peacebuilding* 4 (2): 1–15.

————. 2016b. "(En)gendering Peace: Divergent Post-Conflict Processes for Women in Guatemala and El Salvador" In *Women, Gender Equality, and Post-Conflict Transformation: Lessons from the Past, Implications for the Future*, edited by Joyce Kaufman and Kristen Clark. New York: Routledge Press.

Elson, Diane. 2009. "Gender Equality and Economic Growth in the World Bank World Development Report 2006." *Feminist Economics* 15 (3): 35–59.

Enloe, Cynthia. 2000. *Maneuvers: The International Politics of Militarizing Women's Lives*. Berkeley: University of California Press.

————. 2004. "'Gender' Is Not Enough: The Need for a Feminist Consciousness." *International Affairs* 80 (1): 95–97.

————. 2007. *Globalization and Militarism: Feminists Make the Link*. New York: Rowman and Littlefield.

————. 2014. *Bananas, Beaches, and Bases: Making Feminist Sense of International Politics*. 3rd ed. Berkeley: University of California Press.

Escobar-Lemmon, Maria, and Michelle M. Taylor-Robinson. 2005. "Women Ministers in Latin American Government: When, Where, and Why?" *American Journal of Political Science* 49 (4): 829–44.

————. 2009. "Getting to the Top Career Paths of Women in Latin American Cabinets." *Political Research Quarterly* 62 (4): 685–99.

European Union Agency for Fundamental Rights. 2014. *Violence against Women: An EU-Wide Survey*. Luxembourg: Publications Office of the European Union. http://fra.europa.eu.

Falk, Erica, and Kate Kenski. 2006. "Issue Saliency and Gender Stereotypes: Support for Women as Presidents in Times of War and Terrorism." *Social Science Quarterly* 87 (1): 1–18.

Fausto-Sterling, Anne. 2005. "The Bare Bones of Sex: Part 1—Sex and Gender." *Signs* 30 (2): 1491–1527.

Ferris, Elizabeth, Daniel Petz, and Chareen Stark. 2013. *The Year of Recurring Disasters: A Review of Natural Disasters in 2012*. London: Brookings Institute. www.brookings.edu.

Field, Erica. 2007. "Entitled to Work: Urban Property Rights and Labor Supply in Peru." *Quarterly Journal of Economics* 122 (4): 1561–1602.

Fierke, Karin M. 2007. *Critical Approaches to International Security*. Cambridge: Polity Press.

Fiorenza, Elisabeth Schüssler. 1992. *But She Said*. Boston, MA: Beacon Press.

———. 2001. *Wisdom Ways: Introducing Feminist Biblical Interpretation*. New York: Orbis Books.

Fleschenberg, Andrea. 2011. "South and Southeast Asia." In *Women in Executive Power*, edited by Gretchen Bauer and Manon Tremblay. New York: Taylor and Francis, 23–43.

Food and Agriculture Organization. 2011. *The State of Food and Agriculture, 2010–2011: Women in Agriculture Closing the Gender Gap for Development*. Rome: Food and Agriculture Organization of the United Nations.

Ford, Liz. 2015. "Less Pay, More Work, No Pension: The 21st-Century Woman's Lot Laid Bare." *Guardian*, April 27. www.theguardian.com.

Forest, Maxine. 2011. "From State-Socialism to EU Accession: Contrasting the Gendering of (Executive) Political Power in Central Europe." In *Women in Executive Power: A Global Overview*, edited by Gretchen Bauer and Manon Tremblay. New York and London: Routledge, 65–84.

Franceschet, Susan. 2010. "Explaining Domestic Violence Policy Outcomes in Chile and Argentina." *Latin American Politics and Society* 52 (3): 1–29.

Franceschet, Susan, and Jennifer M. Piscopo. 2008. "Gender Quotas and Women's Substantive Representation: Lessons from Argentina." *Politics and Gender* 4 (3): 393–425.

Franceschet, Susan, and Gwynn Thomas. 2015. "Resisting Parity: Gender and Cabinet Appointments in Chile and Spain." *Politics & Gender* 11: 643–64.

Franzway, Suzanne, R. W. Connell, and Diane Court. 1989. *Staking a Claim: Feminism, Bureaucracy and the State*. Cambridge: Polity.

Fraser, Nancy. 2000. "Rethinking Recognition." *New Left Review* 2 (3): 107–20.

———. 2009. "Feminism, Capitalism, and the Cunning of History." *New Left Review* 56 (March/April): 97–117.

———. 2013. "How Feminism Became Capitalism's Handmaiden and How to Reclaim It." *Guardian*, October 13. www.theguardian.com.

Giddens, Anthony. 1984. *The Constitution of Society: Outline of the Theory of Structuration*. Berkeley: University of California Press.

Gills, Barry K. 2010. "The Return of Crisis in the Era of Globalization: One Crisis, or Many?" *Globalizations* 7 (1/2): 3–8.

Giri, Kalpana. 2012. *Gender in Forest Tenure: Pre-Requisite for Sustainable Forest Management in Nepal*. Washington, DC: Rights and Resources. www.rightsandresources.org.

Goetz, Anne Marie, and Shireen Hassim. 2003. "Introduction." In *No Shortcuts to Power: African Women in Politics and Policy Making*, edited by Anne Marie Goetz and Shireen Hassim. New York: Zed Books.

Goldin, Claudia. 1995. "The U-Shaped Female Labor Force Function in Economic Development and Economic History." In *Investment in Women's Human Capital*, edited by T.P. Shultz. Chicago: University of Chicago Press, 61–90.

Goodhart, Michael. 2008. "A Democratic Defense of Universal Basic Income." In *Illusion of Consent: Engaging with Carole Pateman*, edited by Daniel O'Neil, Mary Lynn Shanley, and Iris Marion Young. University Park: Pennsylvania State University Press, 139–64.

Gosine, Andil. 2013. "Murderous Men." *International Feminist Journal of Politics* 15 (4): 477–93.

Grewal, Inderpal, and Caren Kaplan. 1994. *Scattered Hegemonies: Postmodernity and Transnational Feminist Practices*. Minneapolis: University of Minnesota Press.

———. 2001. "Global Identities: Theorizing Transnational Studies of Sexuality." *GLQ: A Journal of Lesbian and Gay Studies* 7 (4): 663–79.

Gray, Mark M., Miki Caul Kittilson, and Wayne Sandholtz. 2006. "Women and Globalization: A Study of 180 Countries, 1975–2000." *International Organization* 60 (2): 293–333.

Grillo, Trina. 1995. "Anti-Essentialism and Intersectionality: Tools to Dismantle the Master's House." *Berkeley Women's Law Journal* 10: 16–30.

Hallward-Driemeier, Mary, and Tazeen Hasan. 2012. *Empowering Women: Legal Rights and Economic Opportunities in Africa*. Washington, DC: World Bank.

Hallward-Driemeier, Mary, and Ousman Gajigo. 2013. *Strengthening Economic Rights and Women's Occupational Choice: The Impact of Reforming Ethiopia's Family Law*. Washington, DC: World Bank.

Hallward-Driemeier, Mary, Tazeen Hasan, and Anca Bogdana Rusu. 2013a. *Women's Legal Rights over 50 Years: Progress, Stagnation, or Regression?* Washington, DC: World Bank. http://documents.worldbank.org.

Hallward-Driemeier, Mary, Tazeen Hasan, and Anca Bogdana Rusu. 2013b. *Women's Legal Rights over 50 Years: What Is the Impact of Reform?* Washington, DC: World Bank. http://documents.worldbank.org.

Hallward-Driemeier, Mary, Tazeen Hasan, and Sarah Iqbal. 2013. "Historical Database of Women's Legal Capacity and Property Rights." Washington, DC: World Bank. www.wbl.worldbank.org.

Harbom, Lotta, Stina Högbladh, and Peter Wallensteen. 2006. "Armed Conflict and Peace Agreements." *Journal of Peace Research* 43 (5): 617.

Harcourt, Wendy. 2012. "Beyond 'Smart Economics': The World Bank 2012 Report on Gender and Equality." *International Feminist Journal of Politics* 14 (2): 307–12.

Harding, Sandra. 1987. "Introduction: Is There a Feminist Method?" In *Feminism and Methodology: Social Science Issues*, edited by Sandra Harding. Bloomington: Indiana University Press, 1–14.

Haritaworn, Jin, Adi Kuntsman, and Silvia Posocco. 2013. "Murderous Inclusions." *International Feminist Journal of Politics* 15 (4): 445–52.

Hartmann, Betsy. 2011. "The Return of Population Control: Incentives, Targets, and the Backlash against Cairo." *Different Take* (70).

Hartsock, Nancy. 2006. "Globalization and Primitive Accumulation: The Contributions of David Harvey's Dialectical Marxism." In *David Harvey: A Critical Reader*, edited by Noel Castree and Derek Gregory. New York: Oxford University Press, 167–90.

Harvey, David. 2005. *A Brief History of Neoliberalism*. Oxford: Oxford University Press.

Hassim, Shireen. 2002. "'A Conspiracy of Women': The Women's Movement in South Africa's Transition to Democracy." *Social Research* 69 (3): 693–732.

Hewitson, Gillian. 1999. *Feminist Economics*. London: Edward Elgar.

Hill, Danny, and Sabrina Karim. 2016. "Measuring 'Gender Equality.'" Working Paper.

Hill, Felicity, Mikele Aboitiz, and Sara Poehlman-Doumbouya. 2003. "Nongovernmental Organizations' Role in the Buildup and Implementation of Security Council Resolution 1325." *Signs* 28 (4): 1255–69.

Himmelweit, Susan, Cristina Santos, Almudena Sevilla, and Catherine Sofer. 2013. "Sharing of Resources Within the Family and the Economics of Household Decision Making." *Journal of Marriage and Family* 75 (3): 625–39.

Hodson, Piper. 1997. "Routes to Power: An Examination of Political Change, Rulership, and Women's Access to Executive Office." In *The Other Elites*, edited by Mary Anne Borelli and Janet M. Martin. Boulder, CO: Lynne Rienner, 33–47.

Högbladh, Stina. 2012. "Peace Agreements 1975–2011: Updating the UCDP Peace Agreement Dataset." Uppsala Conflict Data Program.

Hoskyns, Catherine, and Shirin M. Rai. 2007. "Recasting the Global Political Economy: Counting Women's Unpaid Work." *New Political Economy* 12 (3): 297–317.

Hrycak, Alexandra. 2010. "Transnational Advocacy Campaigns and Domestic Violence Prevention in Ukraine." In *Domestic Violence in Post-Communist States*, edited by Katalin Fábián. Bloomington: Indiana University Press, 45–77.

Htun, Mala, and Mark P. Jones. 2002. "Engendering the Right to Participate in Decision-Making: Electoral Quotas and Women's Leadership in Latin America." In *Gender and The Politics of Rights and Democracy in Latin America*, edited by Nikki Craske and Maxine Molyneux. New York: Palgrave Macmillan, 32–56.

Htun, Mala, and Juan Pablo Ossa. 2013. "Political Inclusion of Marginalized Groups: Indigenous Reservations and Gender Parity in Bolivia." *Politics, Groups, and Identities* 1 (1): 4–25.

Htun, Mala, and S. Laurel Weldon. 2012. "The Civic Origins of Progressive Policy Change: Combating Violence against Women in Global Perspective, 1975–2005." *American Political Science Review* 106 (3): 548–69.

Huddy, Leonie, and Nayda Terkildsen. 1993. "Gender Stereotypes and the Perception of Male and Female Candidates." *American Journal of Political Science* 37 (1): 119–47.

Hudson, Valerie M., Mary Caprioli, Bonnie Ballif-Spanvill, Rose McDermott, and Chad F. Emmett. 2008. "The Heart of the Matter: The Security of Women and the Security of States." *International Security* 33 (3): 7–45.

Hughes, Donna M. 2000. "The 'Natasha' Trade: The Transnational Shadow Market of Trafficking in Women." *Journal of International Affairs* 53 (2): 625–52.

Hughes, Melanie M. 2011. "Intersectionality, Quotas, and Minority Women's Political Representation Worldwide." *American Political Science Review* 105 (3): 604–20.

———. 2013. "The Intersection of Gender and Minority Status in National Legislatures: The Minority Women Legislative Index." *Legislative Studies Quarterly* 38 (4): 489–516.

Hughes, Melanie M., Mona Lena Krook, and Pamela Paxton. 2015. "Transnational Women's Activism and the Global Diffusion of Gender Quotas." *International Studies Quarterly* 59 (2): 357–72.

Hughes, Melanie M., and Aili Mari Tripp. 2015. "Civil War and Trajectories of Change in Women's Political Representation in Africa, 1985–2010." *Social Forces* 93 (4): 1513–40.

ILO—see International Labour Organization.

Inglehart, Ronald, and Pippa Norris. 2003. *Rising Tide: Gender Equality and Cultural Change around the World.* Cambridge: Cambridge University Press.

Inter-Parliamentary Union. 2000. *Politics: Women's Insight.* Geneva: Inter-Parliamentary Union.

———. 2014. *Women in Politics: 2014.* Geneva: Inter-Parliamentary Union. www.ipu.org.

———. 2015. *Women in Politics: 2015.* Geneva: Inter-Parliamentary Union. www.ipu.org.

———. 2016. *Women in National Parliaments.* Geneva: Inter-Parliamentary Union. www.ipu.org.

International Center for Research on Women. 2014. *Young Men Initiative in the Balkans.* Washington, DC: ICRW. www.icrw.org.

International IDEA, Inter-Parliamentary Union, and Stockholm University. 2016. *Quota Project: Global Database for Quotas of Women.* www.quotaproject.org.

International Labour Organization. 2005. *Sexual Harassment at Work: National and International Responses.* Geneva: International Labour Organization. www.ilo.org.

———. 2012a. *Global Employment Trends for Women 2012.* Geneva: International Labour Organization.

———. 2012b. "Labour Market Gender Gap: Two Steps Forward, One Step Back." *ILO.org,* December 11. www.ilo.org.

———. 2015. *Women and the Future of Work: Beijing+20 and Beyond.* Geneva: International Labour Organization. www.ilo.org.

Jackson, Cecile. 2003. "Gender Analysis of Land: Beyond Land Rights for Women?" *Journal of Agrarian Change* 3 (4): 453–80.

Jacob, Suraj, John A. Scherpereel, and Melinda Adams. 2013. "Gender Norms and Women's Political Representation: A Global Analysis of Cabinets, 1979–2009." *Governance* 27 (2): 321–45.

Jagori, and UN Women. 2011. *Safe Cities Free of Violence against Women and Girls Initiative: Report of the Baseline Survey Delhi 2010.* New Delhi: Jagori and UN Women. www.jagori.org.

Jalalzai, Farida. 2004. "Women Political Leaders." *Women and Politics* 26 (3/4): 85–108.

————. 2013. *Shattered, Cracked, or Firmly Intact? Women and the Executive Glass Ceiling Worldwide.* New York: Oxford University Press.

Jalalzai, Farida, and Mona Krook. 2010. "Beyond Hillary and Benazir: Women's Political Leadership Worldwide." *International Political Science Review* 31 (1): 5–21.

Jayarajah, Carl, William Branson, and Binayak Sen. 1996. *Social Dimensions of Adjustment: World Bank Experience, 1980–93.* Washington, DC: World Bank. www-wds. worldbank.org.

Jensenius, Francesca R. 2016. "Competing Inequalities? On the Intersection of Gender and Ethnicity in Candidate Nominations in Indian Elections." *Government and Opposition* 51 (3): 440–63.

Joachim, Jutta. 2007. *Agenda Setting, the UN, and NGOs: Gender Violence and Reproductive Rights.* Washington, DC: Georgetown University Press.

Johnson, Janet Elise. 2007. "Domestic Violence Politics in Post-Soviet States." *Social Politics: International Studies in Gender, State, and Society* 14 (3): 380–405.

Johnson, Janet Elise, and Gulnara Zaynullina. 2010. "Global Feminism, Foreign Funding, and Russian Writing About Domestic Violence." In *Domestic Violence in Post-Communist States: Local Activism, National Policies, and Global Forces,* edited by Katalin Fábián. Bloomington: Indiana University Press, 78–110.

Johnson, Niki. 2016. "Keeping Men In, Shutting Women Out: Gender Biases in Candidate Selection Processes in Uruguay." *Government and Opposition* 51 (3): 393–415.

Kalantry, Sital. 2012. "Women in Robes." *Americas Quarterly* (Summer). http://scholarship.law.cornell.edu.

Kalpana, K. 2011. "Negotiating Multiple Patriarchies: Women and Microfinance in South India." In *The Women, Gender, and Development Reader,* edited by Nalini Visvanathan, Lynn Duggan, Nan Wiegersma, and Laurie Nisonoff. London and New York: Zed Books, 55–63.

Keating, Christine, Claire Rasmussen, and Pooja Rishi. 2010. "The Rationality of Empowerment: Microcredit, Accumulation by Dispossession, and the Gendered Economy." *Signs* 36 (1): 153–76.

Kent, Lauren. 2015. "Number of Women Leaders around the World Has Grown, But They're Still a Small Group." *Pew Research Center,* July 30. www.pewresearch.org.

Kittilson, Miki Caul. 2006. *Challenging Parties, Changing Parliaments: Women and Elected Office in Contemporary Western Europe.* Columbus: Ohio State University Press.

Kittilson, Miki Caul, and Leslie Schwindt-Bayer. 2010. "Engaging Citizens: The Role of Power-Sharing Institutions." *Journal of Politics* 72 (4): 990–1002.

Klein, Naomi. 2007. *The Shock Doctrine: The Rise of Disaster Capitalism.* New York: Metropolitan Books.

Knight, Kyl. 2012. "Dividing By Three: Nepal Recognizes a Third Gender." *World Policy,* February 1. www.worldpolicy.org.

Ko, Lisa. 2016. "Unwanted Sterilization and Eugenics Programs in the United States." *Independent Lens,* January 29. www.pbs.org.

Kobayashi, Yoshie. 2004. "Has the Closed Door Opened for Women? The Appointment of Women Ministers in Japan." *PS: Political Science and Politics* 37 (1): 63–64.

Kollman, Kelly. 2013. *The Same-Sex Unions Revolution in Western Democracies: International Norms and Domestic Policy Change.* Manchester, UK: Manchester University Press.

Kristof, Nicholas, and Sheryl WuDunn. 2009. *Half the Sky: Turning Oppression into Opportunity for Women Worldwide.* New York: Vintage Books.

Krizsan, Andrea, and Raluca Popa. 2010. "Europeanization in Making Policies against Domestic Violence in Central and Eastern Europe." *Social Politics: International Studies in Gender, State, and Society* 17 (3): 379–406.

Krook, Mona Lena. 2006. "Gender Quotas, Norms and Politics." *Politics and Gender* 2 (1): 110–18.

———. 2009. *Quotas for Women in Politics: Gender and Candidate Selection Reform Worldwide.* Oxford: Oxford University Press.

———. 2016. "Contesting Gender Quotas: Dynamics of Resistance." *Politics, Groups, and Identities* 4 (2): 268–83.

Krook, Mona Lena, and Fiona Mackay, eds. 2011. *Gender, Politics and Institutions: Towards a Feminist Institutionalism.* New York: Palgrave Macmillan.

Krook, Mona Lena, and Diana Z. O'Brien. 2012. "All the President's Men? The Appointment of Female Cabinet Ministers Worldwide." *Journal of Politics* 74 (3): 1–16.

Krook, Mona Lena, and Jacqui True. 2010. "Rethinking the Life Cycles of International Norms: The United Nations and the Global Promotion of Gender Equality." *European Journal of International Relations* 18 (1): 103–27.

Kuiper, Edith, and Drucilla Barker. 2006. *Feminist Economics and the World Bank: History, Theory, and Policy.* London and New York: Routledge.

Levinson, Justin D., and Danielle Young. 2010. "Implicit Gender Bias in the Legal Profession: An Empirical Study." *Duke Journal of Gender Law and Policy* 18 (1).

Lind, Amy, and Christine (Cricket) Keating. 2013. "Navigating The Left Turn: Sexual Justice and the Citizen Revolution in Ecuador." *International Feminist Journal of Politics* 15 (4): 515–33.

Lobasz, Jennifer. 2009. "Beyond Border Security: Feminist Approaches to Human Trafficking." *Security Studies* 18 (2): 319–44.

Lombardo, Emanuela, and Petra Meier. 2008. "Framing Gender Equality in the European Union Political Discourse." *Social Politics: International Studies in Gender, State, and Society* 15 (1): 101–29.

Lombardo, Emanuela, Petra Meier, and Mieke Verloo. 2010. "Discursive Dynamics in Gender Equality Politics." *European Journal of Women's Studies* 17 (2): 105–23.

Lorber, Judith. 2010. *Gender Inequality: Feminist Theory and Politics.* 4th ed. New York: Oxford University Press.

Lorde, Audre. 1970. "Age, Race, Class, and Sex: Women Redefining Difference." Presented at the Copeland Colloquium, Amerst College.

———. 1983. "There Is No Hierarchy of Oppressions." *Bulletin: Homophobia and Education* 14 (3/4): 9.

Lovenduski, Joni. 2005. *Feminizing Politics*. Malden, MA: Polity Press.

———, ed. 2005. *State Feminism and Representation*. Cambridge: Cambridge University Press.

Lu, Kelan, and Marijke Breuning. 2014. "Gender and Generosity: Does Women's Representation Affect Development Cooperation?" *Politics, Groups, and Identities* 2 (3): 313–30.

Luciak, Ilja A. 1998. "Gender Equality and Electoral Politics on the Left: A Comparison of El Salvador and Nicaragua." *Journal of Interamerican Studies and World Affairs* 40 (1): 39.

———. 2001. *After the Revolution: Gender and Democracy in El Salvador, Nicaragua, and Guatemala*. Baltimore, MD: Johns Hopkins University Press.

Maclean, Kate. 2010. "Capitalizing on Women's Social Capital? Women-Targeted Microfinance in Bolivia." *Development and Change* 41 (3): 495–515.

Mansbridge, Jane. 2003. "Rethinking Representation." *American Political Science Review* 97 (4): 515–28.

———. 2005. "Quota Problems: Combating the Dangers of Essentialism." *Politics and Gender* 1 (4): 622–38.

Marchand, Marianne, and Anne Sisson Runyan, eds. 2011. *Gender and Global Restructuring: Sightings, Sites and Resistances*. 2nd ed. London: Routledge.

Matland, Richard E., and Donley T. Studlar. 1996. "The Contagion of Women Candidates in Single-Member District and Proportional Representation Electoral Systems: Canada and Norway." *Journal of Politics* 58 (3): 707–33.

Mayoux, Linda. 2002. "Women's Empowerment or Feminisation of Debt? Towards a New Agenda in African Microfinance." Edited by Gunnar Aegisson. Report based on One World Action Conference, London, March.

Mazur, Amy, and Dorothy McBride. 2007. "State Feminism since the 1980s: From Loose Notion to Operationalized Concept." *Politics and Gender* 3 (4): 501.

Mbembe, Achille. 2003. "Necropolitics." *Public Culture* 15 (1): 11–40.

McBride, Dorothy, and Amy Mazur. 2010. *The Politics of State Feminism*. Philadelphia: Temple University Press.

McCann, Deidre. 2005. *Sexual Harassment at Work: National and International Responses*. Geneva: International Labour Office. www.ilo.org.

McGee, Suzanne, and Heidi Moore. 2014. "Women's Rights and Their Money: A Timeline from Cleopatra to Lilly Ledbetter." *Guardian*, August 11. www.theguardian.com.

McKee, Alan. 2003. *Textual Analysis: A Beginner's Guide*. Thousand Oaks, CA: Sage.

Meier, Petra. 2004. "The Mutual Contagion Effect of Legal and Party Quotas: A Belgian Perspective." *Party Politics* 46 (4): 583–600.

Miller, Alice M. 2004. "Sexuality, Violence against Women, and Human Rights: Women Make Demands and Ladies Get Protection." *Health and Human Rights* 7 (2): 16–47.

Mohanty, Chandra Talpade. 1988. "Under Western Eyes: Feminist Scholarship and Colonial Discourses." *Feminist Review* (30): 61–88.

———. 2003. *Feminism Without Borders: Decolonizing Theory, Practicing Solidarity*. Durham, NC: Duke University Press.

———. 2013. "Transnational Feminist Crossings: On Neoliberalism and Radical Critique." *Signs* 38 (4): 967–91.

Montoya, Celeste. 2013. *From Global to Grassroots: The European Union, Transnational Advocacy, and Combating Violence against Women*. New York: Oxford University Press.

Montoya, Celeste, and L. Rolandsen Agustin. 2013. "The Othering of Domestic Violence: The EU and Cultural Framings of Violence against Women." *Social Politics: International Studies in Gender, State, and Society* 20 (4): 534–57.

Mosley, Paul. 1991. "Structural Adjustment: A General Overview, 1980–9." In *Current Issues in Development Economics*, edited by V.N. Balasubramanyam and Sanjaya Lall. London: Macmillan Education, 223–42.

Moss-Racusin, Corinne A., John F. Dovidio, Victoria L. Brescoli, Mark J. Graham, and Jo Handelsman. 2012. "Science Faculty's Subtle Gender Biases Favor Male Students." *Proceedings of the National Academy of Sciences* 109 (41): 16474–79.

Murray, Rainbow. 2014. "Quotas for Men: Reframing Gender Quotas as a Means of Improving Representation for All." *American Political Science Review* 108 (3): 520–32.

Nabukeera-Musoke, Harriet. 2009. "Transitional Justice and Gender in Uganda: Making Peace, Failing Women during the Peace Negotiation Process." *African Journal on Conflict Resolution* 9 (2): 121–29.

Nagar, Richa, Victoria Lawson, Linda McDowell, and Susan Hanson. 2002. "Locating Globalization: Feminist (Re)readings of the Subjects and Spaces of Globalization." *Economic Geography* 78 (3): 257–84.

National Democratic Institute. 2016. "#NotTheCost: Stopping Violence Against Women in Politics." *NDI.org*, November 8. www.ndi.org.

Norris, Pippa, and Drude Dahlerup. 2015. "On the Fast Track: The Spread of Gender Quota Policies for Elected Office." *HKS Working Paper No. 15041*. https://ssrn.com/abstract=2662112.

Nwankwor, Chiedo. 2014. "Of Democratic Inclusion and Dividends: Women Cabinet Ministers and Women's Interests in Sub-Saharan Africa." *Democracy in Africa*, January 7. www.democracyinafrica.org.

O'Brien, Diana Z., Matthew Mendez, Jordan Carr Peterson, and Jihyun Shin. 2015. "Letting Down the Ladder or Shutting the Door: Female Prime Ministers, Party Leaders, and Cabinet Ministers." *Politics and Gender* 11 (4): 689–717.

OECD—see Organisation for Economic Cooperation and Development.

Opello, Katherine A.R. 2006. *Gender Quotas, Parity Reform, and Political Parties in France*. New York: Rowan and Littlefield.

Organisation for Economic Cooperation and Development. 2012. *Gender Equality in Education, Employment, and Entrepreneurship: Final Report of the MCM 2012*. Paris: OECD.

Paxton, Pamela, and Melanie Hughes. 2007. *Women, Politics, and Power: A Global Perspective*. Thousand Oaks, CA: Pine Forge Press.

———. 2014. *Women, Politics, and Power: A Global Perspective*. 2nd ed. Thousand Oaks, CA: Pine Forge Press.

———. 2015. "The Increasing Effectiveness of National Gender Quotas, 1990–2010." *Legislative Studies Quarterly* 40: 331–62.

Paxton, Pamela, Melanie M. Hughes, and Jennifer L. Green. 2006. "The International Women's Movement and Women's Political Representation, 1893–2003." *American Sociological Review* 71 (6): 898–920.

Paxton, Pamela, and Sheri Kunovich. 2003. "Women's Political Representation: The Importance of Ideology." *Social Forces* 82 (1): 87–113.

Paxton, Pamela, Matthew A. Painter, and Melanie Hughes. 2010. "Growth in Women's Political Representation: A Longitudinal Exploration of Democracy, Electoral System, and Gender Quotas." *European Journal of Political Research* 49 (1): 25–52.

Peterson, V. Spike. 1992. "Security and Sovereign States: What Is at Stake in Taking Feminism Seriously?" In *Gendered States: Feminist (Re)Visions of International Relations Theory*, edited by V. Spike Peterson. Boulder, CO: Lynne Rienner, 31–60.

———. 2003. *A Critical Rewriting of Global Political Economy: Integrating Reproductive, Productive, and Virtual Economies*. London and New York: Routledge.

———. 2005. "How (the Meaning of) Gender Matters in Political Economy." *New Political Economy* 10 (4): 499–521.

———. 2010. "A Long View of Globalization and Crisis." *Globalizations* 7 (1/2): 187–202.

———. 2014. "Sex Matters: A Queer History of Hierarchies." *International Feminist Journal of Politics* 16 (3): 389–409.

Peterson, V. Spike, and Anne Sisson Runyan. 2010. *Global Gender Issues in the New Millennium*. 3rd ed. Boulder, CO: Westview Press.

Phillips, Anne. 1998. *Feminism and Politics*. Oxford: Oxford University Press.

Pierotti, Rachel S. 2012. "Increasing Rejection of Intimate Partner Violence: Evidence of Global Cultural Diffusion." *American Sociological Review* 76 (2): 240–65.

Pinto, Vânia Carvalho. 2011. "Arab States." In *Women in Executive Power: A Global Overview*, edited by Gretchen Bauer and Manon Tremblay. New York and London: Routledge, 10–22.

Plattner, Marc F. 1998. "Liberalism and Democracy: Can't Have One without the Other." *Foreign Affairs* 77 (2): 171–80.

Polgreen, Lydia, and Vikas Bajaj. 2010. "India Microcredit Sector Faces Collapse from Defaults." *New York Times*, November 17. www.nytimes.com.

Puar, Jasbir K. 2007. *Terrorist Assemblages: Homonationalism in Queer Times*. Durham, NC: Duke University Press.

Pui-lan, Kwok. 2009. "Elisabeth Schüssler Fiorenza and Postcolonial Studies." *Journal of Feminist Studies in Religion* 25 (1): 191–197.

Quisumbing, Agnes R., and John A. Maluccio. 2003. "Resources at Marriage and Intrahousehold Allocation: Evidence from Bangladesh, Ethiopia, Indonesia, and South Africa." *Oxford Bulletin of Economics and Statistics* 65 (3): 283–327.

Raymond, Jennifer. 2013. "Sexist Attitudes: Most of Us Are Biased." *Nature* 495 (7439): 33–34.

Razavi, Shahra. 2012. "World Development Report 2012: Gender Equality and Development, A Commentary." *Development and Change* 43 (1): 423–37.

Rees, Ray, and Ray Riezman. 2012. "Globalization, Gender, and Growth." *Review of Income and Wealth* 58 (1): 107–17.

Regan, Patrick M, and Aida Paskeviciute. 2003. "Women's Access to Politics and Peaceful States." *Journal of Peace Research* 40 (3): 287–302.

Reyes, Socorro. 2002. "Quotas in Pakistan: A Case Study." Paper prepared for International Institute for Democracy and Electoral Assistance (IDEA) workshop, Jakarta, Indonesia, September 25.

Rhyne, Elisabeth. 1998. "The Yin and Yang of Microfinance: Reaching the Poor and Sustainability." *MicroBanking Bulletin* (July): 6–8. www.jointokyo.org.

Richards, David L., and Ronald Gelleny. 2007. "Women's Status and Economic Globalization." *International Studies Quarterly* 51 (4): 855–76.

Richardson, James L. 2001. *Contending Liberalisms in World Politics*. Boulder, CO: Lynne Rienner.

Richter, Linda K. 1990. "Exploring Theories of Female Leadership in South and Southeast Asia." *Pacific Affairs* 63 (4): 524–40.

Robnik, Sonja. 2010. "Domestic Violence Against Women: When Practice Creates Legislation in Slovenia." In *Domestic Violence in Postcommunist States: Local Activism, National Policies, and Global Forces*, edited by Katalin Fábián. Bloomington: Indiana University Press, 195–218.

Rosenwasser, Shirley Miller, and Norma G. Dean. 1989. "Gender Role and Political Office: Effects of Perceived Masculinity/Femininity of Candidate and Political Office." *Psychology of Women Quarterly* 13 (1): 77–85.

Runyan, Anne Sisson, and Spike V. Peterson. 2014. *Global Gender Issues in the New Millennium*. 4th ed. Boulder, CO: Westview Press.

Rupert, Mark, and M. Scott Solomon. 2006. *Globalization and International Political Economy: The Politics of Alternative Futures*. Lanham, MD: Rowman and Littlefield.

Russell, Catherine A., and Mark W. DeLancey. 2002. "African Women in Cabinet Positions: Too Few, Too Weak." *Asian Women* 15 (12): 147–63.

Rwanda Men's Resource Center. 2016. "Rwanda Men's Resource Center." Accessed November 8, 2016. http://rwamrec.org.

Sapiro, Virginia. 1991. "Gender Politics, Gendered Politics: The State of the Field." In *Political Science: Looking to the Future*, edited by William Crotty. Evanston, IL: Northwestern University Press, 165–88.

Safri, Maliha, and Julie Graham. 2010. "The Global Household: Toward a Feminist Post-Capitalist International Political Economy." *Signs* 36 (1): 99–125.

Saner, Emine. 2013. "Gay Rights around the World: The Best and Worst Countries for Equality." *Guardian*, July 30. www.theguardian.com.

———. 2014. "Europe's Terrible Trans Rights Record: Will Denmark's New Law Spark Change?" *Guardian*, September 1. www.theguardian.com.

Schmidt, Gregory D. 2003. "Unanticipated Successes: Lessons from Peru's Experiences with Gender Quotas in Majoritarian Close List and Open List PR Systems."

Paper presented at the International IDEA Workshop, Lima, Peru, February. www. quotaproject.org.

Scott, Jessica. 2013. "The Distance between Death and Marriage: Citizenship, Violence, and Same-Sex Marriage in South Africa." *International Feminist Journal of Politics* 15 (4): 534–51.

Scott, Joan. 1986. "Gender: A Useful Category of Historical Analysis." *American Historical Review* 91 (5): 1053–75.

Sen, Purna. 2003. "Successes and Challenges: Understanding the Global Movement to End Violence against Women." In *Global Civil Society 2003*, edited by Mary Kaldor, Helmut K. Anheier, and Marlies Glasius. Oxford: Oxford University Press, 119–47.

Shah, Bina. 2014. "Want to End Sexual Violence against Women? Fix the Men." *Aljazeera*, August 13. www.aljazeera.com/.

Sharipova, Muborak, and Katalin Fábián. 2010. "From Soviet Liberation to Post-Soviet Segregation: Women and Violence in Tajikistan." In *Domestic Violence in Postcommunist States*, edited by Katalin Fábián. Bloomington: Indiana University Press, 133–70.

Shelley, Louise. 2011. "Human Trafficking: Why Is It Such An Important Women's Issue?" In *Confronting Global Gender Justice: Women's Lives, Human Rights*, edited by Debra Bergoffen, Paula Ruth Gilbert, Tamara Harvey, and Connie L. McNeely. New York: Routledge, 35–49.

Shepherd, Laura J. 2008. *Gender, Violence and Security: Discourse as Practice*. New York: Zed Books.

Simmons, Beth A., and Lisa L. Martin. 2002. "International Organizations and Institutions." In *Handbook of International Relations*, edited by W. Carlsnaes, Thomas Risse, and Beth A. Simmons. Los Angeles: Sage, 192–211.

Sineau, Mariette. 2005. "Institutionalizing Parity: The French Experience." In *Women in Parliament: Beyond Numbers, Revised Edition*. Stockholm, Sweden: International Institute for Democracy and Electoral Assistance, 122–31. www.idea.int.

Sistersong. 2016. "Reproductive Justice." *Sister Song, Inc.*, November 10. www.sistersong.net.

Sjoberg, Laura. 2013. *Gendering Global Conflict: Toward a Feminist Theory of War*. New York: Columbia University Press.

Sjoberg, Laura, and Caron E. Gentry. 2008. *Mothers, Monsters, Whores: Women's Violence in Global Politics*. New York: Zed Books.

Sokoloff, Natalie J., and Ida Dupont. 2005. "Domestic Violence at the Intersections of Race, Class, and Gender Challenges and Contributions to Understanding Violence against Marginalized Women in Diverse Communities." *Violence against Women* 11 (1): 38–64.

Spade, Dean. 2011. *Normal Life: Administrative Violence, Critical Trans Politics and the Limits of Law*. Brooklyn, NY: South End Press.

Squires, Judith. 2007. *The New Politics of Gender Equality*. New York: Palgrave Macmillan.

Stetson, Dorothy McBride, and Amy Mazur, eds. 1995. *Comparative State Feminism*. Thousand Oaks, CA: Sage.

Studlar, Donley T., and Gary F. Moncrief. 1999. "Women's Work? The Distribution and Prestige of Portfolios in the Canadian Provinces." *Governance* 12 (4): 379–95.

Swarr, Amanda Lock, and Richa Nagar, eds. 2010. *Critical Transnational Feminist Praxis*. Albany, NY: SUNY Press.

Sweeney, Shawna E. 2007. "Government Respect for Women's Economic Rights." In *Economic Rights: Conceptual, Measurement, and Policy Issues*, edited by Shareen Hertel and Lanse Minkler. Cambridge: Cambridge University Press, 233–66.

Taylor, Charles. 1998. "The Dynamics of Democratic Exclusion." *Journal of Democracy* 9 (4): 143–56.

Thames, Frank C., and Margaret S. Williams. 2013. *Contagious Representation: Women's Political Representation in Democracies around the World*. New York: New York University Press.

Thipe, Thuto. 2013. "Defining Boundaries: Gender and Property Rights in South Africa's Traditional Courts Bill." *Laws* 2: 483–511.

Thomas, Pamela, and Helen Skeat. 1990. "Gender in Third World Development Studies: An Overview of an Underview." *Australian Geographical Studies* 28 (1): 5–15.

Tickner, J. Ann. 2001. *Gendering World Politics: Issues and Approaches in the Post-Cold War Era*. New York: Columbia University Press.

———. 2006. "Feminism Meets International Relations: Some Methodological Issues." In *Feminist Methodologies for International Relations*, edited by Brooke Ackerly, Maria Stern, and Jacqui True. Cambridge: Cambridge University Press, 19–41.

Tickner, J. Ann, and Laura Sjoberg, eds. 2011. *Feminism and International Relations: Conversations About the Past, Present and Future*. London and New York: Routledge.

Tillet, Salamishah. 2013. "Forced Sterilizations and the Future of the Women's Movement." *Nation*, July 9. Accessed October 28, 2016. www.thenation.com.

Tong, Rosemarie. 2009. *Feminist Thought*. 2nd ed. Boulder, CO: Westview Press.

Towns, Ann E. 2010. *Women and States: Norms and Hierarchies in International Society*. Cambridge: Cambridge University Press.

———. 2012. "Norms and Social Hierarchies: Understanding International Policy Diffusion 'From Below.'" *International Organization* 66 (2): 179–209.

Tran, Mark. 2013. "Syrian Women and Girls Allege Use of Sexual Violence in Civil War." *Guardian*, January 14. https://www.theguardian.com.

Tremblay, Manon, and Daniel Stockemer. 2013. "Women's Ministerial Careers in Cabinet, 1921–2010: A Look at Socio-Demographic Traits and Career Experiences." *Canadian Public Administration* 56 (4): 523–41.

Tripp, Aili M., Isabel Casimiro, Joy Kwesiga, and Alice Mungwa. 2009. *African Women's Movements: Transforming Political Landscapes*. New York: Cambridge University Press.

True, Jacqui. 2012. *The Political Economy of Violence against Women*. New York: Oxford University Press.

True, Jacqui, and Michael Mintrom. 2001. "Transnational Networks and Policy Diffusion: The Case of Gender Mainstreaming." *International Studies Quarterly* 45 (1): 27–57.

Tryggestad, Torunn L. 2009. "Trick or Treat? The UN and Implementation of Security Council Resolution 1325 on Women, Peace, and Security." *Global Governance* 15 (4): 539–57.

Tzannatos, Zafiris. 2006. "The World Bank, Development, Adjustment, and Gender Equality." In *Feminist Economic and the World Bank: History, Theory and Policy*, edited by Edith Kuiper and Drucilla Barker. London and New York: Routledge, 13–39.

Udry, Christopher, John Hoddinott, Harold Alderman, and Lawrence Haddad. 1995. "Gender Differentials in Farm Productivity: Implications for Household Efficiency and Agricultural Policy." *Food Policy* 20 (5): 407–23.

UN Women. No date. "MDG Momentum, Gender, and Progress Towards Meeting the MDGs." New York: UN Women. www.unwomen.org.

———. 2011. *Progress of the World's Women 2011–2012: In Pursuit of Justice*. New York: UN Women. www.progress.unwomen.org.

———. 2014a. *Gender Mainstreaming in Development Programming*. New York: UN Women. http://www.unwomen.org.

———. 2015a. "Sluggish Progress on Women in Politics Will Hamper Development." www.unwomen.org.

———. 2015b. "Facts and Figures: Leadership and Political Participation Women in Parliaments." Accessed July 22, 2015. www.unwomen.org.

———. 2015c. *Progress of the World's Women 2015–2016: Transforming Economies, Realizing Rights*. New York: UN Women. www.progress.unwomen.org.

———. 2016a. *Facts and Figures: Leadership and Political Participation*. New York: UN Women.

———. 2016b. *Global Database on Violence Against Women*. New York: UN Women. http://database.unwomen.org.

United Nations. 1975. *Report of the World Conference of the International Women's Year*. Mexico City: United Nations.

———. 1979. *Convention on the Elimination of All Forms of Discrimination against Women*. New York: United Nations. www.ohchr.org.

———. 1980. *Report of the World Conference of the United National Decade for Women: Equality, Development, and Peace*. Copenhagen: United Nations.

———. 1985. *Report of the World Conference to Review and Appraise the Achievements of the United Nations Decade for Women: Equality, Development, and Peace*. Nairobi: United Nations.

———. 1993. *Vienna Declaration and Programme of Action*. Vienna: United Nations. www.ohchr.org.

———. 1995a. *Beijing Declaration and Platform for Action*. Beijing: United Nations. www.un.org.

———. 1995b. *Report of the International Conference on Population and Development*. Cairo: United Nations. www.un.org.

———. 2006. *Ending Violence Against Women: From Words to Action*. http://www.un.org.

———. 2007. "Women and the Darfur Peace Agreement." New York: UNICEF. www. unicef.org.

———. 2013. *Sexual Violence in Conflict: Report of the Secretary-General*. New York: United Nations. www.un.org.

———. 2014. *UN Peacemaker: Peace Agreements Database Search*. Accessed June 10, 2014. www.peacemaker.un.org.

United Nations Development Programme. 2014a. *Fast Facts: Gender Equality and UNDP*. www.undp.org.

———. 2014b. *Millennium Development Goals Report*. New York: United Nations. www. un.org.

———. 2014c. *Sustaining Human Progress: Reducing Vulnerabilities and Building Resilience*. New York: United Nations Development Programme. www.hdr.undp.org.

United Nations Office on Drugs and Crime. 2009. *Global Report on Trafficking in Persons*. New York: United Nations.

———. 2014. *Global Report on Trafficking in Persons*. New York: United Nations. www. unodc.org.

———. 2016a. "Database of Legislation." *Human Trafficking Knowledge Portal*. Accessed August 6, 2016. www.unodc.org.

———. 2016b. "What Is Human Trafficking?" *Human Trafficking*. Accessed August 6, 2016. www.unodc.org.

United Nations Refugee Agency. 2013. "UNHCR Warns of Humanitarian Cost of Syrian Conflict, Especially on the Displaced." *UNHCR*. Accessed October 28, 2016. http://www.unhcr.org.

Vasquez del Aguila, Ernesto. 2006. "Invisible Women: Forced Sterilization, Reproductive Rights, and Structural Inequalities in Peru of Fujimori and Toledo." *Estudos e Pesquisas em Psicologia* 6 (1): 109–24.

Victorian Health Foundation. 2009. *National Survey on Community Attitudes to Violence Against Women 2009: Changing Cultures, Changing Attitudes- Preventing Violence Against Women*. Accessed April 28, 2014. www.ncdsv.org.

Visvanathan, Nalini, and Karla Yoder. 2011. "Women and Microcredit: A Critical Introduction." In *The Women, Gender, and Development Reader*, edited by Nalini Visvanathan, Lynn Duggan, Nan Wiegersma, and Laurie Nisonoff. London and New York: Zed Books, 47–54.

Viterna, Jocelyn, and Kathleen M. Fallon. 2008. "Democratization, Women's Movements, and Gender-Equitable States: A Framework for Comparison." *American Sociological Review* 73 (4): 668–89.

Wallerstein, Immanuel. 1983. *Historical Capitalism with Capitalist Civilization*. London: Verso.

Waters, Hugh, Adnan Hyder, Yogesh Rajkotia, Suprotik Basu, and Julian Ann Rehwinkel. 2004. *The Economic Dimensions of Interpersonal Violence*. Geneva: World Health Organization, Department of Injuries and Violence Prevention. http://whqlibdoc.who.int.

Weber, Cynthia. 2016. *Queer International Relations*. New York: Oxford University Press.

Weldon, S. Laurel. 2002. *Protest, Policy, and the Problem of Violence against Women*. Pittsburgh: University of Pittsburgh Press.

———. 2006. "Inclusion, Solidarity, and Social Movements: The Global Movement against Gender Violence." *Perspectives on Politics* 4 (1): 55–74.

Weldon, S. Laurel, and Mala Htun. 2013. "Feminist Mobilization and Progressive Policy Change: Why Governments Take Action to Combat Violence against Women." *Gender and Development* 21 (2): 231–47.

Whicker, Marcia Lynn, and Hedy Leonie Isaacs. 1999. "The Maleness of the American Presidency." In *Women in Politics: Insiders or Outsiders?*, edited by Lois Duke Whitaker. Upper Saddle River, NJ: Prentice Hall.

Whitford, Andrew B., Vicky M. Wilkins, and Mercedes G. Ball. 2007. "Descriptive Representation and Policymaking Authority: Evidence from Women in Cabinets and Bureaucracies." *Governance* 20 (4): 559–80.

White Ribbon Scotland. 2013. *Attitudes on Violence Against Women: A Snapshot Survey*. www.whiteribbonscotland.org.

Whitman, S. 2007. "Women and Peace-Building in the Democratic Republic of the Congo: An Assessment of the Their Role in the Inter-Congolese Dialogue." *African Journal on Conflict Resolution* 6 (1): 29–48.

Whitworth, Sandra. 2004. *Men, Militarism, and UN Peacekeeping: A Gendered Analysis*. Boulder, CO: Lynne Rienner.

Wibben, Annick T.R. 2011. *Feminist Security Studies: A Narrative Approach*. New York: Routledge.

Willett, Susan. 2010. "Introduction: Security Council Resolution 1325: Assessing the Impact on Women, Peace and Security." *International Peacekeeping* 17 (2): 142.

Williams, Margaret, and Frank C. Thames. 2008. "Women's Representation on High Courts in Advanced Industrialized Countries." *Politics and Gender* 4: 451–71.

Wood, Cynthia A. 2006. "Adjustment with a Woman's Face: Gender And Macroeconomic Policy at the World Bank." In *Feminist Economic and the World Bank: History, Theory, and Policy*, edited by Edith Kuiper and Drucilla Barker. London and New York: Routledge, 142–61.

World Bank. 2001. *Engendering Development: Through Gender Equality in Rights, Resources, and Voice*. New York: World Bank and Oxford University Press.

———. 2006. *Gender Equality as Smart Economics: A World Bank Group Gender Action Plan (Fiscal Years 2007–2010)*. Washington, DC: World Bank.

———. 2012. World Development Report 2012: Gender Equality and Development. Washington, DC: World Bank.

———. 2013. "Violence against Women Exacts High Economic Price, World Bank Says." *World Bank*, November 25. http://worldbank.org.

———. 2014. *Women, Business, and the Law 2014: Removing Restrictions to Enhance Gender Equality*. Washington, DC: World Bank. www.wbl.worldbank.org.

World Economic Forum. 2013. *The Global Gender Gap Report 2013*. Geneva: World Economic Forum. www3.weforum.org.

———. 2014. *The Global Gender Gap Report 2014*. Geneva: World Economic Forum. www3.weforum.org.

World Health Organization. 2013. *Global and Regional Estimates of Violence against Women: Prevalence and Health Effects of Intimate Partner Violence and Non-Partner Sexual Violence*. http://apps.who.int.

Young, Iris Marion. 1997. "Deferring Group Representation." *Nomos* 39: 349–76.

———. 2000. *Inclusion and Democracy*. New York: Oxford University Press.

Yukhananov, Anna. 2013. "IMF Warns of Slow Progress Achieving Gender Equality." *Reuters*, September 23. Accessed July 21, 2014. www.reuters.com.

Yunus, Muhammad. 2005. "Muhammad Yunus, Banker to the World's Poorest Citizens, Makes His Case." Wharton at University of Pennsylvania, March 9. www.knowledge.wharton.upenn.edu.

Zalewski, Marysia. 2000. *Feminism After Postmodernism*. New York: Routledge.

Zentai, Violetta. 2006. "Gender Equality or Gender Mainstreaming?" *Policy Studies* 27 (2): 135–51.

Zippel, Kathrin. 2004. "Transnational Advocacy Networks and Policy Cycles in the European Union: The Case of Sexual Harassment." *Social Politics: International Studies in Gender, State, and Society* 11 (1): 57–85.

Zwingel, Susanne. 2011. "How Do Norms Travel? Theorizing International Women's Rights in Transnational Perspective." *International Studies Quarterly* 56 (1): 1–15.

INDEX

add-gender-and-stir movement, 2, 178; central issues of, 3; gender as a shortcut in, 6

add-women policies, 65, 124, 186; economic development and, 191; gender as women in, 8; kyriarchy and, 187; male domination challenged by, 178; shortcomings of, 188, 206; UNSCR 1325 and, 35; as women's inclusion, 13–14

"advancement of women," 79–80

Afghanistan, 195

African Union (AU), 165

agricultural production, 135–36

analytical gender, 9–10, 45–46; bounded agency and informal barriers and, 188–98; gendered binaries and intersectionality and, 189; masculinities and femininities and, 99–100; neoliberalism and, 190; poor implementation and, 188; productivity trap and, 152; women's inclusion and, 21–22

anti-discrimination, 3, 65, 136; CEDAW and, 79, 87–88, 132; LGBTQ rights and, 201; productivity trap and, 150; protection and, 59

Argentina, 104

Asia-Pacific region, 40

AU. See African Union

Australia: Rudd as Prime Minister of, 184; violence against women in, 175, 176

backlash, 193; electoral violence as, 194–95; to gender quotas, 111; kyriarchy and, 196; of LGBTQ movements, 201; to policies, 20; in post-conflict transitions, 195; verbal harassment as, 195–96; violence against women and, 194

Bangladesh, 45

Beijing Declaration and Platform for Action on Women (Beijing Platform) (1995), 3, 90, 186; conflict and, 94–95; on education, 96; gender-as-women and, 91–92, 95–96; gender quotas and, 92, 104; "gender" use in, 95–96; NGOs at, 91; on poverty, 93; rape as a weapon of war in, 94; violence against women in, 93–94; women as means to an end in, 97. *See also* Commission on the Status of Women

Black Lives Matter movement, 204

Bolivia: economic rights in, 136; sex-segregation of labor in, 138; women in legislative body in, 58

Boserup, Ester, 142

Bosnia and Herzegovina war, 34–35

bounded agency, 109; analytical gender and informal barriers to, 188–98; gendered binaries and, 113–14; gender equality and, 14–15

Bunch, Charlotte: on "double shift," 55; "Women's Rights as Human Rights" by, 88–89

Burkina Faso, 145

Burundi, 165

Canada, 111

capitalism: crises and, 155–56; kyriarchy and, 12; liberal feminism and, 62–63; second-wave feminism and, 61; women's inclusion and, 7, 52, 60–61

ABOUT THE AUTHOR

Kara Ellerby is Assistant Professor in the Departments of Political Science and International Relations, and Women and Gender Studies, at the University of Delaware.